A SERBIAN VILLAGE
IN HISTORICAL PERSPECTIVE

JOEL M. HALPERN

BARBARA KEREWSKY-HALPERN
University of Massachusetts

Waveland Press, Inc.
Prospect Heights, Illinois

For deda Mileta and mala Kajla

Cover Photo: One Orašac household: four generations of villagers plus the anthropologists' family (1970).

All photos in text by Radoje Milivojević, People's Museum, Kragujevac except those on pages 19, 58 and 148.

Maps on page four and page seven, and kinship diagrams on pages twenty-four, twenty-five and thirty-two were prepared by Barbara Kerewsky-Halpern and orginally appeared in *A Serbian Village* (New York: Columbia University Press, 1958).

For information about this book, write or call:

Waveland Press, Inc.
P.O. Box 400
Prospect Heights, Illinois 60070
(312) 634-0081

Copyright © 1972 by Holt, Rinehart and Winston, Inc.
1986 reissued with changes by Waveland Press, Inc.

ISBN 0-88133-209-7

Printed in the United States of America.

Foreword

About the Authors

Joel M. Halpern is a professor of anthropology at the University of Massachusetts at Amherst. His Ph.D. from Columbia University incorporates specialization in Soviet Studies. He has been an Associate of the Russian Research Center of Harvard University and has taught at UCLA and Brandeis.

Barbara Kerewsky-Halpern is an adjunct professor at the University of Massachusetts. Her Ph.D. in anthropology follows a Master's degree in theoretical linguistics. Her research interests in communicative modes in patient/practitioner interactions are applied in clinical medical anthropology.

The authors are the first western social scientists to have worked in post-World War II Yugoslavia, where their research is ongoing. They have also worked extensively in Southeast Asia and have published jointly and individually on social organization in Laos and on peasant life in Eastern Europe.

About the Book

This is a unique case study in that it provides historical perspective for the community and yet deals with changes concomitant with modernization. It also has the great virtue of dealing with the single community in the context of the larger national whole.

The village of Orašac, like so many traditional villages around the world, is caught up in changes that the inhabitants only partially understand. Everything that happens seems to draw the young people away from the land and away from the ways to which their parents and grandparents are accustomed and which they value. Orašac appears very satisfying to the eye seeking a traditional peasant culture. The outward appearance of the village and its older people, at least, is very conservative. The Halperns are able to show in what depth the life way has changed and will change in the immediate future despite this outward appearance.

This case study is of particular interest not only because it is about a modernizing peasant community, but because this community is in Yugoslavia, a socialist country with its own unique cultural and political characteristics. The Halperns give the reader a feeling for these characteristics and their influence upon both village life and modernization throughout the case study, but particularly in Chapter 6.

Many beginning students will find Chapter 2, the discussion of the *zadruga* and its social system ramifications, difficult to assimilate. The zadruga is a basic social unit in Serbian peasant life and deserves serious analysis. It has been treated in this discussion within the framework of professional anthropology. Every effort has been made to make the analysis understandable within this framework, and all specialized terms are available in the glossary. What the authors attempt here is to share with the reader a way of exploring some of the complexities of family relationships.

This case study is enlivened at crucial points by materials drawn from life histories, interviews and conversations, and direct observation, which help to illustrate major features of life, and change in lifeways, among the people of Orašac.

GEORGE AND LOUISE SPINDLER

Contents

Introduction

I N LOOKING AT ANOTHER CULTURE and in seeking understanding, a number of basic dimensions structure our approach. To know who others are we must have a degree of self-knowledge, since it is through our own eyes that we perceive the stranger. A simple statement, admittedly—but by being self-conscious about our feelings and by knowing at least some of their limitations we can best gauge the depth of our perceptions.

The reader has a right to ask: Through whose eyes am I seeing another culture? Is my guide younger or older, man or woman? What are his theoretical or special interests? No investigator is a mere tape-recorder; even a tape-recorder has to be turned on at specific times, and there is also the matter of selection and arrangement.

This account of changes in life ways in a village in Serbia, Yugoslavia, has the following background: As a young couple we first went to Serbia in 1953, living for a year in the village of Orašac and researching material for a doctoral dissertation. This resulted as well in a community study monograph with historical and descriptive emphasis. The village was revisited with our young children during 1961–1962, again in 1964, over the summer of 1966, briefly in 1968 (as honorary godparents of the bridegroom at a wedding similar to the second one described in Chapter 4), and most recently with our family during the early 1970s. Our daughters have progressed from feeding the chickens to more responsible chores of pasturing the lard sow and tending the sheep, jobs gratefully turned over to them by the aging grandmother of the household with whom we live. With each visit they participate more actively in the economy of this household which lacks young people, advancing to helping with sheep shearing, milking, weaving, and the strenuous work of haying, the latter formerly done by men according to the traditional division of labor. A new baby has provided opportunity for attention to changes in child-rearing practices.

Our earlier concern had been to discover what is, to record as completely as possible the state of being of another culture. Later we became more interested in finding out what sorts of changes were taking place and, more importantly, trying to understand the meanings their own culture had for the people of rural Serbia. Over the years one of us has become increasingly intrigued with the structure of the *zadruga*, the South Slav extended household unit, and the new forms it is developing; the other has become concerned with villagers as people, individuals who, as members of a group with specific sets of conditioning values, collectively

1

may represent (or be represented by) a generalization or statistic but who, independently, are unique.

Preparing this book has been a matter of selective description and evaluation, inevitably using to some degree our own covert values as implicit points of reference. Here are we, members of an economically and technologically advanced society, looking at those who have in these ways evolved less. That this is a two-edged sword hardly needs emphasis. There are few of us who, when we think about it, do not ardently appreciate at least certain facets of technological progress. It is hard, for example, to conceive of a person in need of surgery voluntarily opting for nineteenth-century techniques. On the other hand, neither is anyone exempt from a certain nostalgia for ways past. Our observations of the Serbian village scene cannot help but be affected both ways in the retelling.

Ideally, people of another culture should speak to us themselves, even though translation may blur some of the passion and wisdom. We attempt this goal by making extensive use of villagers' casual remarks and autobiographical excerpts as well as of writings by Yugoslav ethnologists. (Of course, in assessing the meaning of what people say about themselves and in placing their statements in an overall and meaningful context we necessarily return to problems of perception.)

There is another level, that at which the specific Yugoslav communist experience is pertinent. Here must be taken into consideration the questioning of the limits of revolutionary change and the sorts of specific cultural factors playing roles in the establishment of parameters within which drastic alterations in life ways can take place.

If it were necessary to sum up the theme of this monograph in a sentence, it would be to say that we are taking a look at the way of life of a people, a national tradition as manifested on the village level, by viewing processes of cultural evolution from the perspective of a century and a half of nationhood, conscious of the interaction of local and national institutions but focusing primarily on the level of the individual life, the kin group, and the ways of gaining a living, and exploring changes which have occurred in order to better understand the situation as it is now and to anticipate at least partially what may be. That in the process we better learn to understand ourselves is a logical consequence of such research.

While this book touches on some of the same points as *A Serbian Village* (originally published in 1958 and updated with data from 1966 for a revised edition in 1967), that monograph's two editions are different in concept from this one. *A Serbian Village in Historical Perspective* represents a further rethinking of the accumulated data, using different illustrative materials. Concern with present and future change has led us into a growing reciprocal interest in historical background. This in turn relates to our desire to place Orašac within the context of the nation-state from which it has evolved. Analyses of social structure and economic factors are considerably more refined here. Some ideas are presented as hypotheses rather than as proven facts, since analysis of material collected in the course of the more recent field trips is not yet completed. Use of the work of Yugoslav ethnographers and sociologists is more extensive. However, since descriptive material is not repeated as such, the reader wishing more background is referred to the earlier book.

Our research in Serbia over an eighteen-year period has been partially subsidized by grants from the National Science Foundation and the National Institute of Mental Health.

Again we acknowledge with appreciation the active and continuing cooperation of Yugoslav scholars and officials and especially of the people of Orašac and surrounding communities who, in addition to being hospitable and open, have been so patient with our persistent efforts to record their ways.

In Orašac and villages like it, all kinds of changes are occurring. Preparing this book has presented difficulties in keeping up with certain aspects of change and especially in pinpointing for ourselves exactly what we mean to convey when we write about "now"—is it post-World War II, mid-twentieth century, or the early 1970s? In many situations "the present" has altered markedly from one visit to the next. We feel uncomfortable making statements about patterns which appear subject to further change. Because of this the last chapter, "Some Reflections on Change," is in a sense an epilogue in which we step out of the role of chroniclers and again address the reader directly. Hopefully we convey a feeling of our own evolving views as well as of the dynamics of technological and political change in a village in contemporary Yugoslavia.

Yugoslavia, with Šumadija in Central Serbia

1

A Land, A People

Šumadija Landscape

IN THE FINE ARTS SECTION OF THE MUSEUM of every larger town in Serbia hangs at least one painting entitled "Šumadija." Sometimes the painting is representational, sometimes more abstract, but instant recognition and nostalgia are there. It is a green and gold landscape, with tall corn and waving wheat, patterns in irregular rectangles; houses, small bright white cubes capped with red tile roofs, are tucked at random into leafy plum orchards and vineyards; in the distance are familiar, identifiable hills.

The Šumadija countryside does look like this, on the surface, from afar. Close-up views as well often do not hint at the multitude of changes happening right now, at a rate more accelerated than that in the past.

Into the bucolic tableau comes a man in sheepskin vest and turned-up sandals, urging a creaking, cow-drawn cart along the lane. He calls a greeting to two women sitting on a grassy knoll tending their sheep. *"Zdravo Vido! Zdravo Seko! Je ste vredni?* (Are you industrious?)"

The hands of the older woman never break rhythm as she replies behind a screen of dark kerchief folded low over her forehead. From a distaff tucked into her waistband and held crooked on her left arm she pulls out grey wool and deftly twists it into a strand, winding it onto a stick spindle rotated in her right hand. The young woman responds by putting down her knitting and pushing her long, unbraided hair off her face. She is seventeen, has completed the eight-grade village school, and wishes she were not here at all but attending the typing class in town. Two people are not necessary for watching six sheep. "This way is all right for you, *Bako*," she asserts, turning to her grandmother, "but for me, I can't wait to get out of the village mud."

Near a curve in the road is a sort of center, a random cluster of village institutions—the school, the church, the marketing cooperative, the new *kafana*, quiet in the middle of the day. In its own way each ties the village to a larger center. The bend is lively at five in the morning, when a blue factory bus picks up workers and other villagers headed for town. Livestock is not allowed on the bus, and people planning to sell animals at market follow on foot, forming a squealing, cackling company in its wake.

For the village of Orašac town means nearby Arandjelovac, reached by traveling several acacia-lined miles up over a hill and down again, along a pitted highroad dating from Turkish times. The road leads past the site of the weekly open market and into the town's single ribbon of cobbled main street, "long as a woman's tongue."[1] It was once lined with a variety of small craftsmen's shops, now increasingly giving way to local branches of national enterprises. At tables set out in front of a new cafeteria, men sit with newspapers and small cups of Turkish coffee. Horse-drawn wagons and cow carts clatter by, now outnumbered by Fiats, trucks, and motor bikes. Shop windows display almost-up-to-date Belgrade goods. A whistle sounds, and workers emerge from factory gates at the end of a workday that began at 6:00 A.M. This is the town in mid-afternoon, an everyday scene seemingly quite detached from the village.

Many of the factory laborers are, in fact, peasant-workers, villagers who return home at the end of the shift to work their land until sundown. Most of the men sitting at the outdoor cafe are from villages too, workers and clerks and students who have chosen not to remain on the land, many of whom return to their villages on weekends or during vacations to help with chores and the harvest.

A Village Boy

Such reciprocity quietly dramatizes aspects of the influences of the town on the village and the village on the town, concepts vital to understanding contemporary Yugoslav society. A young man drinking beer at the end table can be singled out as an example. Appearance to the contrary, Jovan Tomić is a *seosko dete*, a village boy. He is twenty-two, works as a machinist in Belgrade, and every third week or so makes an overnight visit to his family in Orašac. He dresses carefully when he goes home. His slacks hug his hips in the latest style, his fashionable city shoes are shined, and his nails and hands clean. He wears a new leather jacket that cost a good portion of his monthly wage.

After traveling some sixty miles south of the capital into the heartland of Serbia he is refreshing himself before hiking on to the village. The train he took south as far as Mladenovac follows the track used by the Simplon Orient Express. When Jovan boarded his local in Belgrade he saw the green and yellow diesel engine bearing the international train along its route through Yugoslavia. It carries the dual monogram of the Yugoslav State Railway, in the Latin and

---

[1] Here is an example of how quickly things are changing. This chapter was written between visits, before we learned that the Arandjelovac cobbles had just been replaced by a hard-topped road and that the market had been moved to a new, concrete-surfaced site at the other end of town. When we next arrived in Orašac we found (to our pleasure) that the stretch of village road from the cooperative building to town was being widened and resurfaced, with plans to continue the road work as commune funds became available.

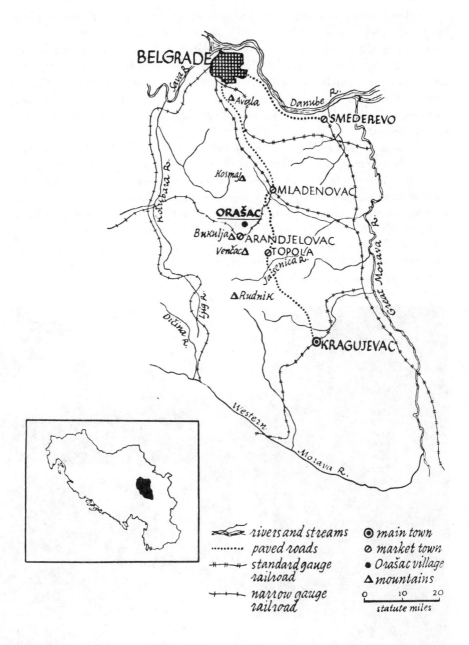

Šumadija

Cyrillic initials of the two official alphabets, with the clasped-hand symbol of American aid. When the impressive engines first arrived they were called *dizelke*, but soon people named them after the late President Kennedy. Jovan muses about such an engine one day carrying him across the frontiers of Yugoslavia to a chance to earn money abroad.

Jovan shared a wooden bench with some peasants and students, knowing by the way they looked at him that they respected his good taste and success in the city. Men and women who had been to Belgrade to sell fruit and cheese swung off at local stops, grasping emptied baskets and enamel pots and shoulder poles. Some carried city purchases, parcels of cloth rolled up in the patterned wrapping paper of NaMa, the People's Department Store. At Mladenovac he changed to the narrow-gauge regional line that wends through fields and pastures and eventually to Arandjelovac.

Jovan finishes his beer. At home there is plenty of homemade wine and *rakija*, plum brandy, but the purchase of a bottle of beer satisfies him more. He knows how to behave in town. Now he leans away from the table and meticulously clears his nose, pinching it with thumb and forefinger. He whips out a comb and runs it through his hair. Tomorrow he'll tell his mother to fix him a vinegar shampoo with rainwater rinse. Just as the young shepherdess is eager to get out of the village, so too was Jovan; but, he reflects as he pushes back his chair, what his grandfather always says is true after all—nowhere is the air better than the fresh, pure air of the village.

Traditional village courtyard

He buys a pack of Morava cigarettes as a gift for his *deda* and makes his way through an alley to the open fields beyond the street. It is almost twilight, and lights are beginning to go on in the new private houses on the edge of town, built by families who have left the village and moved closer to the factories. He reaches the footpath that winds over the ridge. From the crest he sees, on one side, the uneven but unbroken strip of town lights. On the opposite side, beyond the gentler ascent from Preseka Hill, the scattered homesteads of Orašac show up as weak yellow spots of light. Jovan can make out his father's house, out there in line with his uncle's near Misača Creek. He descends, making his way around roots and rocks known since childhood, and comes out on the dark highroad. There is no light, for there are few houses along the road. From Turkish times most people have maintained the custom of locating their dwellings on their holdings. "Stupidity!" he thinks. "We Serbs are still living like primitive men. If people woke up and built their houses by the road, the way they do in civilized places, I'd be home now, screw God."

At the place where a stunted clump of acacia marks the beginning of his lane he turns, stepping cautiously into the darkness. He knows the lane will be muddy and maneuvers instinctively to the higher clay-like mud ridges. A dog barks, not letting up until Jovan is well past the animal's domain, where another dog takes up the warning signal that progresses with him down the lane. The moon rises, and he sees the whitewashed shape of Uncle Miodrag's house. His uncle's dog picks up the barking and his aunt's voice calls, "Who's there?"

"It's I, *Strina*, Jovan."

"Returning home, eh son?"

"Yes, returning."

"*Ako, ako.* So be it."

Jovan skirts the rim of his uncle's cornfield, moving with care to avoid blackberry thorns along the hedge separating it from his father's and grandfather's field. His feet feel for the diagonal packed clay path through the corn which leads to the edge of their compound. Arap, his black dog, yelps with recognition and bounds to greet him.

Jovan caught between urban and rural values, the peasant-workers vacillating from factory to land, a young girl's rejection of village ways and aspirations for a different way—these are merely current aspects of the evolution of Yugoslav society. A generation ago a village girl's dream was to marry into a prosperous peasant household. And with each preceding generation the idea of what constitutes an ideal household varied greatly.

Historical Setting

Central Serbia and particularly Šumadija is an ideal place in which to examine the ongoing transformations of peasant society. There is considerable evidence of neolithic settlement in the area. The modern history of Šumadija goes back to medieval times, when the region had been populated and was part of an early Serbian feudal state. Over the centuries there have been many waves of depopulation and repopulation. When Ottoman forces defeated this state at the Battle of Kosovo, far to the south, in 1389, people migrated north into the region. In 1459 the Turks gained control of Smederevo on the Danube, the last Serbian stronghold, and it has been estimated that about ninety percent of the population of the area later to be known as Šumadija fled to safer areas, many going south and west into upland Dinaric regions and there retaining and even recreating certain social institutions and folk practices which had earlier begun to break down under the impact of the developing state.

The late seventeenth and early eighteenth centuries mark a period of intermittent warfare between the Turkish and Austrian Empires, accompanied by constant population movement. With temporary Austrian occupation in 1718, a gradual weakening of the Turks, and a more favorable atmosphere for settlement, large-scale repopulation again took place. In stages, groups of migrants began to come out of the mountains, settle in closer lowlands, and eventually make their way to the area they called Šumadija, woodland, after the thick oak forests. Orašac was settled in the late eighteenth century. By the early nineteenth century the area was generally, if sparsely, populated, and the woods were felled as population increase proceeded. There were peasant uprisings and negotiations with the Sultan, not resulting in final Turkish withdrawal until 1867. Serbia was proclaimed an independent kingdom in 1882.

History Reflected in Folk Epics

The famous Battle of Kosovo remains a well-remembered date and an event dramatically reenacted in each succeeding generation by means of the still viable tradition of folk epics. These heroic epics, chanted by minstrels and learned by heart, are linked to the same traditions as those of Homer. The Serbs lost the battle but created out of defeat an oral literature which was instrumental in preserving national consciousness during the long centuries of Ottoman rule.

Two features of Turkish control markedly shaped future Serbian society. First, by destroying the medieval Serbian state the Turkish conquest destroyed its ruling nobility as well (the nobility were killed, became peasants or, in some areas, converted to Islam). Second, the Turks granted autonomy to both the Serbian church and to the village community, and so it was around these two institutions that Serbian life, based on a nation of peasants, began to develop anew.

The interplay of these two institutions is well revealed in a folk epic commemorating the First Serbian Revolt against the Turks. Like many uprisings this one began as a petition for the redress of grievances. (It is with this event that Orašac enjoys a moment of glory in Serbian history, for it was here that the leaders of the revolt met in a shaded glen behind the present schoolhouse to plan their 1804 uprising.) These verses are known by every villager, adult and child alike:

> Dear God, what a great miracle,
> When it was time in the land of the Serbs
> For a vast change to occur
> So that others should rule it.
> The headmen do not want to fight,
> Nor do the Turkish plunderers,
> But this is a fight of the poor peasants

Who can no longer bear their burden,
Who can no longer bear the Turks' oppression;
And the holy saints want it.
Enough blood has gushed from the earth.
The time has come to fight,
To shed blood for the holy cross,
Every man should now avenge his ancestors.[2]

That the Turks were not universally regarded as inhuman enemies is reflected in the part of the epic retelling of the story of Kosovo, where both the Serbian King Lazar and the Turkish Sultan Murad perished. The Sultan advises his men:

Brother Turks, counselors and viziers,
I am dying, leaving you the Empire,
Listen carefully to what I say,
So that the Empire may long endure:
Be not bitter to the peasants,
Rather, treat them kindly,
Let there be a fifteen-dinar head tax,
Or at most a thirty-dinar tax;
Do not load them with fines and taxes,
Do not make their life a burden;
Do not interfere in their churches,
Nor in their laws and honor. . . .[3]

Nineteenth-Century Village Life

In the early nineteenth century an outstanding Serbian scholar, Vuk Karadžić, pioneered in Serbian history, ethnography, and linguistics. Based in part on Karadžić's writings, a German historian of the period described Serbian villages as they existed at the time of the First Revolt:

VILLAGES AND HOUSEHOLDS

The villages of Servia extend far up into the gorges of the mountains, into the depths of forests, and sometimes when consisting of forty or fifty houses, they spread over a space as extensive as that occupied by Vienna and its suburbs, the dwellings being isolated, and at a distance one from another. Each habitation contains within itself an entire community. . . . All the members of the family constitute but one household; they work and eat together, and in the winter evenings assemble around the fire. Even when the father dies, his sons, appointing one of their number, the best qualified amongst them, as master of the house, remain together until too great an increase of the family renders a separation

---

[2] Opening lines of the epic *Početak bune protiv Dahija* (Beginning of the Revolt against the Turkish Overlords), translated by the authors in the spirit and meaning of the original but without retaining the characteristic heroic verse form of ten-syllable lines. (For an English translation retaining meter see Morison, *The Revolt of the Serbs against the Turks,* Cambridge University Press, 1942, pp. 34–73.)

[3] Translated from *Početak bune protiv Dahija.*

desirable. . . . The household requires but little assistance from strangers. The men raise their own buildings; construct in their rude manner their ploughs and waggons; prepare the yokes of their draught oxen; hoop their casks; and manufacture their shoes from rough leather. Their other clothing is prepared by the women, who spin wool and flax, weave linen and woolen cloth. . . . Their land yields the food they require, so that salt is perhaps the only article they find it necessary to purchase. The mechanics most in request by the villages are smiths, to make their tools. A mill belongs to several houses cojointly, and each house has its day for using it. The family households, supplying all their own wants, and shut up each within itself—a state of things which was continued under the Turks, because the taxes were chiefly levied upon the households—formed the basis of Servian nationality. Individual interest was thus merged, as it were, in that of the family.[4]

The following passages, translated directly from Karadžić, make explicit the social structure of Serbia in the early to mid-nineteenth century and detail outside influences on the basic economy of the Serbian peasantry:

TOWNS, TRADESMEN, AND CRAFTS

Among the Serbian people there are no people other than peasants. (Those few Serbs who do live in towns as tradesmen—virtually only shopkeepers—and craftsmen, mostly furriers, tailors, bakers, gunsmiths and coppersmiths, are called townspeople. Since they dress as Turks and live according to Turkish customs, and since during revolts and wars they either shut themselves up with the Turks in cities or run away to Germany with their money, not only can they not be counted among the Serbs, but the Serbs despise them.) Serbs, as peasants, live only from their land and livestock. It is true that among them there are traders who buy pigs and all other kinds of livestock, as well as wild game, wax, honey and other minor items, but in their homes they live as do the other peasants. Among the peasants are blacksmiths (who forge and sharpen axes, hoes and plowshares; Turkish Gypsies in the towns mend kettles and other small things), bakers, tailors, furriers, coopers, wheelwrights, carpenters, rope-makers and in some places potters. Every carpenter is a mason as well, and every furrier a tailor. Tailors, coopers and carpenters do not work at home but at the house of the family for whom they are doing the job. Peasants build houses and other buildings even in the towns and market towns. Almost every Serb knows how to do carpentry, although not every man has the tools, for example, for making barrels or carts; but a special craftsman is rarely needed for replacing a metal rim on a wheel or repairing a mill. . . . Spoons, bowls and kneading troughs are usually made by itinerant Gypsies and sold or exchanged for flour and other things. The Serbian women sew, prepare and spin hemp and flax, dye (with indigo, madder, mint, honeysuckle, etc.) and spin wool, weave cotton and woolen goods, embroider knit stockings and gloves. In addition to these women's tasks they also work with the men in the fields; for example, threshing wheat, digging, haying and gathering plums, picking corn and grapes.

FOOD

In the whole of Serbia cornbread is most commonly eaten. It is true that almost everywhere wheat, barley and rye can be raised, but not much of these grains is sown; where they are grown they are more often sold than eaten. Potatoes have

---

[4] Leopold von Ranke, *The History of Servia and the Servian Revolution,* translated from the German by Mrs. A. Kerr, London, Bohn, 1853, pp. 35–36.

become known only recently and very little is grown (more as a curio: necessity), although they could be of considerable value. The veget: commonly grown are beans, cabbage, onions and garlic, plus radishes, t beets and, less frequently, peas and lentils. Kale, kohlrabi, carrots and s_____ unknown. Horseradish grows wild in the fields but is used only as a medicine. Aside from cornbread the ordinary Serbian food during religious fasts is beans and onions; at times when animal products may be eaten there is winter cabbage and bacon, and in summer, milk, cheese, and eggs. The usual drink is water. Wine is generally for celebrations and then only among the richer people; sometimes plum brandy is drunk with food; fortunately it is very mild and so hardly affects the health. The greatest treat during non-fast periods is roast lamb in summer and roast suckling pig in winter, with small wheat buns, hot honeyed brandy, fried onion pastries and cheese pie: on Fridays there is fish (that is, when it is eaten, as it is not always permitted during fast periods) and beans fried in oil.

In all of Serbia, with the exception of the plains and marshes . . . wine as good as any in Hungary can be produced, but today there are few who plant vineyards to produce wine for sale. Many vacant plots of land, both old and new, indicate that at one time more vineyards were worked, but these were probably abandoned due to wars. In Serbia there are plenty of good apples, pears, sweet and sour cherries and peaches. Most commonly planted and cultivated are plums, from which brandy is distilled. Walnuts grow wild and in some places also chestnuts and the fruits of other trees. Although it is possible to earn some money from wine and brandy and the sale of other crops, this is relatively nothing compared to that to be obtained from the sale of cattle and pigs; oxen and cows are bought each spring by Bosnians and Herzegovinians and are then herded to the seacoast; goats and sheep are bought by the Turks; pigs are driven to Germany all the time— they are the truest and greatest pleasure of the people in this regard, first since they are easy to raise in the woods and second since they can be sold at any time of year.[5]

Pig Trade and Social Origins

For more on the significance of the pig trade and the social origins of modern Serbia we turn again to the epic poems. In the following passage, Karadjordje (Black George), leader of the First Revolt, prepares to meet the Turkish foe:

> . . . And Djordje watched and listened.
> When he had counted the Turks,
> He drained his glass and prepared his rifle,
> Took enough powder and lead,
> And went to his pig-pen,
> Among his twelve herdsmen,
> And there aroused the herdsmen
> And spoke to them in this manner:
> My brothers, my twelve herdsmen,
> Get up, and open the enclosure,
> Drive all the pigs out of the pens,
> Let them go where they will.
> And now you, brothers, listen to me:
> Put powder in your gleaming rifles . . .[6]

---

[5] Vuk Stefan Karadžić, *Istorijska Čitanka, odabrani tekstovi za istoriju srpskog naroda,* Belgrade, 1948, pp. 84–86. Translated by the authors.
[6] Translated from *Početak bune protiv Dahija.*

Karadjordje started his career as a peasant, living much as did those described by Karadžić, and becoming a relatively prosperous pig trader. His revolt did not secure independence for Serbia, and he was killed during a second revolt, by Milos Obrenović, a man of similar background, originator of a rival dynasty and founder of the nineteenth-century Serbian state. Of this period and of the important pig trade a British diplomat in the area in 1837 wrote:

. . . The Commerce in Swine is by far the Most Considerable and important in Servia and it is the chief object of domestic economy. The poorest peasant is the owner of some of these animals, upon which he devotes much of his time and attention, to the great detriment of all other agricultural pursuits; the sheep and Oxen are even deprived of all nourishment during the winter months, all herbage or other food being appropriated to the vast herds of swine that overspread the Country. The Servian Government in Consequence endeavored to establish a law limiting each family to the possession of only a Certain number of pigs, but it was not Carried into effect; so great is the prejudice in favor of the Superior profits to be derived in this trade, that the Servian peasantry persist in Continuing it and it is feared that an attempt to enforce such a law might produce a revolt. The trade in Pigs is carried on exclusively with Austrian dealers who Come to Servia in the Spring of each year for that purpose. The sale takes place at this Season when the Pigs are in lean Condition. . . . Payment is made by the Austrian Merchant drawing bills of exchange on Vienna or Pesth [Budapest] at 2 months after date, but they are rarely paid when due, and frequently not at all. . . . the number of Swine imported from the various parts for purchase in Servia to Austria is Annually 225,000. . . .

In Considering the Unemployed resources of Servia the first object which presents itself are the Forrests, Large and Valuable Forrests of Oak are growing in all the Mountains as well as in the Vallies; the Elm, the Ash and the Pine are also abundant everywhere, and although the Cutting of Wood is free to all, there are laws which prohibit the felling of every Species of Oak. . . .

The reasons assigned by the Prince for prohibiting the Cutting or felling of Oak trees is, that he Considers the Revenue derived from the production of the Valonia [acorn cups used in tanning, dying, ink-making] and the letting out of tracts of these forrests to Peasants for the Grazing of Pigs is equal to any revenue that could be procured otherwise—It is much to be lamented that the Prince should have adopted this Opinion as no Country is Capable of producing finer timber (oak) than Servia for Shipbuilding. . . .[7]

The Turkish Legacy

These fragments from historical accounts and from folk literature provide a real sense of the main elements in the historical background of the Serbs: a strong national consciousness accentuated by long periods of foreign domination; a social homogeneity, with the merchant and leadership groups arising from the villages; large household units based on kin, self-sufficient to a very great degree and yet engaged in significant trade with central Europe; and finally a self-reliant pioneering

---

[7] Excerpted from a report by Colonel G. Lloyd Hodges, first British Consul in Belgrade, 1837, courtesy of Public Record Office, London, F.O. 78–312; a more complete excerpt appears in D. Warriner, ed., *Contrasts in Emerging Societies*, Bloomington, Indiana University Press, 1965, pp. 300–302.

experience in settling a frontier area (but one in which the government was already trying to effect administrative controls).

Social distinctions pointed out by the folk historian Karadžić are important in understanding contemporary Šumadijan and Serbian society. Those Serbs who took up town life and imitated the Turks were regarded as strangers by their own people. On the other hand, peasants in the countryside who were also traders profited from their fellow villagers and, of necessity, maintained extensive contacts outside the village; these men were looked upon with favor, and it was from this social background that the political leadership emerged. Thus, in the formation of Serbian society it was not simply a matter of peasants taking over the towns as the Turks withdrew but, rather, of village-based entrepreneurs, often illiterate, assuming leadership, founding dynasties, and subsequently evolving an urban society (with the help of Serbs from across the Danube in what was then Austria) which mirrored both Turkish and European ways. These historic origins later came to play a crucial role in shaping the world view of Serbian peasants.

Perhaps the most important legacy of the centuries under Ottoman rule is the sense of nationalism and heroic tradition it engendered. On every Serb's lips, whether as a reason or as an excuse, is the expression *pet stotina godina pod Turcima,* five hundred years under the Turks. Under Turkish rule the peasantry had a considerable degree of autonomy; village level institutions developed and were reinforced. Of primary significance among these was the *zadruga*, the characteristic South Slav extended family unit, which, having declined in earlier times, now became strengthened. Another direct result of Turkish rule was the strong association Serbs developed toward their own religion, inexorably linking the Orthodox Church and Serbian nationality. On the supravillage level, by the early to midnineteenth century, after the revolts against Turkish control, Turkish models were influential in shaping the emerging state's administrative patterns in law, taxation, and land tenure systems, for example.

Equally as important, and more long-lasting—enduring, in fact, up to the present—is the great influence of Turkish culture on language and material culture. Modern Serbo-Croatian includes a large inventory of Turkish words, particularly of nouns which refer to household items and furnishings, clothing parts, crafts and craft technology, food and food preparation. The traditional folk costume of Šumadija, still worn in modified form by middle-aged and older village men, evolved directly from Turkish garments of the early nineteenth century. The same is true of certain aspects of women's dress that are no longer worn.

With this historical background in mind, we can look in depth at the changing social and economic structure of a contemporary village. Most of the data in this book is derived from Orašac, which affords a representative picture; when necessary, material from neighboring villages is presented for amplification or comparison.

2

The Zadruga

A Classic Account

IN 1827 KARADŽIĆ PUBLISHED OBSERVATIONS on the type of extended family household that has come to characterize "traditional" Serbian society:

The Serbs live mainly in zadrugas. In some houses there are four or five married men, and one-family households are rare. There are as many *vajats* [sleeping quarters used by individual married couples] as there are married men, and the house itself is only for communal eating and the place in which the old women and men sleep; all others sleep each with his own wife and children in his own vajat, without fire in both summer and winter. Around some prosperous houses are groups of vajats and other outbuildings (for example, corn cribs, grain storage sheds and houses with porches) like a small settlement.

Every household has a *starešina* [headman] who governs and guides the household and all its property; he directs the adults and young men as to where they will go and what they will do; he deals with the Turks and attends village and district meetings and conducts business; with the assent of the household he sells what is to be sold and buys what is to be bought; he keeps the money bag and worries about playing the head-tax and other taxes and dues. When prayers are said, he starts and ends them; when guests come to the house (in the larger households scarcely a day passes when there are none), he talks with them and takes meals with them (in the larger households, where there are many members, first the starešina and the guests are served at one *sofra* [low, round Turkish style table], then the men and young men who work in the fields, and afterwards the women and children eat). The starešina is not always the oldest male: When a father becomes old, he turns over the headship to the most able son (or brother, or nephew), even if he is the youngest. If it happens that a starešina does not guide the household well, the household members choose another. In zadruga households each woman spins, weaves, and prepares clothing for herself and her husband and children; as for food preparation, each in turn does the job a week at a time. . . . Usually the wife of the starešina is the woman who all summer supervises the preparation of food for the winter.[1]

---

[1] From *Vukovi Zapisi* (Vuk's Notes), V. Djurić, ed., Belgrade, Srpska književna zadruga, 1967, pp. 63–64. Translated by the authors.

Such is the ideal picture of the Serbian patriarchal household as it existed in the early nineteenth century and continued, with modifications, among more prosperous households up to the time of the second world war.

An expanded definition of the zadruga is a residential kin unit composed of at least two nuclear family units, often including other relatives as well, who work and live together and jointly control and utilize the resources of the household. Usually heads of the nuclear units and others who may be members of the zadruga are related by common descent, mainly in the male line. Thus the zadruga can be considered primarily a patrilocal unit existing within a society which places stress on patrilineal descent and where the formal authority patterns are patriarchal. The term *zadruga*, in addition to referring to such a household unit, is often translated from Serbo-Croat as cooperative or partnership, and this reflects its ideal ethos. Present-day marketing cooperatives or crafts associations are called zadrugas.

Historical Background of Zadruga

The word *zadruga* is not strictly a folk term, having been introduced into the literature by Karadžić in his first dictionary of the Serbian language in 1818. Subsequently, the term was incorporated into legal codes. *Kuća* (household, or, literally, hearth) is more commonly used in rural areas up to the present. Earliest records of the Serbian zadruga date from the thirteenth and fourteenth centuries. We have seen that the Ottoman conquest, by destroying the Serbian medieval state and its urban component, thereby helped perpetuate the zadruga. During periods of great insecurity it had many advantages as a defense unit. The zadruga was also adapted functionally to the mixed agricultural and herding economy that characterized the extensive pioneering efforts subsequently undertaken in central Serbia. In addition, the Ottoman practice of taxation by hearth encouraged large groupings and, from the Turkish point of view, made taxes easier to assess and collect.

Under Serbian civil law, in effect from 1844 to 1946, kinship was the primary basis for the legal definition of the zadruga (nonrelatives could also become members). The zadruga was not exclusively a patrilineal group, since it was possible for men as well as women to marry into it. The ideal pattern, however, was reflected in the fact that a son-in-law was generally looked down upon in such a situation. A widow could return to her natal zadruga particularly if she had no children.

Generally all members resided in the same household compound, which contained the single hearth plus various types of outbuildings similar to those noted by Karadžić. An advantage of the zadruga system was that it permitted adult males to be absent for considerable periods without unduly disrupting the household economy or leaving wives and children unprotected or unprovided for. For example, several men from the same zadruga could be away herding pigs in the woods or taking care of the cattle or sheep in areas considerably removed from the homestead. Similarly, it was possible for peasants to engage in long distance trade in swine and other livestock, as described in Chapter 1. During the slack season some zadruga members could do long-range carting or go to work in towns for considerable periods, knowing that things were being taken care of at home.

Finally, the zadruga was so useful an institution from an organizational point of view that the Austro-Hungarian Empire used Serb military colonies based on the zadruga pattern in Turkish border areas.

Common property holdings were the foundation of the structure of the zadruga. Major holdings were usually in land (although zadruga type organizations also existed among some town merchants). Not all property was held collectively, however: Clothing, bedding, and other small items of personal use were owned individually or by the nuclear unit. Minor economic enterprise could be carried on separately—raising chickens and selling eggs, cheese, garden vegetables, and flax and hemp seeds. In this way mothers amassed the means for their daughters' trousseaus. A dowry of land brought by an in-marrying bride appears to have been a later and disruptive development.

Increase in individual property within the zadruga, the possibility of cash income, and variations in personal consumption patterns placed strain on zadruga ties and were potent factors in bringing about a more accelerated division than that which might normally occur.

But such was the spirit of communal enterprise generated by the zadruga system that even after division, newly separated households continued to cooperate in many ways. Close kin ties were maintained, reinforced by the fact that those who left the parental zadruga often settled on an adjoining plot of land.

The zadruga as an effective collective work unit was also related to the agricultural technology that existed in Serbia during much of the nineteenth century. The forerunner of the wooden plow, a very simple single-handled ard drawn by several yoke of oxen, required the cooperative labor of a number of men in order to be used most effectively. Harvesting grain was done with sickles instead of scythes, a back-breaking, labor intensive practice that continued well into the twentieth century.

The zadruga, like the Russian *mir*, was not only an important part of village organization but also a symbol of national life to which social theorists attached great importance. Svetozar Marković, usually looked upon as one of the founders of socialism in Serbia, felt that the zadruga embodied "the purest form of collectivism" which if perfected would "elevate society from egoism to altruism, from exploitation to justice." At the same time, he felt that the zadruga was breaking up due to bureaucratic abuses and the intrigues of money lenders.[2] For the early nineteenth century one could say that in Serbia the system of social organization was in large measure influenced by the zadruga pattern. In his discussion of the role of the household head Karadžić concludes: "There is a headman who oversees the village or a whole district. At the time of Karadjordje each of his military chieftains was the headman in his district and he himself was the headman in his Serbia."

---

[2] In W. D. McClellan, *Svetozar Marković and the Origins of Balkan Socialism*, Princeton, Princeton University Press, 1964, p. 251.

Some households still bake round wheaten loaves.

The Household Head

Some of the ideal attitudes of zadruga life as well as glimpses of actual behavior are reflected in the writings of a Serb ethnologist of the early twentieth century, Jeremija Pavlović, who studied Šumadija in the period before the first world war. His primary occupation was as a village schoolteacher, and his long residence in the area enabled him to know it well. He observed for this period that, as in earlier times, the starešina was usually the eldest male but might also be an exceptional younger man who was frugal, clever, and honest, who in his work and thoughts set an example for the other members of the household. According to Pavlović the headman was selected on the basis of the consensus of all adult members of the household, although he notes cases of individuals forcefully taking over the leadership. A tyrannical or incompetent elder could instill fear or exploit his position for personal aggrandizement or sexual advantage, particularly if the zadruga were a rich one and employed workers from outside.

The starešina was supposed to be vigorous and industrious; in the phrasing of a folk saying, "He who cannot work cannot give orders." Although he represented the zadruga in its dealings with the village council, the state government, and the church, he was not supposed to sell anything without the explicit agreement of the other members of the household. When he made purchases he was supposed to inform the others of the items and prices.

Usually there was some division of the zadruga on the death of the headman. This could occur along nuclear family lines; often the youngest married male and his family would leave. Patterns of mutual help with housebuilding and agricultural work frequently continued after division.

The headwoman, usually the wife of the starešina, continued to be important. She divided the women's work, kept an eye on household goings-on so that no one took anything to which she was not entitled, and made sure that all contributed in equal measure to the functioning of the household. The other women were obliged to respect her and to accept her advice about the performance of household tasks. She was supposed to act respectfully to the headman who, according to Pavlović, did not single her out from the other women. In keeping with the patrilineal structure, a sister of the household head could openly criticize an in-marrying woman; on the other hand, an in-marrying sister-in-law or daughter-in-law could speak frankly, in private, only to her own husband.

If he so wished the husband could speak openly to others about any problems his wife had within the zadruga group, but she was not supposed to speak of these directly. In addition to the weekly rotation of cooking and baking, other distaff chores continued to include care of the house and courtyard, raising poultry, milking, carrying meals to the men in the fields, and at times helping with the hoeing and the livestock. Running the house was exclusively women's domain. According to a folk saying, "In the house the woman is the head and the man a guest."[3]

Conflict in the Zadruga

There were many potential points of strain. A zadruga member who had a special craft had to turn over his earnings to the household head. If the zadruga sent one of its young men to school, then a conflict about his rights of inheritance might develop subsequently. Although all were supposed to share equally, the person who was given an education and as a result left the village was supposed to give up his hereditary rights or, if the zadruga divided, first to try to sell his land to an interested zadruga or lineage member at a fair price. The zadruga also financed the wedding expenses of its male members, the eldest unmarried male usually marrying first. Generally the first wedding was a large celebration. Traditionally it was a disgrace for it to be otherwise, despite possible objections by some members. Conflict could also arise over the unequal number of children in the individual nuclear families. Each mother was responsible for seeing that her children got all the food they needed. Further complications might arise upon the death of a member. A widower generally remarried as soon as possible, particularly if there were young children. Adoption within the zadruga was common; if both parents died the starešina and his wife, usually the eldest uncle and aunt, acted as foster parents.

---

[3] Excerpted and translated from Jeremija Pavlović, *Život i običaji narodni u Kragujevačkoj Jasenici u Šumadiji* (Folk Life and Customs in Jasenica Region of Kragujevac District in Šumadija), Belgrade, Srpski Etnografski Zbornik 22, Srpska Kraljevska Akademija, 1921, pp. 79–87.

"In the house the woman is the head and the man a guest."

In terms of the quality of actual relationships, in the past as well as today, the most important ties remain agnatic ones, that is, those through the male line. Zadrugas change in composition—a particular individual will almost certainly belong to more than one zadruga in his lifetime, or his zadruga will greatly alter in composition in the course of his life—but the specific kin ties will remain the constants in social relationships. One is always a brother, or a father, but for only a limited period of time is one part of a household with a fixed constellation of members. Serbian kinship terminology reflects overlapping of household (roughly comparable to the mid-nineteenth century zadruga), neighborhood, and village.

The Vamilija

The common descent group, *vamilija*, was not a lineage in the strict sense of the term since it was not a corporate group, nor livestock or landowning group. However, particular vamilijas tended to live in distinct neighborhoods, and even today in Orašac the various neighborhoods generally reflect this fact and are identified as such. Geographic proximity combined with knowledge of relationship in the male line has meant, and continues to mean, that the vamilija has a sense of solidarity reflected in work exchanges, mutual help, and lending, and a general sense of unity reinforced by common attendance at crisis rites such as weddings and funerals. Although vengeance-seeking is more characteristic of the mountainous areas from which they originated, vamilijas very definitely function as common interest groups with respect to other vamilijas in the village and to outside groups in general (see Chapter 3, pp. 70–72). Friendship is often considered to be coextensive with kin ties. With regard to a person he knows and deals with often, a villager remarks, "How can I consider him a friend since he isn't a relative?"

Within the vamilija the adjective *rodjen* is an important classifier, distinguishing one's immediate kin from those more distant. For example, as can be seen by the kinship diagrams (Figures 1 and 2) all cousins, whether matrilineal or patrilineal, can be and usually are referred to in everyday conversation as *brat* or *sestra*, brother or sister. But if the speaker wishes to define exactly whom they are, he will refer to his own brothers and sisters as *rodjeni*, "born," and the others will be defined according to the uncle or aunt who links them to ego; for example, *brat od strica*, cousin, is brother (of one's own generation in a classificatory sense) related through *stric*, father's brother. Similarly a *deda* or *baba* can be anyone of the grandparental generation, either a grandparent or a great-uncle or great-aunt, but a *rodjeni deda* is one's true grandfather. The term *nerodjeni* is used only when it is necessary to be explicit in a negative sense. In more general terms *stric* can often be used to refer to a member of the parental generation within the vamilija, but *rodjeni stric* can only be father's brother.

A traditional way of artificially extending kin ties between individuals of approximately similar age who wish to have a deeper personal relationship is blood-brotherhood. The position of *kum*, godfather, is usually inherited in the male line. *Kumstvo* is a ritual link of highest regard between households, and inter-marriage is not permitted.

Significantly, all in-marrying females are referred to by a common term *sna* (or *snaha, snaja*), whether brother's wife, son's wife, or grandson's wife, reflect-ing to a large degree their common status under the traditional patrilineal zadruga system. From the in-marrying bride's point of view, however, there are specific terms for her husband's brother (*dever*) and husband's brother's wife (*jetrva*). (On the other hand, in the reciprocal relationship her husband refers to her own brother and her brother's wife by the same term, distinguished by sex only [*šurak, šurnjaja*].) From another perspective the patriarchal structure of the Serbian kinship system is stressed by the fact that the same term (*tetka*) serves for both father's and mother's sister, while terms for father's brother (*stric*) and mother's brother (*ujak*) are not only for these relatives but can be broadened to include their wives, children, and close kin, for example: *strina* (father's brother's wife), *brat od stric* (son of father's brother), *stričevi* (close kin of father's brother). In female affinal relations there is only one term, *zet*, to refer to daughter's husband, sister's husband (on either side), and husband's sister's husband. It is clear, then, that patrilineal kin terminology tends to be more specific and matrilineal tends to be more classificatory.

The formally unequal positions of patrilineal and matrilineal lines are symbolized in a village expression attributing to the former links by blood and to the latter links through milk. But it is precisely in the context of these asymmetrical emphases that artificially extended kin ties like the kum relationship and matrilineal kin take on important functions as a means of providing a degree of psychological balance in the network of social relationships, especially in the affective sense. This situation is exemplified by comparing the roles of stric and ujak. As father's brother, *stric* may well be a potentially adoptive father in the traditional zadruga setting should one's own father die, and, especially in a modern context, may be a neighbor with whom one enters into patterns of work exchange as well as a closely relevant model for competitive socioeconomic status. Since father and stric were part of the same household, there usually has been a history of property division with all its attendant conflicts. By contrast, mother's brother, *ujak*, is free of these constraints. Ujak is an honored guest on important ceremonial occasions at the home of his sister's husband, such as the feast day of that household's patrilineal patron saint (which the stric, of course, celebrates on the same day) and the wedding of his sister's and brother-in-law's son, in which he plays a formal role. Like the kum, the ujak can be a counselor in time of need and can freely express affection, unconstrained by potential jealousies among frequently interacting cousins and unrelated to economic self-interest.

The fraternal tie has been stressed as a basis for the traditional zadruga. Also important is the bond between brother and sister. Although the sister married out, her ties with her brother's kin group remained important and indeed gave her identity as an individual, the marital bond implying, as it did traditionally, formal subordination. In fact, in the folk ethos the bond between brother and sister is seen as a sacred one, more binding psychologically than that between husband and wife. This is reflected in folk poetry, much of it declaring sentiments similar to "Nought

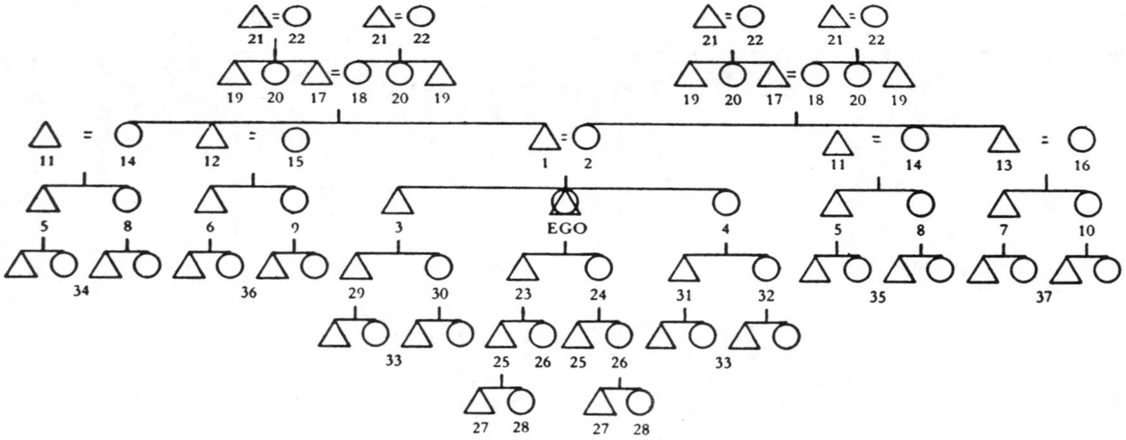

Fig. 1 Serb kinship system

1 Father, *otac, tata,* or *ćale*
2 Mother, *majka, mama,* or *mati*
3 Brother, *rodjeni brat*
4 Sister, *rodjena sestra*
5 Cousin (father's sister's son), *brat od tetke*
6 Cousin (mother's sister's son), *brat od tetke*
7 Cousin (father's brother's son), *brat od strica*
8 Cousin (mother's brother's son), *brat od ujaka*
9 Cousin (father's sister's daughter), *sestra od tetke*
10 Cousin (mother's sister's daughter), *sestra od tetke*
11 Cousin (father's brother's daughter), *sestra od strica*
12 Cousin (mother's brother's daughter), *sestra od ujaka*

11 Uncle (father's sister's husband), *tetak* or *teča*
   Uncle (mother's sister's husband), *tetak* or *teča*
12 Uncle (father's brother), *stric*
13 Uncle (mother's brother), *ujak*
14 Aunt (father's sister), *teka*
   Aunt (mother's sister), *teka*
15 Aunt (father's brother's wife), *strina*
16 Aunt (mother's brother's wife), *ujna*
17 Grandfather, *deda, rodjeni*
18 Grandmother, *baba, rodjena*
19 Great-uncle, *deda, nerodjeni*
20 Great-aunt, *baba, nerodjena*
21 Great-grandfather, *pradeda*
22 Great-grandmother, *prababa*
23 Son, *sin*
24 Daughter, *kći* or *ćerka*

25 Grandson, *unuk*
26 Granddaughter, *unuka*
27 Great-grandson, *praunuk*
28 Great-granddaughter, *praunuka*
29 Nephew (brother's son), *sinovac*
30 Niece (brother's daughter), *sinovica*
31 Nephew (sister's son), *sestrić*
32 Niece (sister's daughter), *sestričina*
33 Grandnieces and grandnephews, *unuci, nerodjeni*
34 Relatives (on father's sister's side), *tetkići* or *rodbina*
35 Relatives (on mother's sister's side), *tetkići* or *svojta*
36 Relatives (on father's brother's side), *stričevi* or *rodbina*
37 Relatives (on mother's brother's side), *ujevići* or *svojta*

24

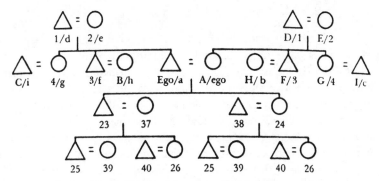

Relationship to *Ego* (male) represented by character left of oblique bar, that to *ego* (female) by character right of bar.

1 Father, *otac, tata,* or *ćale*
2 Mother, *majka, mama,* or *mati*
3 Brother, *rodjeni brat*
4 Sister, *rodjena sestra*
23 Son, *sin*
24 Daughter, *kći* or *ćerka*
25 Grandson, *unuk*

26 Granddaughter, *unuka*
37 Daughter-in-law, *sna, snaha, snaja,* or *snajka*
38 Son-in-law, *zet*
39 Granddaughter-in-law, *sna za unukom*
40 Grandson-in-law, *zet za unukom*

Male Affinal
A Wife, *žena*
B Brother's wife, *sna*
C Sister's husband, *zet*
D Wife's father, *tast*
E Wife's mother, *tašta*
F Wife's brother, *šurak*
G Wife's sister, *svastika*
H Wife's brother's wife, *šurnjaja*
I Wife's sister's husband, *pašenog*

Female Affinal
a Husband, *muž*
b Brother's wife, *sna*
c Sister's husband, *zet*
d Husband's father, *svekar*
e Husband's mother, *svekrva*
f Husband's brother, *dever*
g Husband's sister, *zaova*
h Husband's brother's wife, *jetrva*
i Husband's sister's husband, *zet*

Fig. 2 Affinal relations

heals the heart that mourns a dead brother," which places love for a brother above that for a husband. Such idealized sentiments must be viewed cautiously, but it does seem clear that the strongest and most enduring loyalties were to the household into which one was born. However, when an in-marrying woman became a mother of a son, and as her son grew to maturity, her roles as sister and daughter declined until they became of decisively secondary importance.

In distinguishing contemporary social structure from the traditional zadruga, an important difference is the assertion and coming into prominence of the marriage tie, with a corresponding decline in the brother-sister link. Explicitly, the loyalty and affection of husband and wife to each other has begun to assume at least as great a role as that of the wife as mother to her children on one hand, and of the husband as son to his father and as father to his own sons, on the other.

Zadruga Size

The early Serbian ethnographers tell of zadrugas of thirty to forty members. Karadžić describes one with 62 members, including 13 couples. As interesting as these impressionistic accounts are, we are fortunate in being able to go further in examining past household size and structure, since quite complete census data for the mid-nineteenth century exist for this part of Šumadija. While it is reasonable to take a somewhat critical attitude toward data gathered a century ago from a population that was largely illiterate, in this instance the sample is large enough and the material sufficiently consistent internally and correlative in a logical fashion with materials available later, that it is very useful as a baseline for measuring subsequent change.

The usual picture presented in most descriptive studies of the zadruga is that of the large zadruga unit splitting into smaller nuclear family groups as a result of modernization. According to data from the census of 1863, the largest household in Orašac was composed of 23 members, and five of a total of 214 households were of this size. In 1961 there were no households of comparable size, the six largest (of a total of 453) having ten and eleven members.

Stated another way, in 1863 approximately one-third (32 percent) of all Orašac households with ten or more members contained half (49 percent) of the total population. By 1961 households with ten or more members represented only 1.3 percent of all households, or 3.1 percent of the total population of the village. Over a period of approximately a hundred years the *average* household size declined by almost half (8.3 members to 4.5).

Demographic Variables

Gross size, while certainly important, does not tell much about actual kinship structure of the zadruga itself. It is necessary to explore the demographic variables, age and sex, and to see to what extent they condition or provide parameters for the expression of social forms. By comparing the age structure of the population of Orašac for 1863, 1890, and 1961 we see an expected trend: decrease in size of the youngest age group (ten years and younger), from 42 percent to 32 percent to 18 percent; if age 20 and under are considered, the figures decline from 63 percent to 55 percent to 33 percent, a proportionate decline by about half over a century. On the other hand, in the age-51-and-over group there is over a five-fold increase from 5 percent to 10 percent to 28 percent.

Records indicate that from the 1880s (when age at marriage was first recorded) to the 1960s the overwhelming majority of men and women married between the ages of 16 and 27, most women by 21. An assumption of approximately twenty years between generations seems reasonable. Comparing 1863 and 1961, we can see that the different age and sex distributions make possible contrasting kinds of kin structures. Thus in 1863 the large proportion of the total population in the age-20-and-under group indicates that there were more children, while in 1961 the greatly increased number of people age 51 and over suggests a greater proportionate presence of the grandparental and in some cases of the great-grand-parental generation. In 1961 the over-60 group had 197 women and 141 men; the contrast with 1863 (7 women, 16 men) is dramatic in that during this period the total population only doubled. The relatively greater number of older men in 1863 is probably a reflection of the high maternal mortality rate at that time. The 1961 data reflects war losses and, for women, improved life expectancy after the high mortality rate in childbirth had been largely overcome.

Relationship to Household Head

Taking household members' relationship to headman (or household head, as we can now call him) as a frame of reference for analyzing household kin units, in 1863, out of a total population of 1082, 633 individuals or 59 percent of the population were 19 and under, and approximately two-thirds of these were sons and daughters. The young people were occasionally his siblings or grandchildren or, more frequently, his nephews and nieces. These last two categories again indicate the importance of extended family relationships. The presence of young siblings and married brothers specifically indicates fraternal zadrugas or the possibility of the early death of parents or other elders. (Two of the 131 household heads were women.)

In looking at the kin composition of the households having ten or more members in 1863, we find that of the 529 people in this group 145 are unmarried sons and daughters. When the 42 household heads and 37 wives are added to the latter figure, we see that some 244 or over 42 percent of the kin composing the larger households consist of relationships common to the nuclear family. Looking at it another way, the extended kin component in the descending generation's married sons (32), daughters-in-law (32), and also grandchildren (76) comprise 140 people or some 26 percent of the people in the larger households. (Married sons and married brothers are considered here as extended kin since their status pre-supposes the existence of nuclear family units other than that of the household head.) Laterally extended kin, that is married brothers with their wives (50) and children (83), amount to approximately 25 percent. The remaining 7 percent are siblings of the household head (24), mothers (7), and in one case, father. These are, in a sense, leftover kin ties after the death of the male parental head of the household, where responsibility is assumed by a son, usually the eldest.

If one compares the average number of children for the household head (3.5), his married brother (3.3), and his married son (2.4), it seems clear that the relationship between brothers can be seen as a relatively stable one in terms of family completion, while the married son with his wife will most likely become part of a reconstituted zadruga before their childbearing stage is over. That is to say, the household head's parents or, more probably, his father, will have died before his own son's nuclear family formation is completed. Here a direct comparison with contemporary data is not possible since, as we have seen, only slightly over 3 percent of the population lives in ten or more member households.

Since 1863 a marked transformation has taken place in the overall kin structure of the household unit. This is evidenced by looking at all kin composing the household, as defined by their relationship to the household head. Table 1 lists kin terms found in 1863, 1928, 1948, 1953, and 1961 in order of magnitude. Terms occurring most frequently in 1863 are son and daughter, followed by head of household and, in fourth place, his wife. Beginning in 1928 a stable pattern emerges that carries through consistently to 1953 (despite the incompleteness of the 1928 data and subsequent overweighting of household head, and in spite of the presence in 1948 of a group of German miners and accompanying families who subsequently left by 1953, thereby restoring the village to ethnic homogeneity). The order of frequency becomes household head, son, wife, and daughter. (The earlier pattern seems to reflect the large number of children and, to a degree, maternal mortality.) The newer pattern (1928–1953) indicates that the father-son relationship is the most frequent kin tie. By 1961 this was replaced by the household head-wife dyad. The position of the daughter recedes from second place in 1863 to fourth in 1928, where it remains at present.

What is clearly reflected in these figures is, first, that a daughter marries out as soon as she reaches her late teens or early twenties, and second, that the sons in general remain home, at least for a longer time. As the number of sons borne by individual mothers decreases, as the mother increasingly survives childbirth, as both parents live to a relatively old age, and as sons increasingly leave home, the husband-wife dyad now has a much greater possibility of persisting longer, outlasting that of father-son.

Nuclear Family Relationships

When taken as a unit, the nuclear family relationships among head, son, wife, and daughter consistently constitute two-thirds of the population for all years (percentages vary between 65 and 68). Mid-nineteenth-century Orašac and modern Orašac both evidence extended family ties. The nuclear family relationships, however, have been and remain at the core of village social structure. This occurs despite a drop in the percentage of nuclear family households (31 percent in 1863 to 22 percent in 1961). The relative number of extended families of all kinds also decreased over the century (from 64 percent in 1863 to 58 percent in 1961). There was a similar decline in the number of nuclear units within the extended-family households, offset to a degree by an eight-fold proportionate increase in single individuals and couples (almost all elderly) living alone in 1961 (16 percent) as compared to 1863 (2 percent).

Although relationships within the context of the nuclear family account for two-thirds of the kin terms, clearly they do not account for the high proportion of extended households, where key relationships are those of married brother, daughter-in-law, and grandchildren. The relatively high frequency of married brother (with members of brother's nuclear family) in 1863 testifies to the prominance of the fraternal zadruga at that time. These fraternal family units constitute 13 percent of the total population in 1863; they total 19 percent if unmarried siblings are included. By 1961 these kin represent barely 1 percent of the total population. The

TABLE 1
ORAŠAC KIN TERMS, IN ORDER OF FREQUENCY, 1863–1961

	1863		1928e		1948		1953		1961	
	R.O.a	Abs.#b	R.O.	Abs.#	R.O.	Abs.#	R.O.	Abs.#	R.O.	Abs.#
Household Head	3	131	1	333	1	495	1	464	1	453
Son	1	257	2	302	2	391	2	409	3	350
Wife	4	112	3	227	3	335	3	358	2	367
Daughter	2	203	4	171	4	262	4	254	4	194
Daughter-in-law / Brother's wifec	6	78	5	158	5	174	5	190	5	160
Grandson	7	56	6	131	6	153	6	154	5	163
Granddaughter	10	39	7	108	7	134	7	144	7	152
Mother	12	21	8	47	8	109	8	75	8	78
Brother	5	68	9	32	9	32	9	15	10	11
Brother's daughter	8	46	11	15	12	18		3	11	3
Sister	11	25	12	12	10	31	10	14	10	11
Brother's son	9	43	10	27	11	24	11	13	12	3
Grandmother				3	14	9	12	10	11	10
Son-in-law				2		8	13	8	9	12
Great-granddaughter			13	8		8	10	14	9	12
Great-grandson			13	8		6	13	8	9	12
Father		1		1	13	10		3		5
Otherd		2				22		26		27
Total Population		1082		1585		2221f		2169		2023

a Rank Order.
b Absolute Numbers.
c Same kin term used in Serb-Croatian; in 1863 there were 47 married sons; in 1961, 143.
d All other kin terms and terms for any nonkin included in this category.
e Data not complete for 1928.
f Includes a number of ethnic German miners temporarily resident in village.

importance of fraternally associated ties in 1863 is traceable directly to age structure: At that period, only 30 percent of all household heads were over 50 years of
age but a century later 61 percent were past this age. Therefore, by the time the
eldest brother married and· began to have a family, and certainly by the time his
younger brothers began to found families, their father most likely would have died,
the eldest son succeeding him as head. Increased longevity of the father has been
a factor in the decline of the fraternal zadruga.

The number of three-generation households is proportionately greater in
1961 than in 1863 (42 percent compared to 35 percent). Four-generation households, representing 7 percent of households in 1961, did not exist in 1863. Households of two or more generations increase from a third of all households in 1863
to about half of all Orašac households in 1961.[4]

Correlated with this trend, there is also a more than three-fold increase
in the number of daughters-in-law over the century (with an approximate doubling

[4] Joel M. Halpern and David Anderson, "The Zadruga: A Century of Change,"
Anthropologica, 1970, n. s. 12, pp. 83–97.

of the population), although the percentage of households containing more than one daughter-in-law declined from 8 percent in 1863 to under 3 percent in 1961.

These diverse clues all point the way to a transformation of the extended household from that of lateral extension across two generations to one of lineal extension through three or four generations. Viewed in terms of dyadic relationships, the bonds that have not endured through time are those between married brothers, or between sisters-in-law, regardless of whether we are talking of the fraternal zadruga or the zadruga composed of a father and several married sons; these relationships within the household have, in effect, disappeared. However, the ties between a father and married son remaining in the household have proved stable, as have ties between a mother-in-law and her sole daughter-in-law. Indeed, as in the case of great-grandchildren, or the presence of a mother or even grandmother, these ties can exist across several generations within a particular extended family unit.

It is therefore not correct to think in terms of the dissolution of the extended family. A better term is *reformulation*.

Lineal Extension over Generations

Extension over the generations can occur in two ways (relative to the household head): through the survival of the parents and possibily grandparents as well, or in the case of grandchildren and possibly even an additional descending generation. Both forms have been occurring in recent times. There are almost four times as many mothers of household heads listed in 1961 than in 1863 (78 opposed to 21). In 1961 there were ten grandmothers of household heads listed; there were none in 1863. There are also a few fathers (five in 1961), but only one in 1863. Even more significant is the growth in the descending generations: The 1961 census lists more than three times as many grandchildren (315 versus 95 in 1863) plus an entirely new category, great-grandchildren (24). Obviously, four generations are also contained in households with a surviving mother of household head and the presence of grandchildren.

Thus we now see increasing complexity and variety in household kinship patterns. The fraternal zadruga has in effect disappeared, and fraternal kin ties within the zadruga are now virtually negligible (slightly over one percent). Instead we find, in addition to the totally new four generation household, an increasing presence of people in ascending generations. There is also a small but growing presence of matrilineal kin (1961 records show twelve instances of son-in-law, nine of wife's mother, two of brother-in-law, and four of aunt—none of these categories were present a century earlier).

A Case Study

Such are the overall statistical patterns. But how are they reflected in the structure of real households that existed at the time of the 1863 census? This is possible to check, since many of the more perceptive elder male members of contemporary Orašac society verbally can trace their ancestors back over four generations as well as account for their descendents. Figure 3 shows the 105 male members of the Stojanović lineage, beginning with the founder Stojan. When men reconstruct these genealogies they usually cannot recall in similar detail female kin, consanguineal or affinal. Nor can they reconstruct with accuracy preexisting zadrugas except those in which they themselves (or possibly their parents) participated. Further, comparisons between the early census figures and personal genealogies obtained from elderly informants suggest that males who died relatively young may have been overlooked and omitted, or the total number of children born may be recalled but their sex forgotten. In many cases it appears that only those who survived to adulthood, founded families, and remained in the village are recalled with a high degree of accuracy. This in itself is often quite a feat of memory.

Two 1863 households are illustrated by those headed by the Stojanović cousins Uroš and Radovan, grandsons of Stojan (numbers 6 and 12 in Figure 3; see also Figures 4 and 5). In Uroš' household, where he functioned as the head of a fraternal zadruga, the comparatively large size relates in part to the relatively large number of children borne by his own wife, the wife of a deceased elder brother, and the wife of a younger brother. In the case of Radovan's rather small household, Radovan's father died while most of his children were young; there were only unmarried siblings when Radovan, as eldest son, succeeded to the headship. A new cycle of family formation takes place.

As a household labor force, obviously the former example is stronger than the latter, in fact as well as in potential. The sons and nephews of Uroš will be coming of age and able to contribute substantially, while Radovan in 1863 has to depend on himself and his two younger brothers, with a considerable wait for the next generation of males. In terms of able-bodied males over the age of 15, Uroš' household has four, with five more coming of age in the succeeding decade, while Radovan's household has three (and does not add to its labor force until Radovan's prospective eldest son reaches age 15, an event which will not occur for 23 years; see Figure 5).

HOUSEHOLD AS LABOR UNIT

The real potential for prosperity and status in the traditional Orašac household relates directly to the number of able-bodied males. This is particularly true in view of the fact that all were peasant small-holders; there were no tenant farmers, absentee landholders, or servants, although there was considerable inequality in size of holdings.

In 1910 Pavlović wrote,

When a father has six or seven healthy sons, he truly impoverishes himself while feeding them until they mature, but afterward, if they are only able to get along well together, they will become so prosperous that no one will surpass their level. They will always have workers in their fields, because other households will always be indebted in labor exchange.[5]

---

[5] Pavlović, *Život i običaji narodni u Kragujevačkoj Jasenici u Šumadiji,* p. 82.

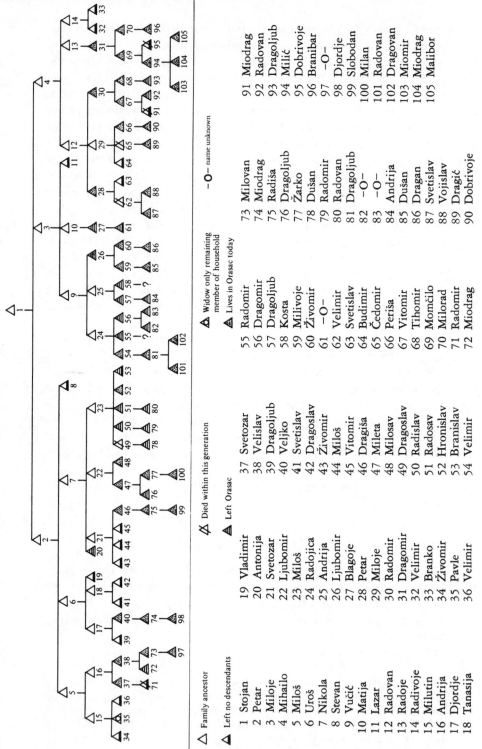

1 Stojan	37 Svetozar	55 Radomir	73 Milovan
2 Petar	38 Velislav	56 Dragomir	74 Miodrag
3 Miloje	39 Dragoljub	57 Dragoljub	75 Radiša
4 Mihailo	40 Veljko	58 Kosta	76 Dragoljub
5 Miloš	41 Svetislav	59 Milivoje	77 Žarko
6 Uroš	42 Dragoslav	60 Živomir	78 Dušan
7 Nikola	43 Živomir	61 −O−	79 Radomir
8 Stevan	44 Miloš	62 Velimir	80 Radovan
9 Vučić	45 Vitomir	63 Svetislav	81 Dragoljub
10 Matija	46 Dragiša	64 Budimir	82 −O−
11 Lazar	47 Mileta	65 Čedomir	83 −O−
12 Radovan	48 Milosav	66 Periša	84 Andrija
13 Radoje	49 Dragoslav	67 Vitomir	85 Dušan
14 Radivoje	50 Radislav	68 Tihomir	86 Dragan
15 Milutin	51 Radosav	69 Momčilo	87 Svetislav
16 Andrija	52 Hronislav	70 Milorad	88 Vojislav
17 Djordje	53 Branislav	71 Radomir	89 Dragić
18 Tanasija	54 Velimir	72 Miodrag	90 Dobrivoje
19 Vladimir			91 Miodrag
20 Antonija			92 Radovan
21 Svetozar			93 Dragoljub
22 Ljubomir			94 Milić
23 Miloš			95 Dobrivoje
24 Radojica			96 Branibar
25 Andrija			97 −O−
26 Ljubomir			98 Djordje
27 Blagoje			99 Slobodan
28 Petar			100 Milan
29 Miloje			101 Radovan
30 Radomir			102 Dragovan
31 Dragomir			103 Miomir
32 Velimir			104 Miodrag
33 Branko			105 Malibor
34 Živomir			
35 Pavle			
36 Velimir			

Fig. 3 Stojanović genealogy

32

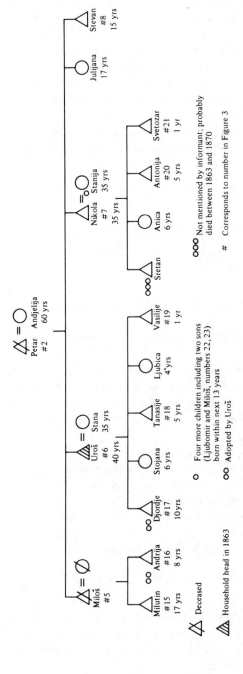

Fig. 4 *Household of Uroš Stojanović, 1863 (18 members, with 5 able-bodied men)*

A village elder reflects in 1970, "A good *gazda* [prosperous peasant] was one who had sons and therefore didn't have to exploit anyone. A man who had no sons was truly poor. This is so even today."

Just as possible wealth may come from a large and well-functioning household, so, for the same reason, has prosperity been threatened by the break-up of the labor group through death or division. There is a folk attitude that the well-being of a peasant household survives fifty years; after this time change for the worse, according to traditional values, is inevitable.

In looking at the history of the extended family in Serbia an important consideration is this: As long as farming was the only realistic means of livelihood for most villagers, and the strength of the family labor unit was effective in increasing production, large fraternal zadrugas and paternal zadrugas with several married sons and many grandchildren made economic sense. With growing opportunities

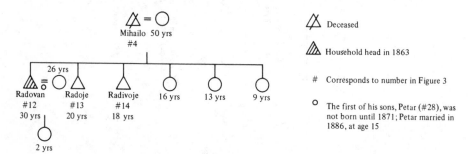

Fig. 5 Household of Radovan Stojanović, 1863 (9 members, with 3 able-bodied men)

outside the village, with the introduction of machinery, even if on a limited scale, and perhaps most importantly with the filling up of the land and the decreasing importance of livestock herding, the large labor units represented by the zadruga became less and less functional. These are some of the causes of reformulation of household kin units.

Earlier the zadruga was an effective production, trading, and defense unit. In more recent times it has largely disappeared in a formal sense. Its general influence persists, however, and has resulted in a useful social form for taking care of the greater number of elderly people as well as for utilizing the labor of the aged by families where the able-bodied male of the middle generation has a job in town while retaining his holding in the village. (This, of course, is not true in all cases, as the growing number of single people and elderly couples living alone indicates.)

THE FAMILIAL CYCLE

Returning to an examination of the 1863 households of the Stojanović cousins Uroš and Radovan and that of a step-cousin, Dimitrije (Figure 6),[6] we see that although size and potential do vary considerably, all three households have in common the fact that the father (and in Dimitrije's case, the step-father)

---

[6] Dimitrije does not appear in the Stojanović genealogy (Fig. 3); he became part of a Stojanović household as an adopted step-son when the brother of the fathers of Uroš and Radovan married Dimitrije's widowed mother.

has died and the mother survives. Because of the age at which the father's death has occurred and the relative ages of the sons, family formation in each of these households is at a different stage. The process is well underway in the case of Uroš, has just begun in Radovan's case, and has not yet taken place in the case of Dimitrije (recorded as having fathered a son in 1870).

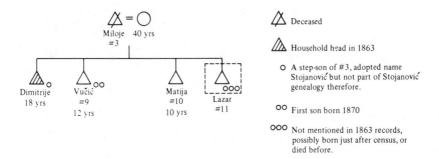

Fig. 6 Household of Dimitrije Stojanović, 1863 (4 members, with 1 able-bodied man)

Following the death of the father, the developmental stages in an extended family household are clear. Fission seems to take place only after the brothers have married and begun to raise families of their own. Analysis of the 1863 statistics reveals that in almost three-fourths of all households in Orašac at the time, there were no daughters-in-law present in relation to the household head (there was, however, one daughter-in-law in almost one-fifth of the households). The characteristic pattern for the period was that of daughter-in-law to a widowed mother whose son was head of the household, as illustrated in the cases of the wives of the brothers Uroš and Nikola.

Not only did the limited life span existing in 1863 structure the kind of kin relationships which were possible, but, in addition, it determined their duration. Most previous writing on the traditional, idealized patterns of zadruga structure make little allowance for these important demographic parameters. For example, the relationship of Dimitrije's eventual wife to his mother, who died in 1879, lasted less than a dozen years.

More than a hundred years later, many new kinds of kin relationships are possible, and because of the increasing life span they are more long lasting.

By viewing household transformation over time one can gain important insights into the basic family unit in Serbian society. A synchronic description of a particular unit is like a photograph that captures a living social institution at a moment in time. Tracing the evolution of one descent group over a century provides a series of images of social process in rural Serbia.

AN INDIVIDUAL CYCLE

Deda Mileta, an Orašac villager in his early seventies, is our guide on a backward look. Based on his recollections and correlated with census data, seven diagrammatic representations of major changes in his household are shown in

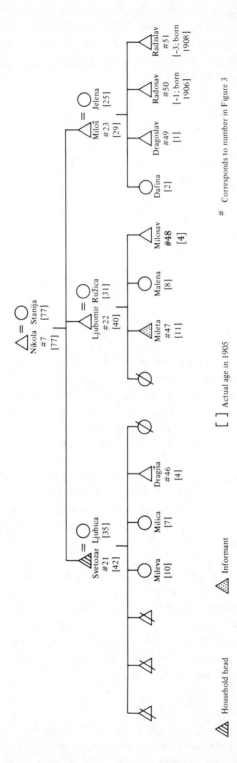

△ Household head

△ Informant

[ ] Actual age in 1905

Corresponds to number in Figure 3

Fig. 7 Composite diagram of household of Svetozar Stojanović, son of Nikola (including children who did not survive), 1894–1909

Figures 8–14. Figure 7, based on memory alone, is not a picture of the household at a given moment but rather a composite, including children who did not survive infancy, from the time of Mileta's birth in 1894 to the division of the zadruga in 1909. The marriage of his younger uncle, in 1900, meant that for about a decade there existed a zadruga of parents, three married sons, and their respective growing

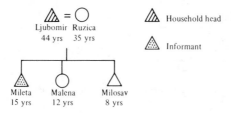

Fig. 8 Household cycle experienced by Mileta Stojanović, 1909 (after uncles divide)

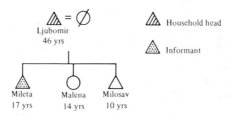

Fig. 9 Household cycle experienced by Mileta Stojanović, 1911 (after mother's death)

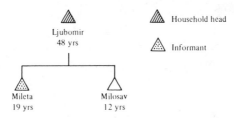

Fig. 10 Household cycle experienced by Mileta Stojanović, 1913 (after sister's death)

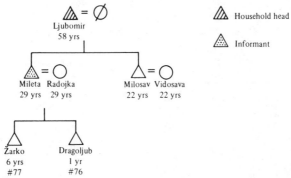

Fig. 11 Household cycle experienced by Mileta Stojanović, 1923 (before brother divides)

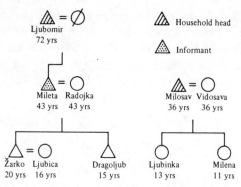

Fig. 12 Household cycle experienced by Mileta Stojanović, 1937 (after brother divides)

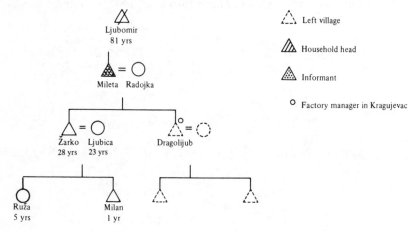

Fig. 13 Household cycle experienced by Mileta Stojanović, 1945 (after father's death)

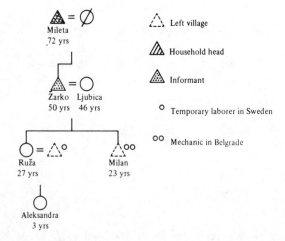

Fig. 14 Household cycle experienced by Mileta Stojanović, 1967

families (Figure 7). This is an example of maximal expansion found around the turn of the century.

FAMILY HISTORY

Deda Mileta is a grandson of Nikola and a grandnephew of Uroš. His personal recollections thus begin with his own deda, Nikola, who apparently became head of the household in 1872, after the deaths of Uroš and their mother (Uroš' sons formed households of their own as they grew up and married).

When recounting his genealogy, however, Mileta likes to begin at the beginning. He adjusts the crown of his fur hat and leans forward. "Listen carefully," he says, "as I tell you how it was." He draws on the cigarette in his whittled holder and begins:

> In the year of the First Revolt, our ancestor Stojan came to Orašac from Montenegro, with his wife and two brothers. He settled in the area that is now near the center of the village. His brothers Andrija and Pavle settled in other sections of the village and founded the vamilijas Andrić and Pavlović. We all share the same patron saint, Archangel Michael. Today people from the three groups can intermarry, but one Stojanović cannot marry another.
>
> Well, listen: Stojan had three sons: Petar, Miloje, and Mihailo. Petar had four sons: Miloš, Uroš, Nikola, and Stevan. Nikola was my grandfather. He had three sons: Svetozar, my father Ljubomir, and Miloš [plus one who left Orašac as a youth]. I was born in 1894, when grandfather Nikola and his wife were already old. My father was the second son, and we all lived together—my oldest uncle, who was head of the house, and his wife and children, my parents and me, and the younger uncle, who was still a bachelor. Nikola was then too old to manage household affairs, just as I, at my age, can no longer go everywhere nor take care of everything.

ZADRUGA OF EIGHTEEN

> Well, Nikola had sixteen hectares and a house with four sleeping rooms plus a kitchen. One room was for him and baba Stanija, and the others for his three sons and their wives and children. No one dared enter deda's room, especially not us children. I remember that after uncle Miloš married we were eighteen together in the zadruga, including ten of us children [Figure 7]. The house was one of the biggest and best in the village. It had beds. All the other houses had oiled paper on the windows, but we had glass, which deda Nikola bought in Belgrade. If I remember correctly, there were also seven outbuildings, including two stalls for our livestock and two corncribs.

Mileta interrupts his narrative. He fits a fresh cigarette into the holder and jabbing with it for emphasis interjects:

> I really ought to mention why deda Nikola was such a cultured person—it was only after he started chasing other women that he started to go bad—well, the reason is, he had a lot of schooling. One of his uncles who had no children of his own decided to school him. At that time there was no school in Orašac, so Nikola finished the four-year school in Bukovik. He did well and continued for three more years in Kragujevac, where he qualified to become a clerk. While working in Topola, then the county seat, he met his wife. She brought to the

family a dowry of 200 ducats, a real dowry in those days. Later Nikola served as a clerk in Orašac, and he held the post for a long time, about twenty years. But after Uroš' death he returned to the land, for he had a good holding. I don't know if all that schooling was really necessary. Look at it this way: his son, my father, had only four years of school. The same with all my uncles. I had four years of school. My own son here had four years.

As I say, Nikola was a good man. And his wife was good, too, a capable and industrious woman. When King Milan visited the village it was her plates and spoons that were used.

HOUSEHOLD ORGANIZATION

Mileta picks up the narrative with his father's generation:

In the evenings my older uncle would sit down with my father and younger uncle and together they talked over what they would do the next day. In the morning the three brothers went about their tasks. Their wives went about their women's work, weaving. In the summer they sometimes helped their men in the fields. Winter in those days was a difficult time for women, because they worked so hard making clothing. Today you can buy whatever you want factory-made. Then, everything was made by hand. They spun and wove all winter long, sometimes almost all night.

Our zadruga was prosperous. We had two wagons, and oxen and horses. We had sheep and a few cows and pigs. We had wagon-loads of wheat. There was enough food for all. Deda Nikola became very old and couldn't do any work. His three sons did all the work. They respected him. They listened to him and to their mother.

That's the way it used to be. Today I, an old man myself, must work and work hard, because my own younger son, with his sons, plus my grandson, son of my elder son Žarko here, have all left the village. I have tried to do some of the work of a younger man.

DIVISION OF ZADRUGA

Some four years after Nikola died, when I was fifteen, our zadruga divided. Why? Because my younger uncle no longer got along with his brothers. He wouldn't listen to them. He wanted to be his own boss. Nothing was written down, they just agreed to divide, and each brother took what was his. The land was fairly divided. Each brother got one sow and about seven sheep. Uncle Svetozar got a wagon, the plow, and a horse. Uncle Miloš got a cow and a horse. He also took the low-lying land and some meadow. Part of the old house was torn down, and Miloš stayed in the other part. Svetozar used some of the old materials to build himself a house on his land, and we did, too, on our land, right where we are now, a few kilometers from the road. Even after division the brothers continued to help one another. We helped in each others' fields and loaned money without interest.

NEW HOUSEHOLD FORMATION

When we came here we were five: my father Ljubomir, my mother, and we three children: I, and a younger sister, and brother [Figure 8]. Together in the zadruga we had all been prosperous. Now, all split up, we were poor. Two years after we divided my mother died, and later, my sister [Figures 9–10]. So for a while we were three. I went to serve in the war and got married when I came home on furlough, so there was a woman in the house. When I returned from service my first son was born.

My brother got married in 1921, and we two remained in one household with our father for 16 years. As it turned out, I had only sons, and my brother had daughters [Figure 11]. He disagreed about several things and after a while he thought the time had come to divide.

Mileta's son, taller than he, with a deeply etched face, wipes his palms on the front of his sweat-stained shirt and sits down on the bench next to his father. "That's the way it goes," he says. Turning to his father, who is content to sit quietly now and smoke, he jokes, "You've told your story, now let me tell mine."

DIVISION AS EXPERIENCED BY SON

Žarko relates:

I grew up in a zadruga composed of my grandfather Ljubomir, my father and my uncle. I was about twenty when uncle Milosav wanted to divide. He wanted to be his own man, the usual story, he thought he could manage better by himself. When we divided, deda Ljubomir remained with his older son, my father. At that time we had seven hectares and 12 ares of land, having slowly increased our holding from the time Ljubomir and his brothers divided. Deda took 80 ares for himself, to be sure he had enough income for his personal needs. Nothing was written down, and we did not go to court. It was all settled at home, between the brothers. The rest was divided between my father Mileta here and uncle Milosav. After deda Ljubomir died they agreed that 20 ares of his land should go to Milosav and the rest stay with us, with the understanding that we, my father and I, would put up a gravestone in deda's name—he died in 1945, at the old age of 81, after he had lived with us and been fed and cared for by us.

The year we divided, I got married [Figure 12]. I remember the division well. Each plot of land was divided in half. We had been living in two simple wood and mud plaster dwellings, not modern houses like the ones we have now, and each brother got one. Uncle Milosav took his apart and moved it over to his piece of land, and since he had to do the hauling he got the wagon and two cows. It was November when they decided to divide, and by March Milosav was already preparing the new site for his house. The pigs, sheep, and chickens were divided. All the utensils and storage barrels, all the containers, were divided. Everything was done by halves, the spoons, forks, everything—one for you and one for you, that's the way it went. Of course, Milosav's bed was his, my father's bed was his, and the items which their own wives and my bride, too, had brought were not included in the division.

WILL, TAXES, AND DIVISION

Since deda Ljubomir did not leave a will, when he was about to die he put his sons on their honor, saying that as he believed in God so his sons should not quarrel and, if that should happen, the one who started it be damned. The land was registered in the names of Mileta and Milosav by mutual agreement, and it was not until ten years later, in 1955, that they were called to court to sign a formal agreement. Up until 1952 our taxes were based on the size of the land holding and the expected income from it, taking into account the number of people in the household; after 1952 taxes were based solely on the amount of land. My uncle realized that under this new system half the taxes were being sought from him. We weren't able to come to an agreement about paying the taxes jointly, as the land was officially in Ljubomir's name until 1954. All this confusion was because we divided just before the war. Who was to say who would remain alive after that horror? Also, before the war legal fees and court action cost a lot, and people tended to put off going to court. Now, of course, that's all changed. Now men and women have equal rights. Before the war only the men had legal rights; girls got a trousseau and sometimes some money, depending on the agreement with the in-laws. After that they had no claim to their family's land or inheritance. But even today they don't insist on their rights, they don't want to claim property from their brothers. It's rare for a woman to insist.

In fact, I don't think my brother Dragoljub will insist on his share, after our father dies. Dragoljub has more schooling than I, he is now a factory manager, he's left the land for good [Figure 13]. The family sent him to school. Our father and I sweated so that he could carry out his wishes. No, I'm sure he won't insist on his legal claim to land.

EDUCATION OF CHILDREN

As for my own children, I have schooled them both equally. Times change. A girl needs an education, too. How things will work out, I don't know. Neither of my children wants to remain on the land to be a peasant. I don't know what they will do and I don't know what I will do.

NEW PROBLEMS

Žarko massages the back of his neck. He looks out over his meadow and is silent. Then:

Mother of God, who ever heard of this problem before? Huh! The way it used to be, the zadruga split, the land and goods were divided in equal parts, and life went on. Who will take care of me and my wife when we are old? Who will work the land? To whom will I leave my land? My brother doesn't need it, and my children don't want it. What will happen if I'm ill and can no longer work? Do I leave the land to someone who will take care of me in old age?

These kinds of problems are new to us. As things stand now, all I know is that a man must work, he must go on. I'll see what is best and then do it, but I surely can't say now how we will finish out our lives [Figure 14].

Familial Cycles and Modernization

These recollections of an old man and the troubled musings of his son bring out many facts. Clearly, zadruga groupings and regroupings have been going on for a long time. The situation has been fluid. Certainly we cannot speak of reformulation of households simply as a result of modern conditions. Basically it is a result of human conditions. These regroupings were taking place in Šumadija and the rest of Serbia (and most of Yugoslavia) long before industrialization began.

The 1863 households of Uroš, Radovan, and Dimitrije illustrate the most frequent cause of a new cycle at that period—death of the head of the household. The bond among brothers was the mainstay of the zadruga. Later, as personal disagreements between brothers developed and as the father began to survive longer, a bond between father and one son became a primary basis for structuring household kin units.

In discussing the zadruga many scholars have spoken of a unit headed by a father as opposed to one composed of brothers heading component nuclear families. As we have seen, these are not mutually exclusive types but are often cyclical stages of household formation which vary through time. The authority of a paternal zadruga head to his married sons is quite different than that of the elected head of a group of brothers. An important qualification is that an older married brother, given the values of Serbian society, would probably exercise as head of the household almost as much authority over a younger unmarried brother as would a father.

In the case of Nikola, although he had in effect yielded power to a son, he nevertheless was probably listed officially as household head. Such is the situation today with Mileta, who despite having turned over most of his actual authority to his son, still continues to be carried on all official village lists as the household head. This follows accepted village practice.

From another aspect, a brother who is head of a zadruga serves at times as a foster father, succeeding to the role of parent as in the case of Uroš where both his father and an older brother have predeceased him. Uroš acted as foster father to the children of his late brother Miloš.

It is difficult to judge the length of tenure of the head of a household. In Nikola's case, he succeeded his brother Uroš in 1872 and approximately twenty years later passed on the role to his eldest surviving son Svetozar. This period of about a generation seems reasonable particularly if one considers effective tenure as opposed to formal occupation of the position.

New Forms

We have mentioned the reformulation of the zadruga. In the early 1970s, in terms of the appearance of four-generation households and the greater percentage and absolute increase in three-generation households, this is, strictly speaking, stretching the term, for in a precise sense the zadruga refers to a household which has at least two nuclear family units. But the essential meaning of reformulation is accurate—the tradition of patrilineal and patrilocal extended household groupings remains viable while land tenure and authority patterns have altered. Notable in the latter regard is the increasing number of female household heads (2 out of 131 households in 1863 as compared with 38 in a total of 453 in 1961).

Of crucial importance for the individual, for village life and, indeed, for the economy of Yugoslavia, is the potential extinction of a particular village household. This is what worries Žarko, not so much for the dying-out of his household as for the very real problem of what will happen to him and his wife.

The successive divisions of zadrugas have taken place within increasingly smaller groups, when viewed in terms of number of members. However, mutual help continues when the group divides; labor is exchanged, equipment is borrowed freely, and money is loaned without interest.

We have seen that dwellings do not survive the social groups that inhabit them. Houses or parts of houses are dismantled and then reconstructed as new houses, much as their occupants split and regroup in new forms.

Kin ties outside the immediate household promote social mobility. In Nikola's case, an uncle provided the means for him to become a clerk. Mileta worked hard as a farmer, and together with his elder son made it possible for his younger son to continue his education past village level and eventually to become a factory supervisor. Žarko has underwritten his two children's departure from the village, aided by partial room and board in Kragujevac provided by his brother, during the years his children were in middle school there.

Modernization does, therefore, explain part of the causes for division. As wage labor becomes more important, conflict increases among nuclear family elements within the zadruga as the child of one unit expresses higher and more expensive ambitions than the child of another. This is what happened in the case of the brothers Mileta and Milosav—within the zadruga, Milosav was expected to contribute equally to his nephew's education.

Another consideration is the increasing closeness of the husband-wife tie at the expense of that of father and son. Formerly, when a villager left to serve in the army, his letters home were addressed to his father or elder brother (it is true that the wife was probably illiterate). Now letters are usually sent directly to the wife, a minor but symbolic gesture.

Households, Houses, and Land

Understanding changing social structural patterns in Šumadija must thus take into account the relationships among individual kin units or households, the actual houses in which they live, and their productive resources in land.

In central and western Europe often one sees farmhouses that are several centuries old. In Orašac occasional houses survive from the early nineteenth century, but these are rare. The common pattern in Orašac seems to have been wooden and mud plaster dwellings which were co-extensive with the particular kin unit, and, as we have seen, when the household divided or reformulated new quarters were built. It is true that Serbian peasant houses of the nineteenth and early twentieth centuries were not imposing structures (as contrasted with the large wood-beamed and stone structures in many parts of Europe), but this in itself is not sufficient to explain the flexible relationship between kin unit and household structure.

To comprehend the matter, the changing size of land holdings also must be understood. (The nature of land use is explored in the next chapter.) It is pertinent to emphasize that the Orašac community evolved in a region that had been forest. Land holdings changed both by expanding cultivated land at the expense of wooded areas and by constant interchange of property, since all sons had the right to inherit. (Areas of Europe in which impartable inheritance existed is where substantial peasant homes enduring over centuries are often found, inheritance patterns having been formalized in written documents, where the kin group can, in a sense, be seen as adapting to the formalized land holding, the substantial dwelling, and the elaborately codified laws.) In Orašac it is the kin unit which appears to have been the central dynamic, with focus on the nature of the household social structure as the primary variable, the dependent variables being the land holdings and physical homestead. A sense of the value of property and the existence of kin conflicts were important here as elsewhere, but the long experience of Turkish rule and the ideal pattern of zadruga organization clearly separate this part of Slavic Europe from neighboring Germanic cultures.

3

Resources, Economy, and Changing Occupations

The Village and the National Culture

T O OBTAIN A VIEW OF A CIVILIZATION IN MINIATURE, as reflected in a specific community, in this case a rural village, we should not lose sight of relationships between what Robert Redfield referred to as the *little tradition* of villagers and the so-called *great traditions* encompassed in national culture, primarily urban life. With urban life in Serbia having grown in significant measure out of village traditions, by looking at the village here we are looking in a very specific way at the genesis of the modern nation of Serbia (subsequently to become one of the major constituents of Yugoslavia at the end of the first world war). Studying a specific community is valuable in itself, and it takes on increasing interest if we know something of the ways in which it is representative of a larger region, or of the rural sector of the nation itself, or how it relates to characteristics of national life.

These are the intended objectives of this chapter. A view of the economic life of Orašac describes the functioning of a specific way of life and presents, as well, a look at an evolving and modernizing culture with deep historic roots. We cannot evaluate the economic patterns of today's Orašac without knowledge of the past, and this may also help to anticipate future change. It is not possible to isolate in neat categories elements which go into the forming of a civilization and influence its subsequent development, but certainly some of the crucial factors can be conceptualized.

The most evident factor for this society originally of herdsmen and farmers is the land, the existing natural base. There are also the traditions and tools, the cultural values and technology concerning the use of these resources, and then the ways of social and political organization including family, household, and nation-state that the population evolved in providing themselves the essentials of life. In a society of nation-state dimensions there is rarely if ever a stable relationship between people, land, and resources; a problem arises as well concerning how the

45

surpluses of goods, and of people, are to be allocated and employed. (Of course, not all nation-states have been successful in the past, but in discussing contemporary peasant societies in the process of modernization, this is to imply that they have a future.) Certain civilizations of the past have disappeared and their populations have become extinct or dispersed. Others have been conquered and out of their political defeat have forged a sense of national identity.

Early History

The Serbs, with their heritage of Kosovo arising from the collapse of the Serbian medieval state, belong to the latter category. A return to central Serbia from the hills of Montenegro was not a migration to a strange place but in a sense a return to an ancestral homeland. As we have seen, resettlement of central Serbia in the eighteenth and nineteenth centuries relates to the decline of Turkish power in central Europe, and equally importantly, coincides with the clashes of Austro-Hungarian, Russian, as well as English and French imperial interests meeting in the Balkans. The Serb nation evolved within this sphere of conflict which influenced all phases of its development.

The lives of the Serbian folk were by no means passive. The frontier theme was present from the beginning, and settlement of the region in which Orašac is located is typified by the experience of Karadjordje, who lived in the nearby settlement of Topola.

Records of Topola date back to the early eighteenth century during the period of Austrian occupation (1718–1738). At that time of relative peace there appears to have been considerable migration into the area. Orašac itself is not mentioned in the records, but Topola is recorded as having six households, and a few other scattered villages in the area having from two to ten households.

Topola and Orašac are located near an old trade route that ran south from Belgrade through Kragujevac to Niš and thence east to Sofia or south to Skoplje. Topola is said to have derived its name from a conspicuous poplar tree near the caravan stop. Orašac, named after a walnut grove, is first mentioned in 1784, and is said to have had a well-built *han*, or inn.

The first inhabitant of Topola and Orašac came from the mountainous Dinaric regions, chiefly the Sandjak and Montenegro. Karadjordje's family migrated to Šumadija at this time, trying several places before settling in Topola around 1781. Later Karadjordje built a house similar to others of that time, little more than a log cabin with a single large room. Because of his active position in resisting the Turks he provided his house with several rifle holes, making counterattack possible if necessary. The eastern side faced the woods, which could be easily reached from a rear door, so that he and his family also could seek refuge in the forest. Like other prosperous villagers, he engaged in livestock trade with Austria and subsequently enlarged his house and holdings. He also had some land and a hideout in a nearby village.

The Nineteenth Century

At that period newcomers as well as older settlers were free to take as much land as they wanted, since the countryside was still relatively empty. In 1808 Karadjordje is said to have mobilized several thousand men for felling the forests around Topola, in this manner to increase his own holdings. The settlement itself grew considerably and became, during the height of his brief rule (he was murdered in 1817), a sort of capital for the new state.

Like his predecessor, Prince Miloš Obrenović used his position to enrich himself, in large part by enclosing lands. He did, however, offer free land to attract new settlers to the area and also granted temporary tax exemptions. In 1820 he ordered his officials to effect a redistribution of land, and this policy became a crucial factor in the political and economic emancipation of the Serb peasantry.

The land began to fill up. From 1834 to 1910 the population density per square kilometer increased from 18 to 60, in a steady upward movement. After 1844 all private land had to be demarcated from village common land and from state holdings. From this time on, it was no longer possible to freely occupy land. New migrants had to get permission of local governments and obtain land through them before they could settle in the region.

Ecological Change

In the United States, when land began to fill up in New England in the nineteenth century, farmers moved to the Midwest and later to the Far West. But in Serbia, once Šumadija was reoccupied there was nowhere to go. Unlike inhabitants of other parts of Yugoslavia, some of whom went abroad for periods of time to seek work or who migrated overseas with their families, relatively few left Šumadija during the nineteenth and early twentieth centuries. Neither did Serbia industrialize, nor did the towns grow to any degree. It is estimated that the Serb population, 94 percent rural and mainly agricultural in 1834, was still 87 percent rural and overwhelmingly agricultural in 1910. The nineteenth century was, nevertheless, a time of dramatic ecological change and of change in the life ways of the peasantry. The cutting of the forest and the increase in the population were reflected first in agriculture. Between 1859, when reliable records were first kept, and the turn of the century all livestock, cattle excepted, declined relative to cultivated areas, on an absolute basis as well as on a per capita basis. Per capita declines of all livestock occurred, in fact, from 1859 through 1949 throughout all of Serbia proper. In Serbia in 1859 there were, per 100 inhabitants, 74 cattle, 164 pigs, and 220 sheep. These figures shrunk to 39, 39, and 56 respectively by 1900, and in 1949 stood at 31, 29, and 96. In absolute numbers cattle remained relatively constant over the 90-year period; the number of pigs declined by more than half from 1859 to 1900 and increased slightly in the twentieth century; the number of sheep remained constant until 1900 and then increased by some 20 percent by 1949. In overall absolute terms there was considerable improvement in livestock holdings in all of Serbia between 1949, when the effects of war ravages were still felt, and 1960. Cattle then increased by over 10 percent and the number of pigs more than doubled.

On a micro-basis with regard to Orašac, comparing the situation on a per capita basis, the number of pigs decreased from 1.7 in 1866 to .3 in 1910 and partly regained the relative proportion of 1.2 in 1960. A similar situation occurred with regard to sheep, the figures being 2.7, .9, and 1.2 for the respective years. Excluding the postwar year 1921, the number of horses also was smaller on both per capita and absolute bases in 1910. In absolute terms, by 1960 the number of horses had exceeded by about one-quarter the 1866 level, but the number of cattle was about 10 percent under that of a century earlier. The number of pigs had increased 10 percent and the number of sheep decreased by about a quarter, with 1910 being the low year in absolute terms for all livestock except sheep. These figures do not reflect the great losses in two world wars and subsequent recoveries.

Figures for agricultural yields are less certain, since they involve more complex estimates. The trend is clear, however, at least in terms of increasing wheat and corn yields in this century. Increases after 1960 as a result of increased distribution of fertilizers and the use of new varieties is particularly marked.

Economic Stagnation

These figures indicate that the latter part of the nineteenth century and early part of the twentieth was essentially a period of stagnation in terms of productivity and potential for a rising standard of living. The drama of pioneering settlement had passed, but industrialization had not yet begun. The forests had been largely cut, the land had filled up and the peasants had nowhere to go. There was neither more land to settle nor jobs in appreciable numbers in the towns.

Yet many old men in the village today, recalling this period of seventy or eighty years ago, talk about the days of their youth as Serbia's golden time: There were no wars, and the popular King Petar ruled.

Summing up the state of the Serbian economy in 1906 a local writer remarked,

> So long as the population was small, land abundant, and capital scarce, extensive farming was suited to the needs of the farmer and of the state, but now that these conditions are changing a transition to more intensive type of farming is desirable and necessary.[1]

Serbia at that time was a classic case of a land of peasant small-holders with minimal class distinctions. In 1908 Belgrade, the capital and largest city, had only 3200 industrial workers. At the turn of the century approximately 85 percent of the population of some two and a half million was rural, and in the villages 90 percent of the people owned their own land. (While the state remained the largest

---

[1] M. Jovanović, "Conservative Peasants (1906)," in Warriner, ed., *Contrasts in Emerging Societies*, Bloomington, Indiana University Press, 1965, p. 309.

landholder, about half the total, most of its holdings were forest. The holdings of the Orthodox Church were comparatively small, only 1 percent of the total.)

Records (in 1897) show that 55 percent of the holdings were less than five hectares in size, with 73 percent between one and ten hectares. In Orašac holdings were somewhat smaller, since there was less hilly and forested land. The average holding for Orašac was 5.4 hectares in 1863 and 4.7 a century later in 1960 (as compared to 8.6 for all of Serbia in 1897). In Serbia at the turn of the century the maximum degree of fragmentation was reached, with an average of 14 parcels per holding. (In Orašac in 1863 there were 1064 parcels or approximately 8 per household. A century later there were 4853 parcels of privately owned land, excluding, of course, the state farm and other government holdings which had markedly increased in size, or an average of 11.5 per household.) Over the century the number of households more than tripled while the number of plots increased more than four-fold. The increasing fragmentation reflects the inheritance pattern of dividing equally among sons.

Village common land, mainly woods, has also ceased to exist. The creation of state farm land after the post-World War II land reform has decreased relative fragmentation by consolidating into several large holdings the land thus acquired. The past century has seen more cultivated land, more holdings, more plots, less woods, disappearance of common lands, and the appearance of socially owned farm land. If village depopulation proceeds, the expansion of the socially owned sector and some concentration of private holdings would appear likely.

The institution of the protected minimum homestead is vital to understanding the stability of the society of peasant small-holders over more than a century. This practice was established by decree by Prince Miloš in 1836, whereby a peasant's home, a minimum amount of land (2.8 hectares was the figure at the end of the century), two oxen, and a cow could not be taken from him for payment of debts. But the law was not always enforced and did not resolve the problem of peasant indebtedness which grew during the nineteenth century, becoming one of the chief political problems of the country by the mid-1800s. Despite the fact that the creditors were not a distinct social class but one developed from the peasantry itself, the oppressive financial burdens were none the less real. The rate of interest for credit for villagers was legally fixed at 12 percent at the turn of the century, but actually they were paying from 12 to 30 percent depending on their bargaining position. Many of the lenders in villages were the more prosperous peasants, although it was considered something of a sin to charge interest when lending to close relatives.

Some Technological Innovations

Developments in Serbian agriculture were from many points of view retrogressive; still, important technological innovations did occur. Particularly important was the iron plow, which replaced the wooden one. Since it cut the land more easily it meant that a yoke of cows could replace several yokes of oxen, a factor which worked in well with decreasing livestock-raising, the need for more intensive land use, and increasingly smaller household size. In Orašac and environs wooden plows began to disappear by the last decades of the nineteenth century, with the multipurpose cow replacing the more specialized ox. In these respects the Jasenica region was somewhat ahead of Serbia as a whole, since in 1897 the older scratch plough, or ard, which only broke up the surface of the soil without turning it, still outnumbered an improved wooden plow and the new metal plow.

Growing population pressure, and the need for increased arable land and for more intensive agriculture, plus specific developments like the improved plow, all influenced the decline in livestock production. In addition, a new forest law enacted about this time restricted the pasturing of the pigs in the remaining forests, formerly regarded as "people's forests," free to all. The general decline in household size also made it more difficult to assign individual family members to full-time chores with the livestock. Finally, since the pigs were the chief export and, as in earlier times, the main market was across the Danube in the Austrian Empire, Austria used the pig trade to exert political pressure on Serbia. Still, the pig remained important. It was usefully adapted to the Serbian rural economy even if it could no longer be grazed in the acorn woods, for it could be fed on corn and kitchen waste, grew rapidly, and required a relatively small investment. The contemporary custom of the lard pig (that is, a selected pig glutted with corn until it can no longer eat, after which it is slaughtered and the abundant lard rendered for cooking purposes) symbolizes the transition from raising lean pigs on acorns and generally extensive livestock-raising patterns more closely akin to ancestral patterns in Montenegro, to the primacy of field crops which are used to feed penned livestock.

With the opening of the twentieth century, Serbian agriculture stressed three different products: grains, primarily wheat and corn; livestock, especially pigs; and fruit, notably plums. The latter formed not only the principal ingredient of the peasants' indispensable plum brandy, Serbia's national drink, but were exported in quantity to central Europe in dried form.

Correlated with the decrease in livestock production was a marked increase in the area devoted to major crops, especially corn. Land in wheat rose from 162,766 hectares in 1889 to 385,584 in 1910, and in corn from 268,423 to 585,226 hectares in the same period. Bread baked from cornmeal was a dietary staple, and corn was also the major pig feed.

There were other important adaptive ecological changes. The oak forests declined and pigs were no longer pastured in them, but the peasants' need for wood for cooking and heating continued. Acacia trees, which today line the roadside almost everywhere in Šumadija, began to be grown at this time, as the peasants to a degree created their own wood product. In the postwar period, particularly as labor has become less plentiful, some vineyards, being very labor intensive, have begun to be replaced by patches of acacia woods.

Agriculture before the First World War

We can turn again to the village teacher-ethnographer Pavlović for a commentary on this period of change, up to the time of the first world war:

Today the people of the Jasenica District of Kragujevac County cultivate these grains: corn, wheat, barley, oats, and rarely, rye. They plant corn for their own food. Wheat is cultivated for sale; they leave themselves only enough for seed and for feast days. Often many prosperous householders do not sell their old wheat until the new crop is in their grain sheds. The poor usually sell theirs immediately for threshing, in this way earning money to buy corn (cornbread lasts longer and is more filling) or they first go and pay their taxes. Usually taxes are not due until the first sheaves are gathered.

Wheat and Corn

Every peasant tries to plant all his arable land. Crops are rotated: where one year wheat is planted, there in another year corn is planted. Before planting wheat, lime is spread. Livestock manure is used on the fields before plowing. For corn, the land is fertilized at the time of planting.

The wheat is sown in April and in July is ready for reaping. Formerly threshing was done by horses and cattle, but today a threshing machine is used. . . . Two hill villages still use the old method. Beans are planted between the cornstalks. When the corn comes up there is a first hoeing, most important since grass is taken out. A month later is the second hoeing, and where the land is particularly fertile a third hoeing. The corn is husked either at home or while still on the stalk. Smaller ears are put aside for the livestock, and the rest is immediately put in the corn-crib to dry. . . .

People say that he who has no meadows should not have cattle, that would be a sin, and he who would have good livestock must have good meadows. No special care is taken of meadows, the grass grows as it will. It is cut when it flowers. Stock are put to graze in the meadows until St. George's Day or until the grass is cut. Sheep are pastured there only in the fall.

Vineyards and Fruits

There have always been vineyards in Jasenica. The old varieties died of blight so today American varieties are used. Older folk very much respected the grape, from which, they say, "God's Law" is made. Grapes are picked in September. They are guarded while they are ripening. A watchman is paid by several people in proportion to the size of their vineyards. The clusters are cut with a knife, piled in the wagon and hauled to each storage basement. When a full wagon pulls up before the basement, one must be on close lookout for the neighbor's children who hover around like grackles to the annoyance of the householder.

People grow various kinds of plums, apples, pears, sour and sweet cherries, peaches, apricots, quinces, and medlars. Fruits are carefully grown, with grafting done in different ways. Not all the fruit trees are within courtyards, some are in the fields. These are looked upon as belonging to everyone and are picked by all. Those in the courtyards are the exclusive property of the household. The children can never wait for the fruit to ripen but eat it green. The peasant does not know how to preserve the fruit for the winter, and fruits are sold as they ripen. Fruit merchants keep visiting the villages as the various fruits come into season, picking up what they want, at the lowest prices. Some old-fashioned households set aside dried fruits for the winter, in order to have "work medicine." During the winter many crave fruit even though they have had too much of it in the summer.

Vegetables

Vegetables are grown in gardens near the house or near streams. In the household gardens beans, peas, potatoes, and all sorts of string beans, corn, onions, cucumbers, tomatoes, and melons are grown, and in gardens near streams, cabbage, peppers, garlic, and beets. Until recently the garden produce was for household use only but today garlic and cabbage are produced for sale. Work in the gardens is mainly done by women or older men who can no longer work in the fields. Flowers are grown in one part of the courtyard and are looked after by the maidens or young girls. The men only see to it that the area is fenced in.

Growing flax and hemp is women's work, and the men see only that the land is prepared. Sometimes in small families where the women can't do all their work the men help them. When it's time for the flax to be sown many pupils don't go to school because they are needed to shoo away the sparrows. Flax and hemp are never sown on Easter Sunday, so that there will not be sadness in the house.

LIVESTOCK

The raising of livestock is of secondary importance, since crops come first. Many men put a lot of effort into livestock-raising, and his best stock reflect an owner's pride. For this select stock the owner puts up a special stall, while the rest of the stock winters in thatch stalls and summers in some fenced area or in a field near the house. The stock are pastured in the spring, beginning in March until the first snows. Oxen, since they plow, must be carefully cared for, and horses as well. The sheep are especially looked after during the lambing season. The pigs are pastured in the oak woods during the winter. There must be a shepherd or herdsman with the stock since they can be grazed in one's own pasture only. But in the fall, when all the crops are harvested, the stock are allowed to go everywhere except in the vineyards and cabbage patches. Then the shepherds get together and play.

Before a cow is milked men like to allow her calf to have more to drink so that it will develop faster, but women like to get as much as possible for the household. When lambs are slaughtered women particularly like the male lambs to be taken so that the females remain for developing the stock. When there are many men in the household, making important the weaving of woolen cloth for peasant jackets and britches, the women suggest that lambs not be killed or sold.

Sometimes the cows are hitched to the plow, where it occasionally happens that they calve in the furrows. In some places one finds a man who yokes a horse together with a cow or ox to pull a wagon. The rest of the world wonders at this and smiles, and asks, "Can this be?"

Raising poultry is women's work. Chickens, turkeys, geese, and ducks are kept. They are used for meat and eggs and also sold. Most money is gotten for turkeys and geese in the fall and winter when they are well fattened. Goose feathers are exchanged with Gypsies for kerchiefs. The poultry is generally kept in the courtyard but during the summer there must be special shepherds for the geese and turkeys who keep them out of the fields.

Beekeeping methods have been inherited from elders. There are many households in which the children know that honey is sweet only from hearing about it. Honey is used as a medicine and a substitute for sugar as well as for sweetening hot plum brandy.

FORMS OF MUTUAL HELP

Peasants most frequently help each other in their work, in the so-called *pozajmica*, that is, today you come and hoe or thresh at my place, and tomorrow I'll help you out. Whoever serves another poorly, if he arrives late or leaves early, no one will then be in his debt. A day of threshing must be returned by three days of hoeing, while a day of reaping is returned with two of hoeing.

In former times people had more oxen, so there was less need for *sprega*, reciprocal loaning of livestock. Then they used the old wooden plow, drawn by three pair of oxen. Today men plow with two pair, and also with one pair, for it is easier with the improved plow. Now, if a loan is necessary, two men get together, usually one with oxen and the other with cows. The oxen lead, with the cows behind. In former times those who joined in this kind of loan stayed together for ten years, but now often they can't keep together even for a year. Usually they quarrel about whose land will be plowed first.

A *moba* is called for threshing or for hoeing corn. Called to take part are those who cannot do their own threshing alone. It is like a holiday. Bachelors, maidens, and young people come. The work begins about 4 in the afternoon. In former times it began at noon, and then it really was true help. At the *moba* the girls and youths sing harvest songs, and usually a flute-player goes with them and plays constantly. The maidens and young men work together and chat. In the evening the head of the household provides supper, after which there is dancing. If someone who is in mourning needs to have a *moba* then the dancing takes place outside the courtyard.

A traditional labor pool for threshing wheat

A husking bee is the most pleasant. But for some it couldn't be worse, when they are beaten with hoes or corn cobs. The *komišanje* is held in autumn when the corn is picked and brought to the courtyard. It begins in the evening and lasts well into the night or before dawn. The corn is put in piles, and those who take part, who are invited or not invited (too bad for them) sit and husk. The young people want to husk in the dark, but the older folk don't allow this and bring lamps or torches.

DAY LABOR

For day labor in the village, pay is sometimes in money and food. It depends on the difficulty of the work. Pay for spring and summer work is almost twice that for winter work, plus food. When the new wheat crop is ready the daily wage immediately goes up. Thus they say, "I won't work for you any longer for 3 *groš*, for I have put a new cross on the door." This means that the season has changed, a wheat cake has been baked from the first grains, and a cross put on the door.

Men who have no livestock must give working days in exchange for the use of stock. For a day of plowing it is necessary to give four to five days of men's work, for a day's use of a wagon, two to three days, and for threshing with horses, three days. Livestock breeding is paid for in work days or in cash.[2]

Changes in Agriculture

A half century has passed since Pavlović made these observations. Were he to return to Orašac today the overall cycle and processes would be familiar to him although there are many new developments that would attract his attention. Wheat and corn remain the principal crops, and the Orašac villager continues to combine agriculture with livestock-breeding. Even on small holdings of five hectares or less, land is allocated to crops, a garden, an orchard, a small patch of woods and a cow or two, several pigs, a few sheep, a flock of chickens, and perhaps some beehives and a few turkeys or geese. The size of the average holding is now somewhat smaller than it was a century ago (4.7 in 1960 as compared to 5.4 in 1863). Despite reservations when dealing with old records, it seems quite legitimate to infer that this part of Šumadija consistently has been a land of small holdings. There are other indicators of stability in a context of ecological change; with regard to the important plum crop, for example, in the Jasenica District in 1847 it is estimated that there were approximately 120 plum trees per household, while in 1953 in Orašac there were 135.

CROP YIELDS

Very important changes have occurred with respect to corn and wheat yields, and especially to the former. In 1893 the entire village of Orašac yielded 2880 quintals (1 quintal = 100 kilograms) of corn, while in 1963 on 71 hectares of the state farm alone the yield almost equaled this amount. The village total for 1963 was 16,763 quintals. Over the same period the gross wheat yield for the whole village approximately doubled. These developments reflect changes on a national level as well. In part the increase in yields is due to the introduction within the past decade of new varieties of seed and the increasing availability of and inclination to use artificial fertilizer.

Equally significant has been the change in consumption patterns. Whereas formerly cornbread was the staple and wheat bread was reserved for special holidays and regarded by the children of an earlier generation as the most delicious treat,

---

[2] Excerpted from Pavlović, *Život i običaji narodni u Kragujevačkoj Jasenici u Šumadiji*, pp. 13–22, 82.

today it is cornbread that is prepared to accompany certain holiday dishes and wheat bread that is used for everyday.

LEVELS OF TECHNOLOGY

Sometimes several levels of technology coexist simultaneously. The state farm maintains a combine for its relatively extensive acreage. Some individual peasants lease out a horse-drawn reaper, and those with smaller holdings still use the scythe. This latter method, most primitive of contemporary technologies, represents, however, an improvement over Pavlović's time when wheat was harvested with sickles. Tractors and other machinery from the state farm, for which the peasants pay a rental fee that includes the services of an operator, is beginning to be used more extensively on private holdings. In the late 1960s four of the more prosperous village households purchased tractors privately, using them on their own holdings and renting them out as well. Since then several more households have bought them.

THE STATE FARM

Making state farm machinery more accessible to the villagers is part of a deliberate government action designed to lead them gradually into closer cooperation with the state enterprises. This policy replaces that of coercive collectivization which was tried in the late forties, after Yugoslavia's break with the Stalinist East European bloc and subsequently abandoned in the early fifties as a result of increasing economic and political liberalization. Today the generalized consumer cooperative in the village, whose office occupies part of the large, unattractive cooperative building in the center, acts as an agent for providing improved varieties of stock, as well as for the purchase of animals, grains, fruits, and vegetables. There is no compulsion whatever, and the peasant is free to dispose of all his produce on the open market in Arandjelovac, if he so prefers. Beef cattle, higher quality grapes, and pigs are some of the items most frequently handled by the cooperative.

OTHER CHANGES

Private agriculture in Orašac, despite improvements in the quality of crops and livestock, better yields, and more government services, such as the availability of veterinarians, still remains small-scale, generalized production, with small capital investment. In the late 1950s electricity began to be installed in parts of the village, and lines have since been extended to most households, largely replacing the kerosene lamps and candles of Pavlović's generation. However, at most houses stock feed is still cut by hand machines, water is hauled up from wells on a windlass, and threshing is most often done with antiquated machinery. All this represents improvement over the days when water was carried from springs and threshing was done by the hooves of oxen or horses. On the level of the small private holding major technological innovation, mechanization, and modernization is still to come.

The enormous changes that have taken place in the life of the Orašac villager in the postwar period are least evident in methods of agricultural production. Rather, they are reflected in change in life styles, values, and the growing significance of nonagricultural sources of income.

The Market Town

To understand the life of Orašac in a meaningful way it is essential to look beyond the boundaries of the village to the nearby market town of Arandjelovac, to the district capital at Kragujevac and, as well, to Belgrade, the capital of Serbia and of Yugoslavia and the major city of the country. From the beginning, starting back at the time of Karadjordje and pig trade with Austria, the Šumadijan village was directly involved in extensive trade even while retaining a primarily subsistence economy. Generally, a greater degree of subsistence was practiced by those with smaller holdings. But even in those early days, craftsmen and other specialists performed services not available within the household zadruga.

In addition to trade and crafts as possibilities for occupations supplemental to or instead of farming, with the start of the formation of the Serbian state there developed limited channels of mobility through the bureaucracy, the army, and to a lesser degree the church. At the opening of the twentieth century industrialization began on a very small scale, not having its principal growth until the post-second-world-war period. The importance of all these activities is well illustrated by the fact that it is a rare man in Orašac who has not had extensive experience in some occupation other than farming during the course of a normal life span. Put another way, there are relatively few households that have derived their livelihood solely from agriculture over the span of a generation. To complete the picture we must also consider those who have left the village and found careers in the city, as well as those who go away for a time and then return or who, although they maintain residence in Orašac, spend varying amounts of their working lives away from their home and holding.

To begin with trade, just as the scene of the peasant plowing with his cows has the look of timelessness, so, too, does the view of his trudging over the hill to market, carrying a basket of fruit, some chickens, or a pig. The market day and market place result from specific and relatively recent historical developments, in this case not technological innovation but deliberate government control of trade and regulation of marketing practices.

Because of its proximity, Arandjelovac is overwhelmingly the most important market center for the people of Orašac, both for the sale of their farm produce and for most purchases. A small general store maintained by the cooperative in the village provides for some everyday necessities.

The Founding of Arandjelovac

The town of Arandjelovac was established in 1859, as a result of a decree of Prince Miloš.[3] At that time it was also made a district administrative center. Prior to then it had been part of the village of Vrbica, adjacent to Orašac. During the Austrian occupation of the area in the eighteenth century, Vrbica was the site

---

[3] The descriptive historical data for this area is based on documents and newspapers in the Serbian State Archives, Belgrade. The help of Stojan Djurdjev and the Archives administration is appreciatively acknowledged.

Women labor in the fields as well as perform housework.

Bringing in the hay.

of a military post of Serbian soldiers serving as border guards for the Austrian Empire. It was also, like Topola, on the old caravan route from Belgrade south to Macedonia and Bulgaria. Later it was the site of a Turkish han.

Prior to its formal founding as a town, the beginnings of a trading center took place in 1837 when Prince Miloš ordered the chief of the Jasenica District, then resident in Topola, to group together the scattered settlements of Orašac and Vrbica nearer the road. At this time merchants and craftsmen from other neighboring villages also began to settle along the natural corridor so evident today in the town's main street. Miloš was temporarily deposed in 1839 and, judging by contemporary settlement patterns in Serbia generally and exemplified by Orašac, his edict did not bring about basic change. What was significant was that even at this early period a real attempt was made at administrative planning and efficient marketing. Planning officials still talk of regrouping scattered village houses.

TOWN DEVELOPMENT

An 1838 directive specified that: "We allow the inhabitants of Vrbica to build stores in their village. They will not have to pay taxes for three years following the establishment of these shops." The following year an official report listed nine stores and three inns. Only two years later there were reportedly 40 shops and inns.

This volume of trade qualified Vrbica to be classed a small town. By then a guild had been established among the merchants, who by petition protested peasant demands that they, the merchants, now pay taxes to the local government. The edict establishing trading privileges and the petition for redress thus began part of a familiar pattern: government policy attempting to regulate trade and determine settlement patterns, simultaneous with the emergence of conflict between farmers and tradesmen. These two factions were certainly not clearly defined social classes but rather conflicting economic interest groups, with the state playing a not terribly effective mediating function.

At about the time the trade and crafts section of Vrbica was formed into the new town of Arandjelovac, mineral springs in the village of Bukovik, at the opposite end of town, were beginning to be exploited. The medicinal properties and excellent taste of the mineral water, combined with the pleasant country surroundings, began to attract visitors to the springs. A hotel was erected in 1866. (Today the Bukovik spa, long since annexed into the town proper, is a regional resort. Its development has had little effect on the people of Orašac.) A much more significant event for the area was the opening of a narrow gauge railway in 1904, branching off from the main line in Mladenovac. The marble quarry in Venčac near Arandjelovac opened in 1912, and about the same time a lignite mine in Orašac, providing an alternate source of employment for the villagers. These enterprises were, of course, made possible in large measure by the opening of the railroad. In addition agricultural trade increased and Arandjelovac became known as a place for the export of plums. But other agricultural products as well were, of course, carried on the new line. It also made it easier for people from Belgrade to visit the spa and so increased the general prosperity of the area.

Prince Miloš' state visit on the occasion of the founding of Arandjelovac was described in the official newspaper, the *Serbian Gazette* of July 21, 1859:

> His trip from Belgrade was a real holiday for the people of the area through which he traveled. Men and women, young people and old, all converged toward the highroad to see and greet "Our father," as they called their illustrious ruler. People greeted their ruler with "Hurrah, hurrah, long life, welcome to our old lord, our old luck." His Highness got down from his carriage every place he visited, politely greeting the people, talking to them and advising them. The entire trip from Belgrade to Bukovik was one continuous celebration. One could see on every face that all were happy with soul and heart to see among themselves "the old leader" who made the fatherland free. The shooting of guns was continuous, and from the hills one could hear merry songs of the happy people. . . . the illustrious Prince allowed the people who had gathered to kiss his hand. Many of them even went twice to touch the hand of the beloved father. His Highness, in desiring to erect a memorial in the town which was built by him, promised to build a church at his own expense. The church was to honor Saint Arandjel and therefore he ordered that from henceforth Vrbica be called Arandjelovac.

TRADE AND CRAFTS

Approval was granted to the holding of a livestock fair in the town on Saint Arandjel's Day. This fair continues to take place on that day up to the present. By 1863, the year of the first detailed census of the town, Arandjelovac had some

89 craftsmen and 33 merchants, aided by 29 assistants and 39 servants, in a total population of 674. The great majority of the people of Arandjelovac were farmers. But even for those who were not, ties with the land remained close. Roughly half the merchants and craftsmen had agricultural land in Arandjelovac or holdings in their native villages, and some had both. Many of those with no land had not yet established households.

Two decades later, in 1883, the total population had almost tripled. Formally the number of craftsmen had increased only by five, but this reflects only those who were admitted to full status in the various guilds. Actually if all traders, craftsmen, merchants, and assistants are taken into account, the total is 295. (By 1930 the population of Arandjelovac had grown to some 2200, with 125 craftsmen and 52 merchants. In 1961, with more than a four-fold increase in population, to 9837, the number of craftsmen is recorded as 46, and 423 people, about 4 percent of the population, are listed as engaged in agriculture.)

Town and Village Merchants

In a sense, Arandjelovac as it existed up to the second world war was of the countryside. Over the years the peasants were often in conflict with the merchants and craftsmen, and these groups existed only to serve the peasant and his needs and to market his crops. This is not to say that the peasants were not exploited by the townsfolk. Continually peasants felt that they were. Most of the merchants, creditors, and craftsmen, of course, were themselves usually no more than one generation removed from the village. Their children more often than not tried to leave the small town for Belgrade or more distant points.

As indicated, in the village a rich peasant might lend money at usurious rates. Also, some merchants continued to be based in the village. Specialization in pig trading continued up until the last decade of the nineteenth century. Some villagers, in the tradition of Karadjordje, bought up stock in the Jasenica region and herded it to Belgrade and by ferry across the Danube into Austria-Hungary, where there were good rail connections to central Europe. With the disappearance of the oak forests, the pigs were herded to areas where corn was readily available and fattened there. In either case, households of peasant traders were respected in the village and it was these households that innovated in the village in many ways, tending to be more active politically and to participate in urban kin and commercial networks.

There was continual battle between the town-based entrepreneurs and those who chose to operate from the villages. Some who did not succeed with their craft or enterprise in town might return to the village to continue operations. From the point of view of government control it was obviously more convenient for commerce and crafts to achieve a degree of centralization. Craftsmen and tradesmen organized into guilds. It was necessary for these town guilds to obtain a charter from the government. This gave them an exclusive monopoly on who could enter into specific crafts. But even within the towns, shops opened and operated without permission of the local guild. The guild, in turn, resorted to petitions to the central government requesting suppression of such craftsmen or traders. In 1899 the Arandjelovac business council protested to the Economics Ministry that village stores in the region were selling sugar, coffee, cotton, wool, and manufactured items in violation of the law and to the detriment of town merchants. In 1901 the carpenters and masons guild of Arandjelovac protested against foreign craftsmen who came from Bulgaria and Bosnia (then under Austria-Hungary) and competed illegally with local craftsmen. They also complained that there were over a hundred unregistered apprentices and assistant craftsmen in the town. If a report from Arandjelovac in 1902 is to be given credence, some craftsmen and assistants not only failed but actually faced starvation. It was reported that several craftsmen who, a few years earlier, had been numbered among the first citizens of the town, had collapsed with hunger on the street after having gone to the guild and then, evidently in desperation, to the local administration requesting financial assistance.

Gypsy smiths, operating outside the system and following a seminomadic life, nevertheless did considerable business in small smithing and woodworking in the villages. The town craftsmen attempted to stop them as well.

In part the strong role of the local guilds and the arbitrating position of the state can be seen as having been influenced by the old Turkish administrative structure, under which the state divided into officially autonomous communities.

An Urban View of Village Life

A characteristic urban attitude toward peasant enterprise is summed up in a 1911 article in the Belgrade newspaper *Pijemont*, on a village adjoining Orašac:

> I don't want to write about peasant matters, for I know that [this newspaper] is not interested in our coarse peasant politics, which in this region are run in the same way as in all areas of Serbia.
>
> Instead of citing the lack of good statistics, on the basis of which it is possible to conclude that our country is advancing, it would be good to make clear for our readers the miserable cultural situation in which the villagers of this region exist.
>
> I take as an example the village of Stojnik.
>
> Oh, how beautiful is this village, in the middle of enchanting Šumadija. Nature is abundant here: beautiful woods, water, fields, pastures, everything necessary to develop into as fine an economic condition as one would wish. Nature has provided all, but that is why the people neglect everything. It seems to one that it was only yesterday that the Turkish feudal lords lost governmental control in this region, so little has been done during the past century of freedom.
>
> In this village, which one might look at as one of our better villages, first of all there are no village roads, or the roads are so miserable that it would be better if there were none at all. When it is sunny it is impossible to stand the dust, and when it rains one cannot move through the mud.
>
> The houses in which the peasants live, people, citizens of Serbia, are absolutely worse than the stalls in which cultured people raise livestock. Many of these houses are filthier than western stables.
>
> The villagers, in any case, lack all facilities and institutions which would make possible their advancement. But here is something to note: In 1905 one kafana was opened as a "slaughterhouse"; in 1907 another kafana took out a license and was opened as a "small shop," in 1909 two more were opened as "small shops," and finally last year one more as a "shop."

Thus one indigent village, where nothing clean exists in the life of the people, has five kafanas.

In all of these taverns, for which permits are easily obtained with the help of "official friends," plum brandy flows like artesian springs. In these kafanas, peasants who have become worthless sit on benches in their torn britches and play cards all day and night. How it was before in this village I don't know, but that is the way it is today.

An elementary school in this village was opened only in 1910, 100 years after the liberation of Serbia.

Is it any wonder that we don't advance?

The reporter with his eyes on the "cultured West" as a model against which to measure Šumadijan villagers seemed unaware of the extent to which nature had closed in on these peasants. To cite an American model, it would be as if no migration would have been possible from New England in the nineteenth century, with no industrialization but with hostile neighbors bent on keeping the area purely agricultural. Once the Serbian countryside had been filled up there was, essentially, no outlet for the surplus population. The towns were overpopulated with traders and craftsmen, and instead of being concerned with expansion they were pre-occupied with maintaining their mini-establishments. With no industry, with the railroad not yet put through, and often with unfavorable conditions for foreign trade, it is not surprising that agriculture remained undeveloped. The peasants were frequently underemployed. The newspaper reporter's condemnation of village kafanas combined with his praising of the region illustrates the urban intellectual's ambivalence toward the countryside: a beautiful place populated by lazy, boorish peasants who should be working.

Yet Arandjelovac, at the close of the nineteenth century, was a relatively active trade center. In an 1893 town report, some 65 shops and 23 taverns are noted in August (and only 18 taverns in September, indicating their seasonal nature). In that year over 1000 head of oxen were traded, plus 300 cattle, 89 sheep, and 70 horses. Over a ton each of wine, brandy, and wool were traded. More than 250 individuals obtained permits to trade merchandise.

Early Migration from Orašac

During the nineteenth and early twentieth centuries there was a small but steady emigration from Orašac into crafts, commerce, and government service. Initially, close kin ties were maintained with village relatives. These tended to atrophy over the course of several generations but, nevertheless, vivid memories of the village past and the consciousness of historic kin ties remain even among those who consider themselves totally urbanized. (Particularly notable is a proud awareness of Montenegrin origins which prevails after a century and a half even though many such ties are no longer directly functional.)

Such is the case of a research scholar in his mid-fifties who has lived most of his life in Belgrade and whose paternal grandmother's family originated in Orašac, his paternal grandfather having come from another village in Šumadija. His account, below, illustrates how kin ties served to bind people and were also the means for promoting social and status mobility (particularly crucial with regard to getting an education). Having a relative in town was a vital asset. Such ties continue to function today.

> After leaving his native village my paternal grandfather opened a kafana in a village near Kragujevac, and there he married, bringing my grandmother from the village of Orašac. It is interesting that both my paternal grandparents are descended from the same lineage in Montenegro, a lineage which is well known for the heroes and prominent people it has produced. A relative of my grandmother became a general who distinguished himself on the Loyalist side in the Spanish Civil War, while another branch of her family contributed a general who fought in the People's Liberation War against the Germans.
>
> Eventually grandfather moved to Arandjelovac where he opened another kafana. On market days and on the slava of the church, when the peasants came dressed in their holiday clothes, they would come with goods to sell, or to see relatives or friends, and usually they would sit in the kafana with a glass of plum brandy or wine and there talk politics, or trade. There were always some who would sit and drink and not pay their bills. Fights started this way. My grandfather was known as an irascible man who would throw such people out. Sometimes a man would spring a knife, because he was drunk. Grandfather would take away the knife, find the man's horse, and tie the drunk on the horse so he wouldn't fall, leading him in the direction of his village until he found some villagers who were returning home from market.
>
> While my father was a child, grandfather had a general store. Later he sent my father to a relative of grandmother in Belgrade to continue schooling. This relative was a prosperous man during the time of King Milan [1872–1889]. So father did not have much direct contact with the village. He studied law and became an official, and was later posted to various towns in Serbia. Remember that we did, nevertheless, retain close ties with my grandfather's village, while we were young, spending every summer or every other summer there. When my father had business in Kragujevac, and that was frequently, almost every month, he always visited his father's village. There he was well received. They were proud that someone in their vamilija had achieved a position of importance. Grandfather's family contributed many intellectuals. We also visited Arandjelovac often.
>
> The ties with Orašac lapsed, however, although I remember listening to the tales of my grandmother's maternal vamilija, particularly a story about one Orašac villager who was known as a politician and fighter against government bureaucracy.[4]

An Apprenticeship

Before the second world war, for most who wished to leave the village an apprenticeship in town was the only outlet. Although the master craftsman might be a relative, the apprentice's life was very hard, in many ways little better than that of a servant. A middle-aged villager recalls:

> My father worked for other peasants because he did not have much land. My parents could not pay much attention to the children. While my father was going to work in distant villages my mother was working at a neighbor's. When I was about ten they sent me to learn the weaver's trade at my *ujak's* place in Mladenovac. So I spent 1934 and 1935 as an apprentice. My ujak treated his apprentices

---

[4] See Joel M. Halpern, "Peasant Culture and Urbanization in Yugoslavia," *Human Organization*, 1965, 24, pp. 162–174.

badly. I stayed for three years but did not learn. In those days the apprentice spent the first two years in the master's kitchen and laid the fires, chopped the wood, hauled the water and also tended whatever livestock he had. He also was nursemaid to the master's children and performed many households tasks. It was not until the third year that he learned something in the master's shop. Conditions were so bad that in the third year I ran home. But then my father sent me to learn the same craft in Arandjelovac, where I worked until 1939, when I returned to Orašac. To be an apprentice then was horrible—the master made a slave of you.

Even those who succeeded and became craftsmen do not have happy memories of the period. Despite the hard conditions it was generally expected that board for the apprentice would be paid by his parents in the village, who were expected to contribute farm produce to help pay for their son's learning a trade. This practice is followed today, when village children board with relatives in town while going to school.

SEASONAL WORK

It was not only children who went to work in town. Seasonally many poorer peasants found work as carters or construction laborers. Others went for periods ranging up to several years to work in Belgrade or other towns. As a result of these diverse experiences it can be said that even before the second world war it was the exception rather than the rule for a villager to have spent all his life involved solely in agriculture. The extent of participation in nonagricultural activities even prior to the period of postwar industrialization can be glimpsed when it is realized that the lignite mine operated in Orašac up to the 1960s, providing intermittent employment to many villagers. In addition, universal military service was compulsory for all able-bodied men.

MILITARY SERVICE

Military service during peacetime provided almost every young man an opportunity to see something of the country, meet people from other areas, acquire a degree of sophistication, and at least be exposed to certain hygiene habits that were not a part of village routine. The Balkan War in 1912, the first world war, and the second world war in turn provided many villagers with their most dramatic life experience. Not the least of these experiences included being taken as prisoner-of-war to such places as Czechoslovakia after the partial defeat of Serbian forces in the first world war and to Germany early in the second world war, thereby exposing Orašac villagers to many aspects of technologically advanced cultures. While they did not enjoy being prisoners they did return with a sense of admiration for the *teknika* of others. This resulted both directly and indirectly in various innovations in village life in matters as diverse as outhouses and ways of reaping wheat. A villager who learned a trade while a prisoner-of-war says, "Each land has its own agriculture, but a craft speaks every language."

Despite the fact that many battles were lost and many comrades ended up in prison camps there persists an intense patriotism among Orašac villagers and a heightened sense of the drama of their wartime activities. Old men still remember the specifics of their unit designations and even the serial numbers of their rifles.

Elements of conventional twentieth-century male peasant costume, ranging from the *čakšire* riding breeches (although most peasants never owned horses) to the *šajkača* caps are derived from military uniforms. Pride in military service had been a well-developed tradition in the nineteenth century as well, as attested to by the gravestone reliefs in the village cemetery, depicting the deceased in their military uniforms. This on-going sense of pride and participation dates from the struggle against the Turks and the pioneering efforts in developing Šumadija.

Villagers asked to recount their life histories often relate the most detailed accounts of periods of military service. A man in his seventies recalls:

> I first served in the army in 1914. I was taken as a young man into the army when the Germans invaded our country. The president of the village took a group of us by ox-cart to a town near Valjevo, where we trained for three months. From there we were sent to Kruševac and then to Priština where we continued our training. After we succeeded in throwing the Germans out of Serbia in 1914, we went to the Bulgarian frontier. There, when the Austrians and Germans invaded again in 1915 we were defeated. King Petar retreated to Salonica and I was taken prisoner by the Germans. But in 1916 I was interned in Czechoslovakia where I worked in a factory. Later I was sent to work for a farmer in Hungary. There I worked as a peasant. In most ways it was like here. But I was impressed by their use of scythes. Here before the war we used sickles to cut wheat. Our people thought that cutting wheat with a scythe would scatter it. They used to grab a few stalks of wheat and cut them. It took many people 10 to 15 days to cut the wheat. Their backs used to hurt because they had to bend over double. I told my father, "Let's go reap the wheat." He said that it would scatter. I said it wouldn't. So this is the way we changed.

The Village in Wartime

During peacetime life for the ordinary farmer was hard enough, but during a war there was great suffering on the home front. A man describes what it was like to be a child just before and during the first world war:

> I remember sleeping with my father and mother in the vajat. It had no windows, neither did it have a stove in wintertime. But people were healthy in those days. In 1911 I began school. I remember going to school in the winter without even a little jacket. For food I had a piece of cornbread in my *torba* and that was it. At home, beside the cornbread we had soup but made without lard. Soak your bread in it and eat. During the winter the soup would be flavored with a bit of bacon.
>
> At that time we were 12 together in our zadruga. The wheat bread that we now eat you could see only about three times a year then. 1912 was the year that we fought the Turks, and school stopped. My father and grandfather went to war and we little ones, 4 brothers and a sister, were left alone. At that time we used to work the land with oxen. But with the war they took the oxen from us and from many others as well. Then we had to plant wheat by using hoes. My father didn't return until 1918. We children didn't know how to work the land or what to do. Those were bad years. There was hunger. There was little bread and we were barefoot and had few clothes. Many people died. I myself was sick for several months with typhus. I had such a high fever I didn't know what I was doing. I ran out to the road. Then my other grandfather put me on the cart and

took me to a doctor. He took off my pants and thumped my little stomach. Then he told my deda, "Stevo, take this one home; he is *gotov* [finished]." But slowly I got better.

Then in 1927 I worked at a storehouse for prunes; it was this same doctor's warehouse. We hefted sacks around, ask God what we did. Then each night one workman had to guard the place. The doctor came to chat with me in the night. "What are you doing?" I told him, "I'm lying on these sacks." Then he asked me if I cared to eat something with lard. I told him, "Sure Mr. Doctor." Then I asked him if he remembered the burned up infant that Stevo had brought him. He remembered and then I told him I was that child.

Serbian Work Values

In spite of their pride, Serbs are acutely aware of their relatively less developed economic status compared to that of western Europe. They want very much to change this situation, and a frequently heard assertion is, "Give us twenty years without a war and we'll make of our Šumadija a little America." Conversely, as an explanation for felt backwardness a standard explanation is, "Well, what can you expect—we were five hundred years under the Turks." Despite strong national identity and consciousness of heroic tradition, the expression *srpska posla,* Serbian business, is used to explain a job poorly done. Similarly ambivalent are attitudes toward work: Heard everywhere, even on the lips of children when there is a hard task to do, is *"Čovek mora da radi* (A man must work)"; but there is also the feeling that hard work does not always bring rewards, as in the expression *"Dobro radi a pomalo kradi* (Work well and steal a little)." And through it all is the attitude that despite difficulties one must persevere—*"Nije lako ali ako* (It isn't easy, but so what)." The sense of drive is also expressed in greetings when villagers meet in the morning: *"Ti si poranio!* (You're up early!)" or *"Jesi vredan?* (Are you industrious, are you with it?)."

Although outside work experience and wide travel during army duty have been common experiences of Orašac men, the economy and nature of the work experience have been particularly affected by two recent developments. These are the increasing availability of education and the growing importance of factory employment.

Town and Village in Retrospect

While there was a growing separation of town and countryside during the nineteenth century, in terms of conflicting economic interests the division was never complete and always overlapped. That is, despite efforts of the town craftsmen and tradesmen to attain a monopoly, trades and crafts remained very much alive in the villages. Further, all the towns in Serbia, specifically including Arandjelovac, contained a good number of farmers, and at least in the beginning, as was seen in the 1863 census, many townsmen had agricultural holdings in their villages or in the town itself. The towns existed almost exclusively to facilitate agricultural trade and to service the rural population.

With the early years of the twentieth century, the opening of a railroad line to Arandjelovac and the beginnings of exploitation of a marble quarry and the lignite mine, the extent of cash income increased. In many ways, work in a mine or quarry was more compatible with a traditional way of life than was employment in a modern factory. In the former, intermittent work for a few years or even seasonally was possible, whereas the conditions of factory work, and particularly the skilled jobs, demand year-round employment over the course of one's working life. An important contemporary consideration here has been the pension and medical and loan benefits that have been available only to industrial workers in the postwar socialist system. While mining and quarrying demand degrees of skill in particular jobs, the overall skill level is higher in industry. In fact, one of the accomplishments of which factory personnel are proudest is the on-the-job training and increases in skill level that former peasants have undergone after beginning factory work.

Movements to Town

A most significant development has been the direct migration of youths, and many younger married men as well, out of the village and into the towns to work in the factories. Population growth in Arandjelovac has been dramatic, burgeoning from 4278 in 1948 and 5745 in 1953 to almost 10,000 (9837) in 1961. Less than 25 percent of the current town population was born there. Further, the villages of Bukovik and Vrbica have become almost like suburbs, distinguished from other villages in the area because over half their present inhabitants were born elsewhere. (By contrast, in Orašac almost three-quarters of the 2024 inhabitants in 1961 were born there, a fairly typical situation for most villages in the area. Those born elsewhere are mostly the in-marrying brides from other villages.) Among approximately three thousand workers in the district, out of a total active working population of some 23,000, over 2000 live in Arandjelovac and others commute daily from the surrounding villages. As of 1961, of some 7400 migrants to Arandjelovac, less than 1200 are of urban origin (those who are consist mainly of technical and administrative personnel with their families); the majority come from villages or small towns, most of them from the Arandjelovac district proper and from the county. Only about 18 percent originate from outside of Serbia proper.

In miniature, this has been the story of much of Yugoslavia in the postwar period: From 1949 to 1960 alone some 2,162,000 people moved from rural areas, or approximately 1/9 the total population (18.5 million in 1961). Most of these migrants are relatively young, while in the villages the percentage of older people progressively increases. In 1961 the group composed of those age fourteen and under represented approximately a quarter of the population in Orašac and two adjacent villages, while in Arandjelovac the percentage was slightly higher (29 percent) and in Bukovik comprised over a third. At the other end of the scale, in the age 60-and-over group the differences are even more striking: Orašac and its two neighbors have some 15 percent of their population in this category while Arandjelovac and Bukovik have less than half as much proportionately (7 percent).

A sandalmaker in town and his village customer

Peddler of sieves on market day

Peasant-Workers

By 1961 some 46 percent of Orašac households derived at least a portion of their income from sources other than agriculture. The largest group of employed workers (79 out of 218) worked at the mine.

By and large the phasing out of the lignite mine operation in Orašac in late 1961 does not seem to have worked any great hardship. The village clerk's incomplete census in 1966, focusing mainly on long-term residents with at least a small amount of land, lists approximately 210 wage earners in 1966, which compares with approximately 220 in the completed census of 1961. But the 1966 list is for a population of approximately 200 less than the 1961 official figure of 2024. Of the 225 people who have left Orašac since 1961, only 67 are out-marrying women, a figure which has traditionally been balanced by those who marry into the village. In addition, 26 nuclear and/or extended families have left, mainly to settle in Arandjelovac. There are also 63 students pursuing education beyond elementary level outside Orašac, many of them in Arandjelovac. Once they have completed their education few if any will return.

Along with a population decrease of about 10 percent, the number of old people increased and, as might be expected, the number of pensioners has similarly increased. In the period 1953–1961 the number of pensioners of all types was about 25; the still incomplete records of 1966 list 69, the majority of whom are ex-miners. The number would be even higher were it not for the fact that some retired miners have relocated with their children, the children having earlier moved to Arandjelovac, or sold their land in the village and built their own house in town. Having a pension does not mean that pensioners do not rely on agriculture. The pension varies with the number of years worked and the kind of job held. For most recipients it represents a supplement to agricultural income. For a minority, however, it does supply the main source of income.

The number of commuters to work outside Orašac (mainly jobs in Arandjelovac) has grown from 74 in 1961 to over 100 in 1966. For these people a special bus service was instituted in the mid-1960s. By 1968 two competing bus lines offered service to town and are much used by peasants going to market as well as by commuting workers.

Expansion of the school in Orašac and the growth of the state farm have provided additional opportunities for employment of local people in state institutions within the village (less than 20 in 1966). Mining has changed from a predominant occupation to a minor one; in 1966 some dozen villagers were employed, about equally divided between the marble quarry and a clay mine for the fire-brick factory. In 1966 only some 185 households of approximately 400 were headed by men whose main occupation was farming or who had children or the potentiality to produce heirs to continue their household as a farming unit. By this date a real revolution in the life ways of the people of Orašac had occurred.

Quantitative Differences among Vamilijas

In discussing Orašac and its economy it is natural to think in terms of units such as the individual, the household, the village. The unit intermediate between the household and the village—the vamilija—also deserves attention. It is not a formal corporate unit in an economic sense, but it is a unit of association with respect to work exchanges and lending of tools and money. This is particularly true in Orašac where the various vamilijas tend to occupy particular sections of the village, so that the functions of neighbor and kinsman overlap. Households within the same vamilija tend also to be competitive, but they are linked by subtle but important economic bonds that have determined their place within the village socioeconomic system over the past century.

Earlier we talked about the variation in economic status of a particular household over the course of a generation and of the vital importance of having sons who remained on the land. But these are not independent variables; each vamilija operates within bounds of varying potentiality that are at least a century old. Table 2 ranks six of the larger vamilijas in Orašac with regard to selected criteria, comparing their relative status in 1863 to a number of analogous categories in the 1960s. The overall trend is indicated by the cumulative rank order scores, which, when population figures are excluded, distinguishes vamilijas A and B as being at an opposite end of the scale from vamilijas E and F. Vamilijas C and

TABLE 2
Six Orašac Vamilijas Ranked According to Selected Criteria, 1863 and 1960s,[a] Compared

1863

Vamilija	Ave. Household Size		Total Vamilija Pop.		Proportion of Village Pop.		Land Holdings 6 Ha. or More		Ave. Land Holding		Property Value	
	#	R[b]	#	R	%	R	%	R	in Ha.	R	in Ducats	R
A	10	3.5	30	5	2.8	5	67	3	8.7	1	212	3
B	10	3.5	31	4	2.9	4	100	1	7.6	2.5	217	2
C	11	2	88	1	8.1	2	75	2	7.6	2.5	232	1
D	12	1	72	2	6.7	1	33	4.5	6.2	4	186	4
E	7	5	29	6	2.7	6	25	6	4.6	6	118	6
F	8	6	48	3	4.4	3	33	4.5	5.6	5	150	5

1960s

Vamilija	Ave. Household Size		Total Vamilija Pop.		Proportion of Village Pop.		Land Holdings 6 Ha. or More		Prop. of Able-bodied Males in Agric.		Male Migrants from Village[c]		Cumulative Rank[d]
	#	R	#	R	%	R	%	R	%	R	%	R	
A	5.0	2	79	5	3.9	5	67	1	90	1	25	1	10/35.5
B	5.5	1	115	3	5.7	2	43	2	78	3	11	4	14.5/32
C	4.4	3	196	1	9.7	1	29	3	67	4	5	5	17.5/27.5
D	3.5	6	116	2	5.7	3	18	4	81	2	21	2	20.5/35.5
E	4.0	4	91	4	4.5	4	17	5	34	6	17	3	32/61
F	3.7	5	66	6	3.3	6	11	6	33	5	3	6	31.5/60.5

[a] Data in last 2 columns from 1966; other 1960s data is from 1961.
[b] Rank order.
[c] Listed in 1966 registry but actually not residing in village; includes students.
[a] Left of diagonal is cumulative rank order excluding population figures (first three categories); on right is total cumulative ranking.

D are the two largest descent groups in the sample, both in 1863 and in 1961. Certain characteristics have remained stable over the hundred-year period, with vamilijas E and F among those with the smallest average household size and lowest percentage of land holdings of six hectares and over. In 1863 they had the lowest average property valuation and in 1966 the lowest percentage of adult males in full-time agriculture.

The size of land holdings correlates with the percentage of men in agriculture, as expectable. For example, in 1966 among 17 households of vamilija F there were only nine full-time farmers, while among the 19 households of vamilija A there were 26. Vamilijas A and B contain prosperous farmers and each have produced a few university-trained professionals among kin who have left the village. There are no professionals from vamilijas E and F, although these groups do contain a large proportion of peasant-workers, some with skills. Among 18 pensioners in the overall sample, in 1966 eleven (including ten ex-miners) come from vamilija E alone. There are no pensioners in vamilijas A and B, nor are there any apprentices in these groups.

Rigid conclusions should not be drawn from these data, but it is obvious that belonging to a particular vamilija does, to an important degree, determine one's chances for success. A member of a less prosperous household that is part of a higher status vamilija is more likely to find it easier to obtain various forms of assistance. There is also the subtle factor of the setting in which one's aspirations are formed. Even political influence can continue within the same descent group. Vamilija A, for example, contains prominent prewar gazdas who were active politically and also whose holdings were subjected to the postwar land reform. At the same time, the long-term secretary of the local Communist party cell that functioned in the village after the war was from vamilija A. Village leaders and party members have also come from among miners in vamilija E. Characteristically, during the 1950s the three most important village functionaries came from vamilijas A, B, and C. No village leaders have come from vamilija F, which is a clearly defined low-status group. Vamilija F has been more prominent recently in terms of premarital pregnancies and for a member arrested for a serious crime (although the latter is rare in the village among all groups).

Rate of emigration from the village seems to relate to vamilija membership but not primarily to vamilija socioeconomic status. The largest numbers of recent migrants have been from vamilijas A and D and the fewest from C and F. The data are suggestive of different paths of occupational and spatial mobility out of agriculture and the village.

Emphasis on farming as a full-time occupation also predictably correlates with higher land holdings. But because of the importance of income and social benefits from jobs in socially owned enterprises, differences in size of land holdings cannot be said to relate closely to marked differences in living standards. Also there are significant differences among households in the same vamilija.

NO SOCIAL CLASSES

Clearly defined social classes have never existed in Orašac. As was indicated in the preceding chapter and particularly in the series of figures illustrating a familial cycle (Figures 7–14), the degree of prosperity can vary significantly over an individual's lifetime and in the past depended largely on the size of the holding and the number of able-bodied workers at any given time. However, as the summarized data suggest, it appears likely that not all individuals experienced the same kinds of familial-household developmental cycles. The ideal types of paternal or fraternal zadrugas were presumably experienced more frequently by those households in vamilija groups with the generally larger land holdings, as was true in the example detailed. Further, land holdings, while not equally distributed in relation to population, are not sufficiently concentrated in any particular groups in a way that would result in markedly disproportionate control of community resources.

The paucity of nineteenth-century written records concerning village affairs (due to the level of economic development, lack of widespread effective literacy, and reluctance of villagers to formalize property arrangements in writing) prevents reconstructing in detail the reasons why certain vamilijas achieved a degree of dominance and others did not. Obvious factors such as the date of settlement by the vamilija founder and subsequent participation in early political and military events were probably significant.

Larger average household size has tended to correlate with larger holdings. Reminiscences by older villagers equate household size with prosperity even though it is possible but less likely that on a per capita basis the amount of land and livestock held by a smaller household might have been roughly equivalent to that of a larger one.

There were other kinds of differences. In 1863 vamilija F had more people than vamilija A and less land. This may well have led to a greater rate of natural increase for vamilija A. The relative population figures for both A and F for 1863 and 1961 are not strictly comparable because of emigration. If recent trends are suggestive of past developments, the relative growth rates of these two groups may be even more contrastive because of the high rate of emigration in vamilija A.

Two features of the data stand out: One is their group characteristic with respect to the total village population and the other is their relationships to one another over the years. These six vamilijas contained 28 percent of the total village population in 1863 and 33 percent in 1961. With the exceptions of vamilijas D and E all groups increased, although at varying rates.

What seems most significant is not the differences but rather the remarkable relative stability of the population and certain aspects of the vamilijas' mutual relationships over a century of wars, natural disasters, migration, and a revolution. Being a member of a particular vamilija can thus be seen as a significant indicator of socioeconomic status and one that has a degree of stability over time but one whose importance should be viewed in an overall perspective, particularly with regard to flexibility of income sources.

Modernization in Peasant Society

Much of the thinking that has characterized modernization in peasant society has revolved around distinctions between rural and urban, parochial peasant and sophisticated urbanite, or viewed another way, corrupt city living and the purity of the village. The source of a nation's essence was seen as originating in its villages,

A house completed in 1970

while leadership and ideas emanated from the city. These generalized dichotomies as described in literary writings go back at least to Roman times and are learned in many parts of the world as the tale of the country mouse and the city mouse. But what is happening in the twentieth century is something unique in the history of the world—the gradual disappearance of a distinctive rural subculture, a peasant way of life. It is not possible to view this change as simply urban influences penetrating village life in the aspect of improved roads, better agricultural methods and crop yields, more educational and health facilities, electrification, and readily available agents of mass communication such as the transistor radio. Rather, change should also be viewed in terms of rural influences impacting on town life in a more dramatic and intense way than has been the case to date, at the same time that the urban influences are affecting rural life. This impact is directly related to the mass migrations from villages to towns, out of agriculture and into industry and other urban occupations. A shorthand expression of this situation is the simultaneous urbanization of the village and the peasantization of the town.

Clearly, this is what is happening in Yugoslavia generally, in Serbia in particular, and specifically in Orašac and the other villages surrounding Arandjelovac. As the history of Serbia shows, the case is somewhat specific in that the towns developed out of the countryside during the past century and a half, so that there is no old urban tradition as such. And all town dwellers can trace their village roots, at most no more than a few generations removed.

VILLAGE IMPACT ON TOWN

The traditional and obvious impacts of the peasant on the town—in terms of the craftsmen who served his particular needs and the important role of the town marketplace—have become progressively less important. Now the new factories and growing tourism are beginning to overshadow the earlier functions of Arandjelovac. At the same time that these developments are taking place, village-derived values can be perceived in many aspects of the lives of the new migrants to town.

For the people of Arandjelovac and the surrounding villages, this is involvement in industrialization the first time around. In the mid-twentieth century Yugoslavia, with contemporary technology and working conditions, the impact of industrialization is quite different than it was in England or America a century or more ago. Further, the socialist system and planning projections have given a particular slant to the Yugoslav experience with modernization.

In addition to the new factory and expanded facilities at the spa, a striking feature of present-day Arandjelovac is the growing number of private homes on the outskirts. Built in the same style as new village homes, these are, for the most part, residences of families who have moved there from surrounding villages, including Orašac. In contrast to many of the civil servants and most of the technicians and professional personnel, who tend to change job locations, the workers, once they build homes on the periphery of Arandjelovac after moving from the village, consider these to be their residences for life.

Not only outward appearance but household furnishings as well are similar to those one sees in the village. The kitchen, with its wood stove, is the focal point of the home, especially in winter, for it is usually the only heated room. Most household activities take place here; the other rooms tend to be used for sleeping only. As in the village pattern, often a bed in the kitchen is used by an older relative or by children. Similarly, the so-called guest room is set aside, as in the village, to display choice items of handiwork, and the walls are adorned with photographs of relatives, dominated by large portraits of ancestors. Occasionally there is a colored lithograph of the family's patron saint. Most of the recent arrivals are relatively young, and many are politically active, factors which would tend to lessen the occurrence of overt religious display.

With electrification, most homes in town now have a radio. Some have a phonograph and, increasingly frequently, a television set. There is usually no indoor plumbing, the water supply coming from a well in the yard or from a shared outside tap. In 1966 water lines and a sewer system were constructed in Arandjelovac. Private home-owners pay to be connected to the lines, and most former villagers feel this is not as necessary a hook-up as that for electricity. Often chickens wander in and out of the kitchen. In the courtyard a pig may be kept, although attempts have been made to ban pigs within town limits. In front of the dwelling there may be a small vegetable garden and a few fruit trees.

The owners of such homes emphatically say that they could not think of "living with strangers," that is, in an apartment house, even if a flat were available, despite the fact that multiple dwellings usually have piped water, indoor toilets, and tile stoves for heating in all rooms.

A worker usually uses his annual vacation time to improve his new house and yard, a process which takes a good many years. As in the village, a house is often constructed in stages, over a period of years, with ground-level kitchen and perhaps one sleeping room ready when the family moves in, the upper level and additional refinements added gradually as funds and time are available.

TIES TO THE VILLAGE

Usually the worker receives considerable help from his village relatives, in the actual construction labor as well as in the use of peasant carts for transporting bricks and cement. His or his wife's parents usually provide him with wine, rakija,

The village clinic

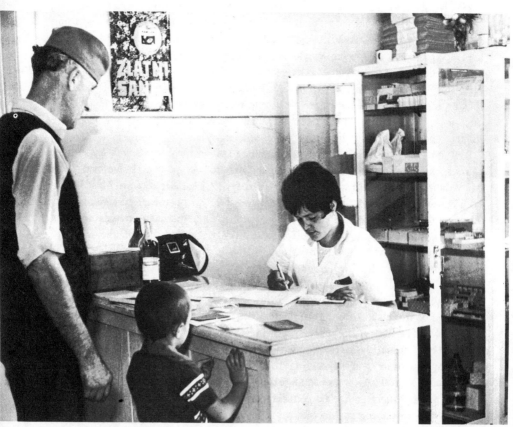

cheese, eggs, fruit, and occasionally chicken and meat. He repays these gifts by helping with farm work in the village on weekends or during part of his vacation. The food contributed by a parent and the ability to thus provide for one's children is a source of pride, and it would be incorrect to say that labor and gifts are repaid in a precisely formulated way. The ties that bind are close, and mutual obligations continue to be strongly felt. When a parent in the village dies, the surviving parent often moves in with the married child in town. There are also informal reciprocal relationships between a brother who has remained on the land and the worker in town. The town brother will often go to the village during his vacation to help with the harvesting, and he will send his children there for vacations. At the same time, if the village brother's child goes on in school he will usually live with his uncle in town.

PULLS TOWARD THE TOWN

A worker is in some cases a member of the party, and his permanent establishment in town, especially if he holds a clerical or minor administrative position, can be facilitated by earlier activity in the former village party cell which enabled him to establish useful connections in the first place. Such an individual is generally more concerned with the larger world than are his contemporaries in the village. Some men are anxious to continue their schooling. Another looks forward to the day when he can buy a car and take his family to Dalmatia "to see the sea." But desires for an electric stove or television, or continuing responsibilities in the village, postpone his daydream. If there are children, the wife usually does not work. A family such as this exhibits strong satisfaction in the successful achievement of having "left the village mud behind." Although there is a strong village flavor in these settlements of ex-villagers, still the working patterns are different than in the village and so are the values. More free time exists and the daily struggle with rounds of chores is not present.

Certainly some aspects of the peasantization of the town are of relatively short duration, as, for example, with respect to lack of water and plumbing. As for keeping pigs and chickens and raising vegetables, this is in part related to current price levels; it is often felt to be more economical to fatten a pig and then have the meat and the year's supply of lard. Also, it is hard to learn to make extensive and repeated cash purchases after having lived on a subsistence based economy, especially since in the early years of settling in town there is the need to save as much as possible for completing the house.

Municipal authorities are naturally concerned about the persistence of village patterns in town. Factory managers are dismayed when the new migrant puts forth his best efforts in nest-building and not in the job. Further, Yugoslav factories emphasize the active participation of workers in the management process, and all attention drawn away from participation in factory affairs, to build a house or help relatives in the village, is obviously regarded as counter-productive. And of course it places greater strain on the worker, who has less energy for the job. This is much less a problem for the ex-peasant residing in town than for the peasant-worker who continues to maintain his village residence and holdings. In either case, however, participation in the totality of urban existence is diminished.

Many factories maintain rest homes and hotels in vacation areas. Peasant-workers rarely take advantage of these facilities, but the newly settled migrants are beginning to do so. It will be interesting to see how ex-villagers integrate themselves into town life over the next few decades. What has been witnessed in Arandjelovac during the 1960s essentially has been part of a settling-in process slowed in part by lack of district government funds to provide adequate housing, paved streets, enough school facilities, and other urban amenities to meet the rural influx. This situation is becoming familiar the world over.

Many of the initial features of peasants settling in town will pass. We are discussing here a small town of some 10,000 people, with the villages of origin nearby. The experiences of a villager who moves to Belgrade or even to a medium-sized town such as Kragujevac, the district seat, vary somewhat. In Arandjelovac kinship and friendship ties are easily preserved, although even with respect to a move to Belgrade the total size of the country in both area and in population make possible a kind of continuity not possible to maintain to the same extent in larger countries.

There are more subtle aspects of peasantization that relate to changes in behavior over a period of generations and not decades. In a sense these are parallel to problems faced by first- and second-generation immigrants in America, many of whom came from peasant backgrounds in Europe. The first-generation town dweller is preoccupied with the struggle to establish himself in town in a psychological sense even though the outward material adjustments may be made more quickly. This is reflected in choice of recreation, ways in which surplus money is spent, aspirations for children's education, and judgments regarding the important things in life. Also important is his attitude toward village life and agriculture as an occupation: He either will feel still strongly bound to the village or will consciously reject many of the values associated with farming. He will rarely be indifferent. Further, part of the psychological urge to establish oneself in town is a felt need both to over-compensate and to become more "urban," often in a particularly demonstrative way.

An Ex-Peasant's Comments

The situation of the man whose comments follow is illustrative, although he was perhaps poorer than most. He is 41, his wife is 37, and their three daughters are 13, 8, and 6. His mother has remained in the village with his brother who commutes every day to a job in town. Before the war the household of the two brothers and their father was among the poorest in the village with less than a hectare of land. He served in the war for a year and was wounded several times. After his father died in 1945 he became apprenticed to different masons in Arandjelovac.

During the past eleven years I have been a party member. My first job in Arandjelovac was with the Pioneer Construction Enterprise and the next for a building cooperative. Then I got work at the electro-porcelain factory, where I still am. In 1955 I took and passed the exam to become a master mason. As a foreman I now have some 7 masons and 6 unskilled workers working under me.

In addition to my salary I also receive a children's allowance. In order to build my house I took out a loan through the factory which I will repay over the next 30 years. About a fourth of my salary—including the children's allotments—I use to pay the mortgage. [This is much higher than the usual percentage.] I sometimes take out credit to buy clothing, things we need. The salary of the director of the factory is only about three times mine.

I met my wife at the market fair in Arandjelovac. She came from the village of Markovac, from a rather poor household. For a dowry she brought only one wardrobe closet and bedding. We then rented a room and a kitchen on the main street in Arandjelovac. The morning after our marriage we had nothing to eat. My wife went to her father in Markovac to ask for help. Her father was angry claiming that he had thought she was marrying into Orašac and not Arandjelovac. He said he thought he had married his daughter in a village and not in town. When she lived at home he had been very hard on her, making her get up at midnight to cut cornstalks for fodder. On that first visit home her mother gave my wife a pot, two plates, two spoons, two forks, and one knife. This was in 1951.

After several months we bought a bed, two chairs, and a table. For two years we lived in our room. Then I found a plot of land for sale on the main street. It was only 13 *are*, small, but enough. We agreed to economize and eat less in order to have the money to buy it. In 1953 I began to build a house. My wife helped with the labor and so did relatives from Orašac, who also provided some of the wood. I made the bricks myself. While construction was going on I had a liver attack and had to spend six months in the hospital. My wife visited me every day. When I got out relatives and fellow workers helped with the roof.

After my first daughter was born my wife said that we didn't need more than one child because we were poor. I still wanted to have a son. A second daughter was born and later a third. But now we have enough children. We would like our oldest daughter, now in the fourth grade, to be either a typist or seamstress, but if she were a good student we would be willing to send her further in school.

My older brother in the village would like to adopt my oldest daughter since they have no children. Now he has to get up at four every morning to go to work. If he would move to Arandjelovac I would allow him to adopt our daughter. But my sister-in-law says she doesn't want to move to town. She says she wouldn't like having to go to market every day to buy everything. She claims that in the village she has everything she needs. My mother would like to come and live in town, but my brother has not yet decided, because of his wife's influence. I have already signed over to him my land in the village, but if he were to come here I would help him build a house. If my mother were to move to town and live with us she could watch the children, and then my wife could work. She could be something like a janitress in a school and so earn some money so that we could live a little better.

We make great efforts for our children and we live for them. But when the children grow up they will not worry about their parents. I went through a lot to build the house; if I die the house will remain and the children will have a roof over their heads.

His wife comments:

I look after the children and I'm concerned about their schooling. But I can't do much since I have only two grades of school myself. I watch them while they do their lessons. There are so many costs involved—copy books, pencils, drawing books, materials for handicrafts, and the mid-morning snack. Sometimes, when there is a parents' meeting, they decide to buy something for the school, and because this is a group decision all parents have to pay a share even though it is difficult for some. But no one wants to be an exception and not pay.

The man continues:

When the children grow up I will sell this house and get an apartment [room] and live there with my baba like a pensioner. I built the house here because here it is possible to have pigs, chickens, and a little orchard. In this way we can live more cheaply.

The Peasant as Employee

The peasant-worker living on his holding and commuting to a job outside his village is an important component of the Yugoslav labor force. According to a special agricultural census in 1960, it is estimated that there are some 1,306,000 peasant-workers in a total labor force of 2,985,000. The presence of these peasant-workers and the departure of primarily young people from the village have significantly altered the age structure of the full-time agricultural labor force. Between 1953 and 1961 the age-50-to-64 group increased its proportional representation in the total agricultural labor force from 15 to 22 percent, while the age-15-to-19 group declined from 18 to 12 percent. Even more striking is the contrast in age structures of the agricultural and industrial labor forces. Of the total number of male workers (miners, industrial workers, and craftsmen) in 1961, 54 percent were 20–34 years of age, 22 percent were 35–49 years, and only 12 percent were 50 or over, as contrasted with 33, 21, and 35 percent, respectively, for agricultural workers. The peasant-workers were by and large the younger men; 58 percent of agricultural workers were under 40 as contrasted to 73 percent of peasant-workers. Further, the agricultural work force now has more women than men, if part-time workers are included and peasant-workers excluded.[5]

The peasant commuter is usually enmeshed in a conflicting situation: He wishes to work and at the same time to operate his small farm. In the prewar period and earlier, when a member of a peasant household went to work in a nearby town or even went off to a distant city for considerable periods the matter was not as crucial as it is today. Then the household was larger and the loss of his labor less keenly felt. A brother, cousin, or physically mature son could take over most of his chores.

During the past few decades there has been a decrease in the size of the household, more aged members, and an accompanying fragmentation of land. In the postwar period not only has the status of agriculture as a way of life declined, but the economic advantage of the agricultural producer has decreased. Although recent official policies have attempted to halt these trends, the segment composed of migrants and peasant-workers is not confined to those who have small holdings.

---

[5] Joel M. Halpern, "Farming as a Way of Life: Yugoslav Peasant Attitudes," in Jerzy F. Karcz, ed., *Soviet and East European Agriculture*, Berkeley and Los Angeles, University of California Press, 1967, pp. 364–365.

Strains on Families of Peasant-Workers

According to the 1960 census, 217 out of 454 Orašac households had members actively employed off the holding (many worked in the then functioning lignite mine). Although the majority of these households had less than 5 hectares, 56 of the 102 households in the village with holdings of 5 or more hectares contained peasant-workers. Much of the burden for running the farm, especially while the men are at work, has fallen on the younger women, who have distaff duties to attend to in addition to the new farm chores, such as feeding and watering the livestock, a task formerly done by the men. The major agricultural tasks such as plowing, reaping, or threshing are difficult for them because of the nonmechanized technology and necessity for sheer physical strength. When women are relied on for these tasks the strain is great and the quality of production low. Further, since factory working hours usually run from 6 A.M. to 2 P.M. in the summer and an hour later in the winter, Monday through Saturday, it is sometimes necessary to get up three hours before work starts to allow time for commuting. In Orašac a minimum of an hour's walk is required each way. Despite the new bus service, for most workers the scattered pattern of village houses means that they have to walk a half hour or so to reach the road. Arriving back in the village at 3:00 or 4:00 in the afternoon, the worker hardly feels refreshed. Obviously the strain shows, in both the on-the-job performance in the factory and the quality of his agricultural labors at home. The conflict is greatest during seasons of peak agricultural work. Then "epidemics" break out, there are many absences for illness and production is seriously affected.

In the past the policy has been to encourage peasant-workers to move to town, but adequate housing has not been available.

The overall picture is not a very satisfactory one, and government planners are much concerned. A crucial factor is that the desertion of agriculture is more rapid than the replacement of their labor by mechanization, with a resultant growing scarcity of quality labor in agriculture. However, with the overburdening of the cities by migrants from the countryside and the slowing down of the tempo of industrialization in Yugoslavia in the sixties, there is a growing tendency to induce farmers to remain on the land.[6] The peasantization of the town, urbanization of the village, slowly increasing mechanization of agriculture through the state farms—these are all part of the long-term general process of diminishing distinctions between town and countryside in terms of standard of living and value systems. It was never possible to talk about rural and urban dimensions as separate ways of life in Serbian culture; it is even less so now. Different kinds of specialists in education, agriculture, and health are coming to Orašac in increasing numbers, while some of the village's most able sons and daughters go to Arandjelovac. Looking toward the future one cannot talk about a changing Orašac against a background of a modern Arandjelovac; rather, both communities are rapidly changing together. The traditional Arandjelovac of a century ago, with its small craftsmen and merchants, is just as much a part of history as is the Orašac described by Pavlović.

---

[6] Rudolf Bičanić, commentary on Halpern, "Farming as a Way of Life: Yugoslav Peasant Attitudes," pp. 382–384.

Women must do more farm work

Government Planning

It would certainly seem premature to speak of a postindustrial society with reference to this area of central Serbia. However, it is not unreasonable to attempt to envision the outlines of future change. One of the principal theoreticians of Yugoslav communism, Edvard Kardelj, conceives of the problem in broad terms, citing automation and the relative decline of the number of industrial workers while at the same time foreseeing new jobs, services, and social activities:

> It is quite clear that relatively speedy transfer of the labor force from the countryside to non-agricultural activities will continue to be not only our task but also a condition of economic progress. . . . Neither must we lose sight of the fact that this problem is solved, or at least reduced, by speedier development of agricultural production, given the ever-expanding and comprehensive cooperation of the socialist sector with individual producers, and given the improvement in general economic conditions of life and work in the countryside.[7]

Specifically intended by government planners is the expansion of existing large-scale socially owned farm enterprises by a process of land purchases from

---

[7] Edvard Kardelj, quoted in Halpern, "Farming as a Way of Life: Yugoslav Peasant Attitudes," p. 367.

owners leaving agriculture. Their overall role is still small in terms of size (they encompass about 14 percent of total arable land in Yugoslavia in 1966, representing a doubling in a decade; in Orašac it is still less than 10 percent). However, with their intensive use of machinery and fertilizers these socialist farms are now producing most of Yugoslavia's wheat. There is no doubt about the possibility for a future for private farming: The 1963 constitution is specific on this point, stating that individuals have the right to own arable land up to a maximum of 10 hectares per household, exempting woods.

Optimum Private Agriculture

We saw one aspect of the future in the migrant from Orašac who settled in Arandjelovac. Another aspect can be seen in the comments of a villager practicing a type of highly commercialized, specialized farming that does not yet exist in Orašac. He is from the prosperous village of Vinča, near Topola, not far south of Arandjelovac. His remarks point up the continued vitality of the zadruga and the way in which, under certain conditions, a maximum of full-time labor can be combined with modern production techniques, on the maximum-sized permissible private holdings. His account therefore represents the optimum in private production. One of the couples in this fraternal zadruga lacks children, and this may lend stability to this extended family household.

There are nine members of our *zajednica* [local term for zadruga]: my older brother and myself (I'm 42), my son (22), daughter-in-law and grandson (7 months), my daughter, our two wives, and our old mother (79). We have 10 hectares of arable land and three hectares of woods. We have three concrete houses forming a courtyard, which we built here by the roadside during the past five years. At the moment we have an old truck and a Volkswagen truck. In the first house we have an entry room, a large reception room, and one room for sleeping, plus a pantry and a bathroom. In the second house we have two sleeping rooms, a room for guests and a balcony. In the oldest building, which has the summer kitchen, a section is used as a smoke house, and there is also a sleeping room for workers who come for a few days to help us. We often transport them here in our small truck.

Of our arable land we have 2 hectares in vineyards and 4 in orchards, with the rest of the land planted in wheat and corn. We sell our products in Belgrade and also in Vojvodina. Where we sell depends on the price. We sell grapes and plums for export. Last year we sold 13 tons to the zadruga [marketing cooperative] here. We cooperate with the zadruga for spraying and buy artificial fertilizer from them. They plow our land with their tractor. Here in Vinča it's not as hilly as other parts of Šumadija, and we could have our own tractors, but since peasants here concentrate on vineyards and orchards tractors aren't really economical—our orchards and vineyards must be plowed gently, with a horse.

Our zajednica is fairly large, but one here in the village has 17 members. It is also headed by two brothers, but unlike ours theirs is now thinking about dividing. In our household we all eat together at one table and decide what we will do the next day. When dawn breaks each person knows exactly what he has to set out to do. There is no looking at each other and talking. The women, too, divide up their work. One week one woman is in the kitchen and the other milks the cows and works in the fields. The next week they change. Baba is in charge of the kitchen. Each wife prepares her own sleeping quarters. There is no separate family budget. All the money goes into a common fund and then we spend for what we need. My children like their uncle and aunt more than they like us.

My daughter finished the eight-year school and then she took a seamstress course. She wasn't happy in school. My only son finished four grades of elementary school, served in the army, and then came home to be an agricultural worker. This is the same amount of education my brother and I have had.

If a peasant is more literate or has finished more schooling, then he is no longer a peasant. Those who have finished middle school are neither peasants nor city people. If they return home, they can only spoil a peasant household. Such people have learned city ways, and it is hard for one of them to accept being a hard-working peasant. You have to get into the dirt and have calluses on your hands. Many households here in Vinča have fallen because of this—the son returns home, but one day he decides not to be a hard worker and to enter state employment. Then his household's land and production fails. He has accomplished nothing. Neither has he secured a good position for himself in town nor has he resolved his problem with the land.

We, in our household, have had success only with what our blistered hands and sweat have earned. In the future we would like to have a good barn for our cattle, a modern brick one. It would also be good to have piped water so that we can lessen the burden of watering the stock. At present we have only a well. If we had piped water we could raise pigs as well, you know, rig up what they already have in foreign countries, where the stock are watered right in the barn and feeding the cattle is mechanized.

Some people, instead of putting their capital into greater production, want to live better. We in our household are aggressive about improving production. Relocating our house near the road is more convenient for us since we now have our whole complex of land behind the dwellings. This year the commune will pave the road and we will be able to get to town more easily.

Physically our work is very hard. We work 18 hours a day during the season, not seven or eight. In summer we get up at three, feed and water the livestock and then go to work in the vineyards. When one wants to have greater productivity, that productivity requires more work. For instance, this year we hoed our orchard twice, plus two sprayings plus applications of artificial fertilizer and manure. Otherwise the yield would not be every year but every fifth year, as in former times. Of course, labor today is not what it was earlier. You can't find workers who will help you. Our surplus labor has gone to work in industry.

For my daughter, I would like her to be able to escape this physical work. To save her from this she should go somewhere in town, where life will be easier. When I was a pupil I asked to go on in school, but my *stric* didn't permit me. He said that we had land, and for whom was the land? My father was together with his older brother, the starešina. I was a good pupil in elementary school but when the elder ordered it one had to listen.

It is not necessary only to produce. We must also sell our produce. Our country has to export, and so it is with us peasants: we have to market our produce. Without this we cannot build a house, buy a TV, or get a truck tomorrow. Harvest time is hardest of all. One must work the whole day and then on into the night, driving to market with the crop. I have worked for 2 months and not for one night of this period did I lie down in my own bed. I go to market and then work till 12 or 1 and then return home and load up again. As agricultural producers we must work hard in our younger years to have what we need to live on when we get old.

It is in crucial areas such as this production of fruit crops that the government is attempting to encourage the individual farmer. Technologically advanced specialization, as this household practices it, where the use of big machinery is not feasible, is obviously part of the future picture for the agriculture of this region. It remains to be seen, however, whether price incentives alone will be sufficient to motivate the younger generation to stay on the land and whether sufficient suitable mechanical equipment can be made available to lighten the physical burden so that farming may become more attractive, perhaps even to those with specialized training in agriculture.

4

Living Out Lives

B Y MEANS OF HISTORICAL RECORDS and our field data the preceding chapters
have presented analyses of the social and economic bases of Serbian village
society. In this chapter and the one following, we want to bring the village
to life, to populate the setting and to glimpse aspects of everyday life and special
occasions. Descriptions of the annual holiday cycles and transition rites in an
individual's lifetime have been published earlier,[1] and here we want to detail, within
a time perspective, ways in which some individuals go through certain ritually
embellished life crises. We also want to highlight a new one, the direction a village
youth takes on completion of the eight-year school.

Through participation in religious and secular ceremonies villagers reaffirm
membership in the household and extended kin group. In addition there are other,
less public, beliefs and practices by means of which individuals or entire households attempt to exert control over those who might harm them or might not
conform with their wishes.

We want to try to express the context in which these events take place, to
convey how villagers feel about change, how they make decisions, and react to
important alterations in their lives. People follow cultural patterns, but they do so
as individuals. To supplement autobiographical excerpts already presented, we
include here fragments of true conversations.

In Yugoslavia there is also the postrevolutionary framework of very rapid
social and economic change. In a relatively stable peasant society the most vital
questions revolve around succession to family headship and inheritance of rights
to the land. Today in Yugoslavia the ways in which members of each household
articulate themselves to the expanding nonagricultural, industrializing town as
part of their society are more crucial.

---

[1] Joel M. Halpern, *A Serbian Village,* New York, Harper & Row, 1967.

Infancy

Orašac villagers over age 50 recall that when they were children, many infants did not survive the first year. Today infant mortality is greatly reduced.[2] Since the early 1960s most village women have been having their babies in the maternity ward of the health center in Arandjelovac. Those who are *moderni* have gone to town for monthly checkups. There is no charge for maternity care, and any village woman can take advantage of the service; the only drawback is one of logistics—readying a cow cart or horse-drawn wagon or paying a villager with a car to make the trip to town. The value of prenatal care is recognized but often considered not worth the effort.

Once home in the village the tightly wrapped infant, having received standard postnatal care at the health center, is immediately subjected by its grandmother to time-honored precautions, just in case. The baby is unwrapped and gently rubbed with warm melted lard. It is securely swaddled from armpits to toes with a length of brightly colored braided yarn. It is placed on a bed, where relatives and neighbors can come to admire it and wish the parents and grandparents well. In order to discourage the evil eye, a clove of garlic is put on the infant's forehead, and as a further barrier two hand-forged iron wool combers are placed spikes outward on either side of the tiny head.

The birth is registered with the village clerk, and those parents who wish to, or whose own parents or grandparents urge them, arrange for a traditional christening service at the church. The infant's godfather, who plays an honorific role throughout his lifetime, has the privilege of choosing the name. The combination naming and baptism takes place in the cold basement rectory of the church, where the priest pours water over the naked infant. The kum, receiving the baby in a linen towel, proudly pronounces the name he has selected. A small piece of the infant's hair is snipped off and rolled into a ball together with wax from a candle used in the ceremony. Swinging his censer, the priest leads the godfather and father in a prayer around the ceremonial table. The sign of the cross is made over the infant, and a crucifix is touched to his forehead, lips, and genitals. Finally the kum spits lightly over his godchild, "to confuse the evil eye."

Babies are swaddled until they are about six months old or ready to start creeping. When asked why, a new village mother replies, "I don't know. I do it to please my mother-in-law." Says the mother-in-law, "We swaddle so that his legs will be straight and so that he will be *miran* [peaceful]."

Until the mid-1960s there was no question about nursing procedures. All babies were breast fed, if not by the mother then by a relative or neighbor. Now, however, glass·nursing bottles are coming into fashion as more young mothers desire to be up-to-date and also to assert themselves especially with respect to their mothers-in-law. "Look at it this way," says one, "this is one thing that I and only I have control over. My mother-in-law can't tell me what to do."

---

[2] In the 1880s over 40 percent of deaths were of infants under one year. By 1950 the figure fell to 25 percent, and the 1970 rate is much lower.

Special attention is given to the baby's diet until the first teeth appear, after which he is fed what the adults eat except for extremely greasy or spicy foods. Free advice is available from a children's dispensary in town, and as a result the more diligent village mothers now daily squeeze shredded carrots in order to prepare a vitamin drink. As in the past, a healthy baby is a fat baby, and affection is shown by continually offering tidbits of food. A common endearment for the ideal round-headed, plump-cheeked Serbian baby is "little pumpkin."

One grandmother watching her four-month-old grandson getting wiped and powdered shakes her head and says, "In my day, plunk him down in the cradle, tuck a little fresh straw underneath, a little scrap of rag between his legs, and *gotovo*, finished! Today, my God, a little blanket, a little pillow, a little white diaper. Powder! When I was young who would have thought of such things."

Reacting to her daughter-in-law's determination to take a toddler for periodic checkups at the clinic another village grandmother remarks, "It used to be, when a child fell or stepped on a thorn, pour on a little rakija, that's all. But now, hu ha, right away run to the doctor!"

Older villagers recall that children used to be fed cornmeal mush from a common wooden bowl at a low table in a corner of the kitchen. They never ate with grownups and never dared interrupt the men. "The trick was to keep your eyes on that wooden bowl and your mouth open only to shovel the mush in as fast as you could. In those days we didn't dare look up for fear of missing a spoonful or of making a grownup angry." Children were disciplined with spankings, cuffs on the shoulder, and ear and nose tweaking. One agent of discipline which has survived the generations is "Mirko," an anthropomorphic willow switch that resides above the door lintel and starts to twitch and jump off its perch in the presence of a naughty child.

Bringing up Children

Now small children are often reasoned with as a first resort before applying hand or switch. A grandfather exclaims, "Good God, now even a little child is born with an eighth-grade diploma! Who ever heard of talking sense with children? I like it better my way. All whippings are heaven-sent."

Around the household compound small children are dressed in nondescript layers of cut-down clothing. When taken out in public they are dressed as elaborately as possible. Children are status symbols, and the appearance of a child in a hand-knitted outfit and immaculate white stockings is instant testimonial to the industry and *kultura* of his family.

Language is used freely as a vehicle of emotion in Serbian village society. Children early learn to curse as part of the normal process of language acquisition. A well-brought-up child is one who is respectful of elders, does not talk unless spoken to, and is not restless in adult company. For whatever reason, if such a child starts cursing in the presence of people outside the family, the parents will excuse him with a nervous laugh and a remark that this behavior is learned from children down the lane.

A chicken wanders into the kitchen where four-year-old Dušan is munching a slab of bread smeared with lard. It falls on the floor and the chicken pecks it up. "Screw you, you wretched chicken," mumbles Dušan.

Going to School

Going to school used to be a great privilege and completing the four-year village school an accomplishment. Since the end of the war, education has been compulsory. The Orašac school has been expanded into a full eight-year school, and it is now necessary for all village children to attend until they complete the eight grades or are sixteen years of age. Most villagers between the ages of 30 and 50 are literate and have finished fourth grade.

School starts with first grade when a child is seven. This milestone coincides with his assumption of household responsibilities. As the composition of the household changes and contracts in size, small children have to participate more and more in real tasks. They are counted on now to do things other persons might have performed when there were more people living under one roof. It is more than a matter of gathering kindling and fetching things. Young children watch the cows, sheep, and pigs, feed the chickens, help in the vegetable garden and around the house. Even for small children it is sometimes difficult to get one's chores done on time. "Mother of God, I don't know how I can manage," an eight-year-old was heard to declare as she dashed from the sheep hutch to collect her striped woolen school bag and go off to school.

Formerly childhood was the time when training began for sexual division of labor. But girls are no longer taught to spin on a distaff. Now they learn some woodworking in school, and boys learn to do simple knitting and cooking. This would have been thoroughly unacceptable to fathers and grandfathers a generation ago. The trend toward lack of labor division extends all the way to heavy work which was formerly exclusively men's. This includes swinging a scythe in the hayfields; many teen-age girls are today learning, of necessity, how to handle one. This shortage of able-bodied men in peasant agriculture may represent a transitional stage in the modernization process, but its social impact is strong.

Special Role of Grandparents

Combined with responsibility is the knowledge that children are loved and needed. There is an especially warm relationship between grandparents and grandchildren, with much kissing, stroking, and verbal manifestation of affection. Often a child and grandparent share a bed, for warmth and security as well as for convenience.

Grandparents have played a special role in reciting the old epics and folk songs and transmitting these to their grandchildren along with a fervent sense of national identity and pride in ancestry. Village elders would enchant children for hours when playing the single-stringed *gusle* as an accompaniment to the measured chanting of the heroic tales of the Serbian kings and the struggles against the Turks.

A special warmth between grandparents and grandchildren

These poems are now readily available in printed form, and although children still love to hear their grandparents' recitations and songs, on most other themes they are sure they know more than their elders do.

Preparation for the Future

Parents have mixed feelings about their children's futures. Always one hears doubts expressed about the value of more than four years of school for a village child: "Give a boy more than four grades and it ruins him for peasant farming. We'll pay the penalty tax and pull him out of school next year. He's needed here on the land." Some say, "The peasant's way of life is one of constant suffering. I want to give my son opportunities I never had." Many parents' ambitions for their daughters are to find ways to help them escape from village life. But if a girl is not a good student or if her labor is needed at home in the years before a marriage is arranged, then there is little she can do but "stay home and dig."

The curriculum at the village school is based on a semester plan prepared by an education committee for the Republic of Serbia. Many innovations have been introduced, such as excursions and visual aids, but instruction remains basically learning by rote. Children are not taught how to learn but what to learn. In the earlier years, a good part has to do with classroom technique. One pupil is called to the portable blackboard while the others write in their copy books. When initiating this procedure, which is used throughout elementary school, the teacher intones, "In your left hand, sponge; in your right hand, chalk. Write!"

Finishing the eighth grade marks a crucial turning point. It is tacit recognition that the boy or girl has some talent and will probably not remain on the land. Out of 32 recently completing eighth grade, only three or four had no plans other than to stay in the village. Some were going to learn a trade, and twenty had hopes of going on to a middle school. Of this number their teacher estimated that about twelve would make it. There are three alternatives to staying in the village: to be apprenticed to a private craftsman or to a state enterprise which offers on-the-job training, to be enrolled in a middle technical school or, rarely, to go on to the *gimnazijum*, the academic high school in Arandjelovac.

DOBROSAV

Dobrosav is seventeen. He completed the village school with an undistinguished record and with no plan for further schooling. His father's holding is small, something over two hectares, and without enough work to keep a young man occupied. The farm work such as it is is done mostly by his mother; his father works in a factory. Through connections in his mother's village, arrangements were made for him to be apprenticed to a stone-cutter there. This craftsman deals mainly in custom-made tombstones and also handles incidental jobs such as granite steps. Dobrosav gets room and board plus 20 dinars a day (approximately $1.60 in 1970). Dobrosav and his parents consider this a very good deal. He does not have to help his master's wife with household tasks.[3] He is proud that he

---

[3] Compare with the recollections of an apprentice in 1934–1935 (see Chapter 3, p. 63).

has progressed from working on steps and cornerstones to beginning to do lettering on tombstones: "My *majstor* does the stars and angels, but to speak frankly, I'm more literate than he is, and it's a great help to have me with him. When you work in stone you have to do it right the first time." Dobrosav walks the three hours home to Orašac every Saturday to spend the weekend. He is proud to be self-sufficient, and as a mark of his wage earning wears the latest in flared slacks and tapered lace-cloth shirt.

ZORICA

Zorica's family permitted her to complete the village school because her labor was not needed full-time on the land, and especially because they wanted to enhance her possibilities for a marriage outside the village. With this in mind they encouraged her to enroll in the four-year commercial course at the middle technical school in Smederevska Palanka, where she could board with relatives of her godfather. Her parents' plan was for her to find a job in Arandjelovac at the end of her schooling, so that she could work there and live at home until a suitable marriage could be arranged. An important part of the scheme was that Zorica's income-producing potential plus the impressive fact of twelve years of schooling would figure importantly in the dowry inventory. Currently she is in her third year at the middle school, and there are aspects of Zorica's higher education her family does not know about. She has a boyfriend in Palanka and last month took off two days to go to Belgrade for an abortion. "My father and grandfather will kill me if they find out," she confides, "but truly it's their fault. They are trying to plan out my life for me."

JOVAN

Jovan, whom we met earlier and who is employed in a machine shop in Belgrade, was graduated two years previously from a vocational training school. He considers himself lucky to have gotten a job just a few months after receiving his machinist's certificate and attributes this not only to his skill but to his family's contacts. "Everything depends on *veze*, connections, who you know." Once Jovan's move off the land became an established fact, however, his father and grandfather had misgivings. As a strong young man in a household with enough land to support him, his labor is now sorely missed by an aging grandfather and by a father already past his prime. Dragutin, Jovan's father, blames all that goes wrong on the fact that his son has left the village. He often says bitterly, "Look at me. A man without a son. My own father was right. We made a big mistake. We over-educated the boy and he is no longer good for village life." Dragutin's father sums it up this way: "Youth today is ruined, no good. There is nothing more one can say."

VELJKO AND MIRA

A village grandmother agrees. She says of her two urban grandchildren,

Take Veljko now. A seventeen-year-old boy, and he can't pass mathematics. I tell my daughter and son-in-law, "Why do you keep the child in gimnazijum if he can't pass mathematics?" And do you know how they pamper him? They hire a tutor, 60 dinars for two hours. Dear God! And look at the boy, thin, pale, no interest in anything but that transistor he carries next to his ear. When I was young a boy his age would be strong, capable of doing a man's work.

With my granddaughter, Mira, it's a different story, thank God. They spoil her, too, but she's a girl and a medical student. Poor child, studying is a very difficult occupation. You can't even have a boyfriend. She even had to cut off her long hair because she had no time to take care of it. When my granddaughter is studying for exams, my daughter keeps the apartment quiet and runs to Mira every hour with coffee. Imagine, a student has to struggle to stay awake! She refreshes the child by soothing her temples and wrists with a handkerchief dipped in cologne. But it takes courage and nerves to be a medical student. For the kind of work I was raised to do, all it takes is strength.

The Choices

The real crisis, then, in the course of growing up in Orašac is the crucial decision about finishing the village school and about what happens afterward. Whatever the outcome, it vitally affects the young person concerned and all members of his household as well. For those who do not complete eighth grade, either because they cannot keep up with the school work or because their families do not want them to continue, dropping out tends to separate them from their age mates who continue. Girls who are not in school tend to stay home, and boys are increasingly finding unskilled jobs as day laborers for agricultural work or in menial maintenance work in Arandjelovac. Often these young people together with some older village women make up the bulk of the seasonal labor force for the local cooperative farm.[4]

For those who finish eighth grade and especially for the ones who go further, the factors determining these moves are complex. Academic ability is certainly significant. Also it is important to come from a fairly prosperous household which can afford the expense of supporting a student away from home. At the same time, coming from a household with a fair-sized holding (five hectares or more of arable land) can increase pressure on a boy to remain in the village, especially if he is an only son. If the youth has ability the family is confronted with the familiar dilemma: Many parents want to give their children opportunities that did not exist when they themselves were growing up, and at the same time there is a fervent desire to continue tilling the family's land.

Sometimes a compromise of sorts can be reached, when a son is able to get a job of some skill in town and continue to live at home, contributing cash plus labor to the farm economy. This is becoming more common as employment opportunities in Belgrade, Arandjelovac, and other places become tighter, and as Orašac becomes recognized (by young people) as not so bad after all, now that the pitted road through the village is partially paved and one can easily get from village to town by motorbike or bus.

---

[4] The Orašac Cooperative Farm is actually currently set up as a socially owned enterprise with an organizational structure similar to that of the factories in town, except for the farm's large number of temporary workers.

The household of deda Milivoje, who is close to 70 years old, has been carefully grooming grandson Radisav to take over one day. This conservative and industrious three-generation household went to great expense to build a new house near the road, an innovation which surprised many villagers, despite the increasing trend to do so, but which Milivoje and his son knew would please Radisav. Ten years ago, when Radisav finished fourth grade, they decided to let him stay in school a little longer. "Why should the boy dig when he can be learning? We don't need his labor now." At that time, of course, the boy's father was in his prime, in his mid-thirties. Radisav was permitted to continue in school one year at a time, and when he passed the gimnazijum entrance exam his proud family let him enroll. In part bending to eventual family pressure, the young man did not complete high school, and after his compulsory army service he returned to the village and got a job in the new supermarket in town.

The large unoccupied sleeping room in the new house is called Radisav's Room. His mother and grandmother like to plan where the bride's dowry furniture will be placed, for it is fully expected that as an obedient and dutiful son of a traditional family, when he marries he will bring his bride home to his father's and grandfather's house.

Marriage as a Contract

To Šumadijans marriage is the only natural way of life. Marriage always has been viewed not as a contract between two individuals, but between two households or extended family groups. A young woman does not marry a bridegroom; she marries into such and such a household. As was brought out in Chapter 2, traditionally the tie between brother and sister or father and daughter was considered closer than that between husband and wife.[5] The marriage bond has always been a serious one, nevertheless. In the village divorce or separation was rare and continues to be the exception. Since the union and the obligations were clearly between households, for one spouse to desert the other would reflect badly on both households.

Marriages in the past were usually arranged. Many Orašac couples in their forties and fifties recall that they had scarcely seen one another before their wedding. There were various means of getting acquainted, however, such as at spinning or

---

[5] The primacy of these relationships over the marriage tie is a recurrent theme in folk poetry. In one poem a young man is wounded, and the mountain spirit demands heavy compensation in order to save him:

Her white hand demands he of the mother,
Of the sister all her silken ringlets,
Of the wife he asks her pearl-strung necklace.
Freely gave her hand young Jovan's mother,
Freely gave her silken hair his sister,
But his wife refused her pearly treasure:
Nay! I will not give my pearl-strung necklace,
For it was a present from my father.

Servian Popular Poetry, translated by John Bowring, London, printed for translator, 1827, p. 198.

threshing bees and at dances held on special market days or the day of the village's patron saint. Wedding festivities at the households of relatives or neighbors provided other opportunities.

Traditional Courtship

Before the first world war, Pavlović described the courtship pattern when young people attended fairs in Arandjelovac and Topola, from one to five hours' walk from the surrounding villages:

> Some members of almost every household go to the fair, the mother together with her daughter-in-law and daughter, while the young man of the house goes with members of the same vamilija in his age group. . . . The young men bring most money to the fairs. They prepare for this about a month in advance, for they need it for buying drinks (usually they drink beer), for lunch (in a tent or kafana), for paying for leading the kolo and for buying cakes for girls. The bachelors go all dressed up, while the daughter-in-law and daughter wrap new dresses in kerchiefs which the mother carries. When they are near the fair they get dressed, arrange their hair and rouge and powder their faces, and the old clothes are tied up in the kerchiefs which the mother again carries, and these bundles are left with some relative near the fair or in a kafana. In the evening when they return home they change into their old clothes. It is because of this dressing up, making up, and primping in the mirror (which each carries) that the women go separately.
>
> Arriving at the fair all dressed up, the girls are taken by the hand and invited to the kolo where they join in the dancing while the mothers watch from the sides. In the course of the dancing some bachelors might treat a group of maidens to lemonade or slices of melon, and they know that in the evening each girl will receive a cake from her boyfriend, the larger the cake the greater his affection.
>
> When it is time to go home things usually get rushed. The mothers are naturally happy when their daughters can dance longer, but the men come to summon them and to curse. One hears, "Come on, we're leaving now!"—"Wait 'til we find Mile. Hey where did he lose himself?"—"Never mind, he'll come home." When they do leave everyone hurries, especially the women, for much work awaits them at home. The bachelors go in groups chatting animatedly and holding hands, and the girls try to stay near them and smile at them.[6]

Contemporary Courtship Possibilities

Fairs and dances are still held. Today there are in addition independently organized village dances which, interestingly, go by the old term prelo (spinning bee). The pattern is remarkably similar to that of sixty years ago, the young people attending separately, in groups of friends, and the mothers watching from the sidelines. The young men may wear stiff new kaubojski (jeans) in place of the once proudly worn folk costume. The girls, in flowing hair and pants-suits, may use lipstick instead of dabbing their cheeks with bits of moistened red crêpe paper. The boys, linking arms, still circle the clusters of girls to look them over, and the girls still blush. The dancing and music are much the same. Few village youths

---

[6] Pavlović, Život i običaji narodni u Kragujevačkoj Jasenici u Šumadiji, pp. 42–43.

know how to do contemporary western dances (although they know about them), and all continue to enjoy the traditional kolo circle dancing.

On the surface the pattern seems unchanged. But there is a difference. Teen-agers are now more relaxed in each other's presence. Most of them have gone to school together more than twice as long as did young people of their parents' generation. Many have been together on school excursions, and there are other opportunities for contact away from the parental eye.

Youth brigade volunteers in Orašac

In the summer of 1970 a youth brigade, mainly of teen-age volunteers including many from Orašac and surrounding villages, lived together at the village school, temporarily converted into a dormitory with separate sleeping quarters. They were organized on a quasi-military basis, with both sexes sharing heavy construction work. At meals and during evening socializing the atmosphere was informal. Along with work details and political slogans, walls were posted with signs of casual match-making. Many of their songs recalled Partisan struggles of the last war, when men and women served together. The atmosphere of this kind of work group symbolizes many of the changes that have occurred in male-female relationships in the postwar period. There is formal political and legal equality and a sense of easier social interaction, although the patriarchal tradition still survives in a diminished sense.

"Love, Village Style"

The most popular television program of 1970 on the Belgrade channel was a weekly comedy serial, "Love, Village Style." Proper village parents of the period in which Pavlović wrote would be distressed by the show. The story line is the bringing about of an arranged marriage in a village like Orašac. Satire has to ring true if it is to appeal, and the enormous popularity of this program reflects the current truth in terms of the contradictions in rapidly changing village values. Urban people, themselves not far removed from village origins, and villagers too, watch with avid attention, frequently calling out commiseration or encouragement to the characters on the screen.

The hero is a strapping village youth who refuses to be forced by his extended family into a marriage for which he feels unprepared. At present he is more concerned with reading and his hobby of repairing sewing machines. The girl's parents raise questions about his masculinity, and in one episode he is dragged to the clinic in town and interviewed by a particularly voluptuous lady doctor. In the comic scenes it is always the elders who are made to appear ridiculous while the young couple, who are developing an affection for one another, begin to work matters out in their own way. These themes—the ludicrous inability of the respective families to formalize arrangements and the use of the supposed lack of virility of the boy as subjects for comedy—reveal some of the ways in which marriage patterns have altered. Family ties and property remain significant, but parental generations are now unable to use these as direct levers for obtaining their will; instead elders are in the role of cajolers and pleaders. The pretensions that both households bring to the marriage negotiations are also portrayed, but perhaps what is most important is that despite everything love, village style, remains very much a family affair.

Marriage Arrangement

In actual fact, marriage arrangement and ritual follow in form many of the old traditions. The most desirable characteristics of a prospective daughter-in-law are that she be industrious, healthy, and from a good family. The latter means not only that the girl's family be of reasonable wealth, expressed mainly in terms of land, but also that her family be regarded as conscientious and of good character. Deficiencies will tend to offset positive considerations. If the girl's family has a large holding but her father drinks too much or beats his wife too regularly or obviously, or if a sibling is a cripple, such facts are rationally noted and reckoned on the mental balance sheet. The political views of the respective households may also be a consideration. Often villagers prefer to consider a match with a poor but virtuous household, especially when there is a wage-earning potential. Naturally, all defects are not immediately apparent, particularly if the partners are from separate villages; and marriage brokers sometimes participate or relatives on both sides may act as intermediaries. If a successful marriage contract is concluded, further links between the two households may follow. Vamilija exogamy is the main marriage restriction.

Weddings generally take place in the autumn after the harvest is in and before the series of religious fasts prior to Christmas. With a decline in the religious aspects of weddings, including increasing disregard for fasting prohibitions, some of the forms are altered. The following description of a type of wedding observed and participated in by us dozens of times in the 1950s and 1960s still holds for more traditionally oriented households "making a wedding" in the early 1970s.

A Traditional Wedding

Two weeks prior to the marriage a formal betrothal ceremony takes place at the village church. A few days before the wedding day the groom's father, dressed in holiday clothes, sets out through the village to invite the wedding guests. Participation in one another's weddings and funerals is reciprocal, and the guests are prepared for his coming. The most important guest is, of course, the family's kum, who will be godfather as well to the children resulting from the marriage. Also important is the chief witness, usually the bridegroom's maternal uncle. At each household the father ceremoniously offers the head of the household a sip of brandy from his flower-garnished flask.[7] In return the invited person refills the father's flask with some of his own rakija, so that in going from house to house the father always has a full flask. Over his shoulder he carries a striped woven sack, to which each guest pins a small gift such as a towel or a handkerchief.

Early on the wedding day the groom's relatives and guests assemble in his father's courtyard. Horse-drawn carriages are borrowed or rented for the occasion and trimmed with garlands of autumn flowers. The horses have chrysanthemums twined through their bridles and long towels attached, which stream in the breeze as the party trots over village lanes to the bride's father's house. Many of the men carry pistols to shoot off and bottles of home-made brandy in outstretched hands, and they sing and shout lustily along the way. Riding in advance of the procession is a young man on horseback, a sort of jester who tells jokes and puts everyone in a festive mood. His cap is decorated with a long braid of flax and colored ribbons, and he wears a necklace strung with garlic cloves, small red peppers, and corn kernels. The origin of his role is as a parody of the bride, designed to deflect the influences of the evil eye from her person. Behind him ride the official leader of the party and the standard-bearer carrying the Serbian flag. The young bridegroom rides in the first carriage, between his godfather and chief witness. In the next carriage is his best man, a brother, cousin, or close friend, with a white sash draped across his chest. Then come relatives and guests, often with Gypsy musicians riding along playing and singing.

As the lively wedding party approaches the girl's father's homestead, the leader urges his mount ahead in order to offer brandy to the bride's father and to formally be admitted to take the bride. Usually an obstacle must be overcome before the party can enter the courtyard gate. A swaying willow pole topped with

---

[7] Traditionally this was a carved wooden flask in characteristic folk design but today is often an old army canteen or a beer bottle.

a small pumpkin and a white flag may be strapped to a tree outside. The leader, assisted by the clowning antics of the jester, must retrieve the trophy and can then, to the accompaniment of wild cheers, gallop into the courtyard. Here the bride's female relatives are assembled, straining to catch a glimpse of the groom and singing stylized songs of grief about the bride's mother's feelings on the departure of her daughter.

The groom's father, godfather, and witness are seated at the head of a long table in the yard, and the party is served drinks and food. His sisters or girl cousins carry gifts to the bride, including the bridal outfit and often a practical winter coat and pair of sturdy shoes. In former times a necklace of gold coins was presented as well. They help her dress in her new finery and as she is led outside, pistols are fired in the air. She greets her bridegroom and respectfully kisses the hands of all her new in-laws. When the meal is over she bids her parents farewell and is put in the care of the best man, who serves as her guardian until the marriage ceremony. He helps her into the first carriage and sits beside her. As the bride's family watches silently from their gateway the party disappears down the lane, out of sight but not out of earshot, the singing and shouting gathering momentum as the procession approaches the village church. The bride sits alone with her thoughts, a frightened stranger in the midst of the noisy merry-makers.

THE CHURCH CEREMONY

Before entering the church, the mother-in-law loosens the girl's shoes "so she will bear children easily." During the ceremony the bride and groom stand gravely before the priest, with the godfather and witness behind them, all four holding tall beeswax tapers trimmed with flowers. During part of the Orthodox rite the couple must join hands, and for this the groom's mother provides a scarf to discreetly cover the clasped hands, since "It would be shameful if everyone saw." The priest blesses silver wedding crowns which the young couple kiss before being crowned in marriage. They sip wine from a ceremonial goblet which is then offered to the principals in the party. The ceremony is a tense affair for newlyweds only, for the others laugh and talk during the ritual and even ask outright for more wine.

Leaving the church as man and wife, the couple joins in a kolo in the churchyard. Usually dancing in the yard continues while the principals escort the bride and groom to the office of the village clerk where the marriage is officially registered. When a wedding is held during a fast or when the bridegroom is politically active, the church ceremony may be eliminated entirely, and the civil ceremony suffices.

THE WEDDING FEAST

When the lead carriage bearing the newlyweds enters the groom's father's compound, the bride is not permitted to get out until she is given a baby boy to kiss three times. In her married life she will become a full member of the household only after she has borne a child, preferably a son. Then she steps down onto a sack of grain and tosses corn kernels in four directions. As a final symbol of fertility and prosperity, she enters her new home for the first time with loaves of bread tucked under each arm and a jug of wine in her hand.

At the head of the series of tables set end to end in the courtyard the godfather and witness preside over the festivities. The others take their places along the tables according to age, sex, and relationship to the groom's family. The bride, groom, and best man stand at the head of the line of tables during the entire feast, which may last up to eight hours. Before the wedding meal there is a presentation of gifts prepared by the bride for her in-laws. For this much enjoyed ritual the jester acts as master of ceremonies, making everyone laugh as he describes each gift and tosses it to the recipient: "Here's a fine shirt sewn by our lovely bride for her good father-in-law, if he can ever fit it over his belly! And here's a beautiful pair of socks for her brother-in-law. What! They smell like he's already been wearing them."

A large ceremonial loaf is brought to the head of the table and passed down from guest to guest, each of whom slaps money on it and shouts out good wishes for the newlyweds, the larger the sum the louder the gesture. After the first round of feasting, dancing begins. The kolo leader, waving a white handkerchief, shows off nimble footwork. Older men try to keep up with the younger ones.

Toward dusk the bride and groom retire into the house. Celebrating continues in the dark courtyard. Sometimes the jester climbs on the roof and sets fire to a bundle of straw. The others encourage him as he capers around the roof and threatens to burn the house down unless the bride comes out and tosses him a gift.

The bride's relatives arrive the next day and are honored with special hospitality. More recently, when wedding celebrations tend to be shorter they may arrive later on the same day. The groom's father personally serves them, and the two families become *prijatelji*, a relationship of deep respect and friendship.

Jovan's Courtship and Marriage

Jovan Tomić is returning home to the village again. He picks his way along the darkened lane, smiling to himself and quickening his pace. He wants to reach the house before Dragutin goes to bed, for he has big news for his father. He is engaged to be married. Jovan, however, does not know that the young lady he chose is actually the result of many months' maneuvering on the part of both sets of parents, manipulating the young people to the advantage of all. In the morning, sitting at the oak plank table and tearing chunks of brown bread to use as pushers for his fried eggs and onions, he looks up between mouthfuls and tells his parents, "I tell you, she's a good, strong girl! Healthy teeth, good breasts, a good body for bearing children. A worker in the city doesn't need a wife who can pitch hay, but I know what counts. A strong wife is a good thing."

Several months earlier, the landlady where Jovan rents a small furnished room had informed him that her nephew was moving to town and needed the room. Housing in the capital is very difficult, and Jovan was unsuccessful in finding another place to live. Dragutin, who goes to Belgrade regularly to sell cheese and brandy, had for some time been asking around among customers and acquaintances about a possible wife for his son. As a village father he was particularly concerned about his son's new freedom: "It's a dangerous thing for a young man Jovan's age to be without responsibility and at the same time to have money burning in his pocket. And that's not all that's burning in his pants. He's ripe. He needs to be married or he'll start carousing."

He told his wife and father that the room problem came just at the right time: "I heard about a family with a 19-year-old daughter, a peasant family that's been in the city a couple of years. The father is a mason. He was able to buy a plot on the outskirts and has built his own house. There's a room in it for the elder daughter who's already married and a room for this younger one. A nice, empty room for her and Jovan, and it's not far from where he works."

In the course of negotiations Dragutin had agreed to contribute to the match an electric stove and a small refrigerator. This entailed selling one of his cows, a fair exchange, he figured, in return for rent-free lodgings plus a wife for his son.

Once arrangements and obligations had been settled, Dragutin again had second thoughts about contributing to the severance of Jovan's ties to the land. "Why, in God's name," he shouted at his wife, "can't we all live here together under one roof in the normal Serbian way? That's what I really want, all of us here in the village in one heap. Screw the sun! If we're living under socialism, let it be a socialism that works for me. Why should my son work his ass off for another boss? Let him work for me. Let's work together!"

Through a mutual acquaintance of the young couple a meeting had been arranged and a brief courtship followed during which Jovan, too, was very much aware of that empty room. In a short time the couple decided to marry, agreeing to discuss with their respective families their plan to have a big wedding in the village and then to live in the girl's father's house in town.

Jovan is not a party member, and the decision to dispense with the church ceremony is not so much a political act as a matter of convenience and of doing things in a modern way. A new and rather elegant municipal office serves the neighborhood in which the bride's family lives. Because the couple will be residing in that precinct and not in the village, it is agreed that the official marriage registration will take place there.

THE CIVIL CEREMONY

On the wedding morning, members of the party arrive at the village homestead in carts and cars, some borrowed. They regroup so that the more important members can fit into the available cars to make the trip to the city to fetch the bride and escort her to the civil ceremony. For the bumpy and circuitous two hour drive, villagers unaccustomed to car travel have taken the precaution of swallowing motion-sickness tablets provided by Jovan. After arrival in the city and an impromptu kolo in the street, wedding members and urban neighbors alike stare as the bride is escorted from her father's house. Modishly attired in a street-length wedding dress, she carries white gladioli wrapped in cellophane. The store-bought bouquet crunches noisily as she shifts it from hand to hand, but it is the latest in correct wedding accessories and much preferable to the home-grown bouquets of red and yellow dahlias wrapped in wet newspaper, as carried by village brides.

The party collects on the steps of the municipal office—a noisy group of relatives and friends, including Jovan's godfather, his ujak, his young cousin as best man with traditional white sash, and a friend from the machine shop serving as jester, complete with garlic necklace and a live, squawking hen.

One room in the building has been designated a marriage chamber. It is arranged with rows of chairs and a strip of maroon carpeting leading to an official desk where a male and a female clerk officiate for the civil ceremony. At the entrance to this chamber there is animated argument with the chief clerk. He requests that the hen and the standard bearer's large flag be left outside in the corridor.

The clerk performs the ceremony, questioning the kum and the ujak, in his honored role as *starojko*, and asking all assembled if the information is correct as given. The relatives in the audience respond heartily. A brief statement on the legal and moral responsibilities of married life is read. The couple is pronounced officially married in the eyes of the state, and the clerks smile automatically and tell the newlyweds they may now shake hands. An assistant hurries the party out of the room through a different doorway, reminding the jester to go back and retrieve his hen.

Urban Ways and Rural Values

Now the wedding party is confronted with a dilemma. This concerns the protocol of getting back to the village. With open carriages there is no problem. Here, however, the standard bearer can carry the flag aloft only if he rides in the sun-roof Volkswagen belonging to one of the bride's cousins—but who ever heard of a member of the bride's family leading the procession? The godfather, who should rightly be near the head of the line, has come in an aging Moskvitch driven by a relative, and it cannot keep up with the Fiats and Opels belonging to Jovan's urban friends who by rights should rank last.

For weeks before the wedding, Jovan's family had been busy, and his grandfather, acknowledging the substantial expenditure of funds and energy, says "Even though our Jovan has left the village, it is necessary for us to make a proper wedding. I wouldn't think of doing anything else. We owe a real party to all the people whose weddings we have attended over the years." Dragutin agrees. "We're Tomići. Of course we have to make a wedding."

He had gone out with his flask to invite the guests and, again in accord with village custom, had invited especially capable neighbors and relatives to be helpers for the wedding feast. Being a helper involves three or four days of hard work, arriving at the host's homestead by 5 A.M. and often not leaving until 7 or 8 in the evening, as well as serving all day the day of the wedding and being on hand for a full day afterwards to help clean up. It is, however, an honor, obvious recognition of one's capabilities. Those called rarely refuse. The biggest imposition is that it means rearranging one's own household schedule, which is especially hard when a husband and wife are both invited to be helpers.

As the line of cars straggles into a pasture near the haystacks, the guests can tell that in spite of the young bridegroom's urban ways this is to be a real wedding. Long wooden tables borrowed from throughout the neighborhood have been arranged to seat about a hundred guests. At the head table, places are set with dishes and cutlery. Down where the women and children sit slabs of bread serve as place settings, with wooden spoons with which people can help themselves from a common bowl. Helpers dart everywhere, keeping fires going, hacking roasted pigs and sheep into serving portions, running from cellar to courtyard with pitchers of wine, and ladling out festive dishes. As an indication of their honored roles they wear gifts presented by the host. Formerly such gifts were a pair of socks or a length of shirting prepared by the groom's mother and stitched to the server's shoulder so that all could see. At this wedding the women helpers have been presented with lace-trimmed nylon slips, suggested to his mother by Jovan himself, and these are tacked with thread to the back of their sweaters and jackets. The men have been given drip-dry shirts which, intact in plastic wrappers, are affixed in place over the recipients' shoulders.

Gypsies, long regarded in villages as the best musicians, are on this occasion replaced by a group chosen by the bridegroom on recommendation of a co-worker. It includes the usual accordion, violin, and bass fiddle and plays tunes based on folk themes made popular by Radio Belgrade. The new songs are familiar to all, but the older guests request more traditional music.

Jovan and his town friends are immaculately turned out in suits and ties. Their wives or girlfriends wear mini-skirts. Comments one village guest, "Mini-skirts! There ought to be a law against them. I bet the Russians don't permit it. Besides, you can get rheumatism that way."

Older village men wear the Šumadijan folk costume, lovingly preserved in laurel leaves for events such as this. Jovan possesses no such outfit, but he is pleased by the way his grandfather looks in brown home-spun woolen britches, jacket, and over-vest trimmed with black braid, by his black sheared lamb hat and pigskin sandals with turned-up "noses." On this day Jovan's father wears the same outfit in which he himself was married, of fine blue wool trimmed with elaborate black silk braid.

In the midst of the feasting and drinking, Dragutin in his holiday finery goes down to the meadow to bring up clover for his cows, carrying the heavy load precariously balanced on a pitchfork on his shoulder and moving directly past the rows of tables toward the barn. Jovan knows the cows have to eat on schedule but ruefully wishes his father had gone around the outside of the courtyard instead of right through the party. Then he realizes that this is a silent rebuke: His father is clearly telling him, "Look at me, doing the work that rightfully you should be doing. You've left the land and I still carry on, and on top of that I make you a wedding to do us all proud."

Features of Contemporary Nuclear Families

A bride is not called a woman until she bears a child. Most brides are therefore anxious to have a baby as soon as possible in order to establish a position in the household. During pregnancy there are some restrictions on food and ceremonial activities, but work continues around the house and in the fields until the last possible moment. Although the first child and a second (especially if the first is a girl) are welcomed, there are extremely strong feelings about limiting family size. Since the war, very few couples have had more than two children. If traditional contraceptive methods fail, various local means of abortion are practiced. These are frequently self-induced and are usually effective, according to village women in their thirties and forties. Reliable data are, of course, difficult to obtain (since it seems to be a point of pride to relate the details and numbers of abortions one has sustained), but it appears that abortions exceed live births. Contraceptive techniques in use for decades elsewhere in Europe are only now gradually coming into use, and more contemporary devices are unknown. Tradition, cost, lack of privacy, lack of sanitary facilities, and lack of information have been factors inhibiting their use.

The special relationship mentioned earlier between children and their grandparents is in some respects a new feature of village social structure. With the increasing age span grandparents are simply around longer, and new types of relationships can develop which were earlier the exception. Much has been written about the decline of patriarchal authority, but part of what is actually happening is that there are now more older people living, and they are often too old to take active economic roles.

Let us look briefly at statistics and again take Orašac in 1863 and 1961 as points of departure: In 1863 there were 40 extended households headed by a starešina, with his wife, and containing three generations. In 1961 there were 165 households (as stated earlier, the population approximately doubled in the intervening century). In 1863, 22 of the household heads were over age 50 and none were over 70; in 1961, 111 were over age 50 and 16 were over 70.

As the situation of Jovan illustrates, migration of young people has resulted in a reduction in the number of couples in the child-bearing years and consequently in the proportion of children in the total population. However, compared to a century ago, the growing number of old people represents a significant development both in absolute and in relative terms. If there were no migration, and given modern health facilities, the number of old people would be approximately the same (but would of course form a smaller percentage of the total population). A hundred years ago there were fewer old people in the villages.[8]

Dyadic Relationships

In considering the life cycles of individuals in a patrilocal system it is important to know for how long specific dyadic relationships such as father/son, mother-in-law/daughter-in-law, grandfather/grandson, or grandparent/grandchild generally will probably endure. It is obviously quite a different situation than when, for example, one or both parents are likely to die during the course of the child's

---

[8] These points are dramatically illustrated in Table 3 (percentages are rounded).

TABLE 3

AGE STRUCTURE OF ORAŠAC POPULATION IN 1863 AND 1961

| | 1863 | | 1961 | |
Age	Number	Percent	Number	Percent
0–10	456	42.3	358	17.7
11–20	221	20.5	302	14.9
21–30	189	17.4	271	13.2
31–40	114	10.2	346	17.0
41–50	53	5.0	177	8.6
51–60	39	3.7	268	13.1
61–70	10	1.0	190	9.4
71 and over			111	5.2
Totals	1082		2023	

SOURCES: Serbian Statistical Bureau and Serbian State Archives, Belgrade.

growing up and thus, as was seen in the zadruga cases from 1863, the children are then raised by a paternal uncle and his wife; or whether the mother-in-law/daughter-in-law relationship is likely to endure while the daughter-in-law is raising her own children to maturity; or what the opportunity will be for a grandson to get to know his grandfather. In the past, discussion of these problems has been handicapped by use of selected instances that tended to support idealized patterns.

With the statistics phrased in terms of household head, we can look for a moment at the ages of daughters-in-law in the two census years. In 1863 there were 50 daughters-in-law in 131 households, 15 percent of whom were over age 30; in 1961 there were 160 daughters-in-law in 453 households (more than the proportionate increase in population), 57 percent of whom were over 30. Age at marriage for both bride and groom has remained relatively constant over the hundred-year period. Taking the bride's age as 20 and her father-in-law's as something over 40, in the earlier period the father-in-law was likely to die by the time the daughter-in-law reached 30. A century later the relationship endures more than a generation. Similarly, grandfathers today generally live to see their grandsons mature. The stretching out of these dyadic relationships obviously affects their quality, especially as they occur in the context of smaller household groups combined with a higher standard of living.

Evaluating Changes

How can one evaluate these changes? Can it be that the veneration of elders in former times reflected at least in part a respect for their exceptional staying power, their survival ability? Today, with many older villagers on pensions and with medical care accessible to all, old age is not so much of an achievement. Is it possible that interpersonal relationships were more intense because they tended to be shorter, that the attachment of a mature son for his father was tempered by the implicit realization that the father would not be around much longer? Was the respect shown by a daughter-in-law toward her mother-in-law conditioned by the fact that within a decade or so she would succeed to the older woman's place?

Of course, these are generalizations based on a typology of relationships and

not on particular cases. Data are available to document how long individual relationships lasted, while we can only infer the consequences. Analysis of mortality in
Orašac in the periods 1871–1875 and 1957–1961 yields total deaths of 146 and 90
respectively, the latter figure including those who died in hospitals outside the
village. In the earlier period, 44 percent of deaths occurred before age 5 and 10
percent over age 60; between the ages of 16 and 60, 30 percent of deaths occurred,
and of these most were women in child-bearing years. In the latter period 68 percent
of the deaths were in age 60 and over, and only 6 percent in the under-age-5 group,
with 26 percent in ages 16–60. High infant and maternal mortality in the earlier
period and deaths in the old-age group in the latter period are all expectable. What
is more important in the data is that they demonstrate conclusively several important
factors: First, since each child born now has a better chance of survival, women
spend less time bearing children, and more time is devoted to individual children.
Abortion became more common in part as health conditions improved, but now the
slow but increasing use of contraceptive devices will probably decrease the number
of abortions. Further, kin ties through birth or marriage are more likely to last
longer. It may well be that one of the factors involved in the decline of patriarchal
authority in particular and the authority of elders in general is that today a physically and emotionally mature son or daughter-in-law is much less easily sub-
ordinated to an aging parent, whereas because of the demographic parameters such
confrontations were considerably less frequent a century ago. Today the grand-
parental/grandchild relationship is able to develop much more fully. This explains
the creation of new roles and shows how the extended kin group acquires a new
flexibility and a new lease on its continued cultural existence.

In talking about these changes Smiljka, an energetic matron in her early
forties, says

> I have to smile when I think about how I came to this household as a frightened
> girl 25 years ago. I remember all that my own mother and grandmother had
> instructed me about serving my mother-in-law, about treating my in-laws with
> utmost respect, about learning about how the household was run since I would
> some day run it. Their instruction was good, of course, but times change. I never
> had to wash my father-in-law's feet. My mother-in-law was kind to me and now,
> in her old age, I am good to her.

Smiljka is the mother of Radisav, in the new house near the road. She
confirms: "I know young people want to have separate households today. But if
only our Radisav brings a bride here, everything will be fine. I will be a friend to
her, not a boss, and in that way my husband and I will be taken care of when we
are old, too."

Death in the Village

When death comes to the village, if it is the death of a child or a person
in his prime, and particularly if it occurs unexpectedly, it is regarded as a great
tragedy. The decease of old people is viewed as a normal event. Their time has
come; they are ready. An elderly villager explains, "I as an old man work a little,

"I as an old man work a little, drink a little brandy, and slowly wait for death."

drink a little brandy, and slowly wait for death." He is not depressed but contemplates his end with equanimity.

At death the body is dressed in the deceased's best clothes. Many villagers carefully preserve the folk costume to be buried in. All windows are closed so that the soul of the deceased cannot return to the house. Sometimes an older woman leads a child around the death-bed three times, placing a candle near the head and chanting, "I give you this white candle. You give me long life." After a funeral ceremony at the church, the church bell tolls and marks the procession of mourners as they make their way up the road to the graveyard. The women wail loudly and constantly in stylized lament. When the coffin is lowered into the grave each relative throws in a handful of earth. Some money is tossed in as well, to help the deceased on his way. The priest pours red wine in the form of a cross over the grave, and the mourners, particularly the women, call to the departed soul to relay greetings and messages to other deceased relatives whom it will soon be joining.

The bereaved family brings food to the burial, to be eaten near the grave. In part this practice is related to the belief that whatever is put near the grave will be received by the dead person in the other world. A ceremonial dish of boiled wheat, chopped walnuts, and sugar is prepared, and all the mourners are called to the graveside in order of kin and social rank to eat a spoonful of it in memory of the deceased. Wine, brandy, and a roast are served to all. On the Sunday following the burial a more elaborate meal of soup, stew, meat, cakes, and fruit is brought to the grave.

It is believed that the deceased wanders for 40 days, visits the places he has been to during his lifetime, stops at Jerusalem and Mount Athos (the Orthodox sacred site in Greece), and finally ascends to Heaven. Thus on the fortieth day and again after six months and a year, similar graveyard feasts take place. In addition three times a year, during Lent, at Christmas, and in the summer, special memorial feasts are held. This frequent graveyard feasting and the elaborate preparations it involves are very costly in time and money. Many villagers contend that they cannot afford to bring so much food to the cemetery, but they also feel it would slight the souls of their deceased to be neglected. Strongest of all is a desire to keep up appearances, for the graveyard is the one public place where all villagers come, and one household would be disgraced if it could not put on as big a spread as another.

If the deceased is a party member or from a household which has for economic and political reasons sloughed off religious observances, the rites associated with the funeral still follow the traditional pattern in most respects. Instead of the priest officiating at the graveyard, a eulogy of the deceased as an exemplary communist or as a worker in a collective enterprise is given by a fellow employee or by a member of his firm's workers' council. Meanwhile, the relatives of the deceased busily lay out the usual collation of food and drink. The women break into their ritualized wailing, and the family makes plans for an appropriate tombstone that will add distinction to their vamilija's section of the cemetery.

5

Aspects of Ritual Life

Views of Peasant Life

SOCIAL THEORISTS HAVE LONG DEBATED the nature of village life. A view expounded by certain nineteenth-century political philosophers and reformers in Russia and the Balkans was that it consisted of idyllic cooperative institutions which were the capstones of civilization. As was pointed out in Chapter 2, they sought to distinguish their Slav cultures from what they characterized as the decadent West. Svetozar Marković stressed the zadruga as the essence of Balkan social organization. In opposition to this concept is a notion of peasant life as one with limited resources and bitter struggles for existence, one neighbor jealous of whatever success accrues to another. This idea is related to certain Marxian analyses of peasant society which see more prosperous villagers always taking advantage of poorer neighbors. (In some ways, contemporary Yugoslav government reforms can be viewed as attempts to introduce an atmosphere of cooperative harmony into village life; this is discussed in the concluding chapter.)

Both points of view are complex. In the discussion on the zadruga we tried to show that, in terms of kinship structure, factors of cooperation and competition functioned at different levels and in different situations. We have seen the extended household as a unit of economic cooperation and solidarity with respect to outsiders, but within it suffered, and continues to suffer, conflicts among component nuclear family units and between individuals. Households in the same patrilineal descent group form a unit in important kinds of relationships with the rest of the village; yet among households conflict exists, albeit often discrete, because of a desire to surpass one's close kin in material possessions and accompanying status and also frequently due to disputes originating in shared land inheritances.

These complementary tendencies of cooperation and competition, important characteristics of Serbian village life, also appear in aspects of the ritual life of the community.

The Slava

The *slava*, feast day of a descent group's patron saint, is a ritual celebration common to all households in the vamilija. This shared observance is a major source of group identity, but it is celebrated by each household individually. The separate household celebrations serve to honor and reaffirm ties with matrilineal kin, almost always from a different neighborhood and often from a different village, as well as to maintain bonds of friendship with unrelated fellow villagers.

The slava (*slaviti*, to glorify, to celebrate) is today uniquely Serbian and gives rise to a proud folk saying, "*Gdje je slava, tu je Srbin* (Where there's a slava, there's a Serb)." The institution stems from pre-Christian times and is founded in ritual beliefs shared by many Indo-European peoples. In pagan times each descent group had its own particular deities, similar to protective household gods among ancient Romans and others.

In the twelfth century St. Sava, the first Serbian archbishop, advocated adopting existing practices into the Serbian Orthodox faith. The Orthodox Church of the period was opposed to assigning Christian saints the protective properties of older deities, but over the centuries this practice became an integral part of customary religious activity.[1] The slava is the most important ritual observance in Serbian life although, interestingly, there is no special prayer or church service for the occasion.

It is celebrated exclusively in the home, with two minor aspects of church participation which can be seen as affirmation of church sanction. Some days before the slava the village priest comes to the celebrating household to sanctify the house and bless water to be used for baking the slava bread. On the morning of the slava the loaf is then carried to church to be blessed.

PREPARING THE HOUSE

Around the household compound, preparations begin weeks in advance. The ritual usually represents a household's biggest yearly outlay for ceremonial purposes. Most households use the slava as impetus for an annual general house-cleaning. This includes carrying all furnishings out of the house room by room, preparing buckets of lime and water, and whitewashing walls and ceilings. If the house is of wattle-and-daub construction, the exterior is whitewashed as well. Rough plank floors are scrubbed, and earthen floors are sprinkled and swept. Window-panes, kerosene lamp chimneys, and fly-specked light bulbs are vigorously cleaned with newspaper soaked in rakija. The so-called guest room, which normally serves as a repository for unused dowry items, is made ready. This room contains a long table with benches, built especially with the slava feast in mind. As soon as the fresh whitewash is dry, the framed colored lithograph of the patron saint is rehung in its place of honor. Sprigs of sweet basil, a holy plant among Serbs, are tucked around the frame. Nearby are hung family photographs, usually including a large portrait of the deceased elder with a carefully draped, hand-loomed towel around the frame.

---

[1] S. Kulišić, P. Ž. Petrović, and N. Pantelić, *Srpski Mitološki Rečnik*, Nolit, Beograd, 1970, pp. 175–178.

PREPARING THE FOOD

The necessary kitchen activity frequently means that women of the house must stay up for several nights. Serbs say that to eat well is to eat full, and great quantities of food are prepared. The slava feast includes specialties that have to be made in advance. Dough for home-made noodles is mixed, cut into strips, and turned out onto a sheet. For days this sheet of drying noodles may be shifted from bed to floor as other household needs require the space. Plates of hogs' hock jelly, the grayish gelatinous mass enlivened by circles of hard-boiled egg and ground paprika powder, are set out in a corner to congeal, to the accompaniment of warnings not to step in them. A rooster is stewed for broth. Mounds of raw cabbage are shredded for salad. Chopped pork and rice are rolled up in pickled cabbage leaves for *sarma*. Cookies are decorated with jam and sprinkled with coarse sugar. The main torte, usually a big sponge cake requiring 16 or more eggs, is laboriously whipped into shape by children of the household who take turns.

Preparing the roast meat is men's work, and depending on the time of year the slava roast can be a sheep or pig or sometimes both. It is mounted on a spit, basted with fat, and slowly turned over a pit of hot wood coals, until the skin is golden brown and meat juices begin to run out and hiss onto the coals. The women strip the intestines and stuff them with liver and heart chopped with garlic, saving this pungent dish to bake last, after the cakes and cookies have been made and removed to another room. The outdoor bread oven must be fired. Village housewives usually bake once a week, for the entire week, and on this occasion double amounts must be prepared. Finally, the special slava loaf is made. It is actually two loaves, a flat, unleavened bread upon which is placed the high, round holiday loaf, with the seal of the Orthodox Church impressed in the center.

PERSONAL PREPARATIONS

On the eve of the holiday members of the household take time out to ready themselves. "This is *my* general housecleaning" quips a villager as he strips to the waist and takes an infrequent sponge-bath. Men who shave once a week strop their razors and give their mustaches extra attention. Women wash their hair with rainwater. Holiday clothes are brought out of dowry trunks and wardrobe closets where they are stored from year to year in newspaper and laurel leaves. The straps of the men's sandals are polished with melted lard, and their fur hats get a good brushing.

CELEBRATIONS IN GOOD AND BAD YEARS

The abundance of food now prepared for the slava, which certainly reflects the improved economic position of the villager in more recent times, should be compared to Pavlović's discussion of slava preparations. He makes a point of describing the different types of celebrations held according to good and bad harvest years:

> In "lucky [good harvest]" years, all are happy. When the slava comes it is possible for them to entertain beloved guests abundantly. In these years all are glad to increase the number of guests. After the slava they usually say, "So and so had the largest number of guests. Lucky for him!"

. . . in a bad year . . . everything must be purchased for money. . . . Those who want to observe the old customs must borrow and then for the whole next year must pay off the debt. Then they curse the slava which has brought them to this sorry state. In these years few guests come, and the domaćin doesn't go [to other slavas] and doesn't invite people to come to him. Many think then that it is necessary only to ceremonially break the slava bread, and nothing more. There are then many houses which instead of killing a sheep prepare only a chicken.[2]

The strongly reciprocal nature of slava invitations made the lessened expenditures easier to bear, although there was probably considerable individual variation, as the problem of indebtedness indicates.

On the slava morning a member of the household who has not participated in slaughtering the animal for the roast takes the holiday loaf to receive the priest's blessing. Children of the family must attend school on this day, much to their disappointment, although younger pupils, who attend the earlier of the two shifts, are home again in time to participate in most of the festivities. They often accompany the older sibling or grandparent carrying the slava bread to church and then run across the rutted wagon trail that separates church property from the schoolyard.

SLAVA GUESTS

Even before noon guests start to arrive. The situation is similar to that reported by Pavlović:

Eagerly the await the arrival of *ujak* [mother's brother], *ujna* [mother's brother's wife], *teča* [father's sister's husband], *pašenog* [wife's sister's husband], *zet* [son-in-law, also sister's husband], *šurak* [wife's brother], and if someone hasn't yet come, all assembled fret, "Why isn't he here yet?"[3]

Today matrilineal relatives arrive from Arandjelovac and even from Belgrade, as well as from other villages. As urban in-laws appear, their clothing, jewelry, and hairstyles are carefully appraised while kisses and greetings are exchanged.

In addition to these relatives who represent most of the household's guests, also invited are the kum and favorite neighbors who are not members of the vamilija. To be "best neighbor" is something special, a reciprocal relationship with important functions. It is true that villagers sometimes define relatives and friends as synonymous. Still, as has been pointed out, various kinds of conflicts do occur within the vamilija, and since matrilineal kin are often comparatively far away, cooperative neighbors can play an important (if supplementary) role in village social interaction.

THE RITUAL

As guests arrive they are served in turn *slatko*, traditional sweet preserves offered as a gesture of hospitality, then hot or cold rakija, followed by Turkish

---

[2] Pavlović, *Život i običaji narodni u Kragujevačkoj Jasenici u Šumadiji*, pp. 89–90.
[3] Pavlović, p. 89.

coffee. Children of the household greet guests by kissing their hand, the traditional form of respect to elders, and by uttering as well, *"Ljubim ruku* (I kiss your hand)." The guests are ushered into the special room, and when all are assembled the *domaćin*, in his role as host and household head, begins the celebration by lighting a beeswax taper and crossing himself three times. The gathering falls silent as he prepares to supplicate his patron saint for the well-being of his household. Hot coals from the oven are carried in by his wife, and these he puts in an earthenware holder along with pellets of incense. He stands gravely before the saint's picture, letting the fragrance rise, and then moves around the table wafting incense toward himself and toward each guest, individually welcoming and blessing each. Guests reply with toasts to the health and prosperity of the household, everyone around the table punctuating the wishes with murmurs of "God grant it!"

A young girl of the household or a ritually clean woman ceremoniously carries in the slava loaf, now adorned with a candle in the form of a flat cross with the four ends bent up and lit, a serpentine candle, an apple, a sugar lump, and small sprays of basil, and places it before the host. With the assistance of the guest of honor, who may be a respected in-law or the best neighbor, he performs the important ritual of breaking the bread. The loaf is cut along the lines of a cross, turned by both pairs of hands, and broken into quarters. Red wine is poured on the cut surfaces and the men, solemnly kissing each other on both cheeks and on the lips, chant in unison, "Christ is in our midst now and forever, Amen." The ritual is repeated three times, manifesting with the symbolism of bread and wine the presence of the Father, the Son, and the Holy Ghost.

This ritual in the individual home, repeating modified church observances, symbolically links simultaneously a Christian faith and a strong sense of ethnic identity with the basic kinship unit, the household, while asserting ties to the household deity of a pre-Christian past. The brief act is at the very core of Serbian cultural and social identity.

The ceremonial loaf is sliced and distributed to all. Each man also gets a bit of the basil to tuck behind his ear, and the mood changes from one of solemnity to conviviality. According to Serbian protocol, in his role as host the domaćin remains standing throughout the ensuing meal, moving around the table making certain his guests' glasses are never empty and constantly urging them to help themselves to choice bits of food—"Take, take, help yourselves freely!"

Long after the women and girls of the house have carried in all the platters of festive dishes and the formal feast has ended, the company remains at table drinking and singing. With pocket knives men whittle at cubes of creamy fat overlaid with crackling pigskin, and women snack on cookies and wedges of cake. Toward nightfall the hosts join their guests at the benches around the table, reminiscing and story-telling. Small children curl up on the bed in the corner. Older children, heavy with food and wine, nod sleepily at the lower end of the table.

Guests who live too far away to return home are expected to spend the night. By arranging cornhusk-stuffed mattresses on the floor any number of overnight guests can be accommodated. Before they go home the next day their hosts press on them gifts of roast meat and cake wrapped in newspaper. Guests who live in the neighborhood are urged to come back the following day to share the remains of the feast.

Reflecting on Serbian hospitality and the need to keep up appearances, one exhausted domaćica confides after her slava, "I could do very well without having guests here again tomorrow, but it wouldn't be right for us not to be hospitable, and besides, we've got to use up all this food."

Easter

A major theme of Orthodoxy is the Resurrection and the Transfiguration, and Easter is the most important holiday in the Eastern Orthodox religious calendar.

Unlike western Catholic countries, and the Catholic parts of Yugoslavia as well, where the parish church is often the most imposing building in the village, in Serbia rural churches were usually built of wood and were small and low. This design is often explained in terms of the centuries of Turkish domination and the desire to avoid attracting attention. In addition, as we have just seen, the most important ceremonial center is the home. A secondary center is the graveyard. During Turkish times the priests who served the peasant population were relatively few, often with little more education than the villagers themselves. Given these historical factors, the church itself is modest, and regular church attendance does not occur.

Easter is the one exception. The ritual observances in the village church follow closely those prescribed by the Orthodox Church. On this occasion the Orašac church is filled to overflowing. The holiday is preceded by the seven weeks of Great Fast during which people formerly were expected to forego all meat and dairy products. Explains a villager, "Nobody follows the Great Fast any more except the priest with his family, and of course he has to." Adds another, "Today most of us just keep a token fast, from Palm Sunday to Easter Sunday. As for myself, God forgive me if I fast in spirit only, because to tell you the truth I can't take my bean gruel without lard."

On the evening of Good Thursday villagers stream into church, mechanically crossing themselves as they enter. For most this is their first visit since the previous Easter. The majority who go to hear the story of the Crucifixion read are women, young and old. They bring bouquets of early spring flowers to offer to the icon on the altar before standing in small kin clusters on the stone floor. After kissing the silver altar cross the men present casually congregate to one side. An undertone of talking and visiting continues even after the priest appears from behind a three-part altar screen and prepares to read the Sufferings of Christ. "Is this not *our* church and *our* priest?" a woman asks in response to a query about church decorum. Everyone holds a small candle which is alternately lit and extinguished at prescribed times during the service. The glow of candles shimmers on the walls, and the heavy smell of incense and hyacinths fills the small church.

Traditionally on Good Friday there is a livestock market and fair in Arandjelovac. This has always heightened the holiday mood, even for those who do not participate in the religious observances. Holiday clothes reserved for weddings and slavas are taken out and brushed up. Younger people, who prefer to alter their dress with the seasons, show off new clothing or at least a pair of new shoes. The main street of Arandjelovac on this day becomes a showplace of evolving peasant fashion. Today it is often not possible to distinguish village young people from their urban counterparts.

On this day, too, grandmothers and their grandchildren share the fun of making Easter eggs. Commercial dyes are available, but most village households enjoy making homemade colors with huckleberry juice, boiled onion skins, and boiled walnut shells. The tinted eggs are rubbed to a sheen with a rag dipped in lard.

To be at the sunrise service on Easter morning villagers complete their rounds of early chores and leave their homesteads while it is still dark. Every household brings along an Easter breakfast, and as the family enters church each housewife stops to hang her striped woolen sack or willow basket on a picket of the churchyard fence. Quickly the church becomes filled. Latecomers shove and crowd near the door. When the service is over tapers are lit from the altar candle, and amidst more pushing and tugging and cautious shielding of one's own blinking taper, the congregation forms a procession as it emerges from the church. The familiar contours of the landscape take form against a rosy sky. The sexton proudly carries the faded church banner at the head of the procession, and the priest's polished censer leaps forward on its chain leaving a pungent wake of incense. The congregation moves three times around the church and is then shepherded inside for Holy Communion. The priest and his assistant methodically shred off pieces of bread, popping some into each communicant's mouth, pressing the wine goblet to his lips, wiping his chin with a plaid handkerchief, and gently pushing him on to keep the line moving.

People step out again into the churchyard as the sun spills over the vineyards on the hill. They call to one another "Christ is risen!" and respond "Indeed He is risen!" Men urge neighbors and friends to celebrate with a sip of their best rakija. Hand-loomed blankets are spread on the grass and families share a picnic breakfast and egg-tapping games. Easter morning is a rare occasion when, if possible, all members of the household go out together. It is also an infrequent time when villagers gather together from their scattered homesteads. The nature of religious activities and the dispersed pattern of settlement make such all-village gatherings uncommon.

Distinctions between the Slava and Easter

Many important distinctions can be noted between the ritual observances associated with the slava and with Easter. As we see, the slava is basically a pre-Christian ritual which has been adapted into an Orthodox context but remains a ritual of the home with minimal formal religious associations. In contrast, Easter is celebrated with conventional religious observances and little folk ritual (other than that associated with the symbolism of Easter eggs, a custom common to most Christian peoples).

Christmas

Christmas, while an important Orthodox holiday, has evolved in Serbian peasant culture in something of an intermediate position and is focused primarily in the home. This is the holiday village children say (out of earshot of their teachers) they like best, because of the many beloved folk customs performed at this time. Christmas falls on January 7 (December 25 of the Gregorian calendar of the Orthodox Church) and so some of the anticipation is now dulled by the fact that the modern New Year has been celebrated earlier in the week. New secular customs, discussed below, are playing an increasing part in village life.

The day before Christmas a man of the household goes to the woods to cut down a young oak tree. Toward nightfall the domaćin carries in the ceremonial *badnjak* or yule log that has been cut from this tree and uses it to light the hearth. Today the hearth is usually the wood-stove in the kitchen, and the log is thrust in with an end protruding. In the several village households which now have small electric stoves, the wood-stove, still used in winter for heating and cooking, is ceremoniously lit. The head of the household calls out "Christ is born!" and the family replies "Indeed He is born!" Dry logs are carried in and lit in the name of the Father, the Son, and the Holy Ghost. The domaćin kisses the badnjak and crosses himself, intoning "As I kiss the yule log, so may the cow have calves, the ewe lambs, the sow piglets, the hen chicks, and may every soul in my household have good luck and a productive year."

For the Christmas Eve meal straw is spread on the kitchen floor, incense is prepared, and the family prays together before taking the last fasting meal on the floor. A feature of this meal is the small loaf of bread each member receives, prepared especially for him. The loaves for the males are in the form of domestic animals, and those for the females are usually in the shape of braids.

It is felt that an undesirable visitor on Christmas morning is an omen of bad luck for the coming year, and this is avoided by having a child of the household, preferably a boy, go out and rap at the door to gain admittance. He is warmly received as he enters under a shower of grain. He kneels before the yule log, striking it to make sparks fly and chanting a prayer for the well-being of the household. With the "first arrived" in the place of honor the family sits down to a holiday meal with roast meat. The meal is shared by the family itself, without guests, since all the other households are also celebrating. This meal features a loaf of bread with a coin baked into it, and whoever gets the coin will have especially good luck in the coming year. In many Orašac households the coin is stuck to the ceiling with a bit of dough and is considered a good sign as long as it remains there.

The Christmas celebration, coinciding as it does with the winter solstice and the new year's hope for good fortune, contains many pre-Christian and later observances related to fertility and the welfare of the household. Also present are elements related to cults of the dead and to animistic beliefs. The yule log is a symbolic representation of the forest spirit. Fertility is symbolized in the Christmas Eve loaves. Some of the rituals are more elaborate: for example, the "wheat demon" has to be exorcised, in order to insure a good crop in the coming year, and so a rooster is sacrificed (the significance of the roast for the holiday meal has also been linked to sacrifice[4]); the blood is let over the last haystack in the courtyard, where the demon is presumed to reside, and it is this straw which is taken into the house to spread on the floor.

However, many customary beliefs of this type, related to raising animals, cultivation, and the agricultural cycle generally, have largely disappeared from the consciousness of contemporary villagers. "What is the meaning of the straw on the floor?" we ask. "Why do you do it?" Here are some answers offered as explanation:

"Because Christ was born in the straw."
"*Pitaj Boga*, ask God!"
"It's an old Serbian custom."
"Well, if you leave the Christmas straw on the floor for three days and three nights without sweeping it, then you won't have bugs in the kitchen in the summer."

In recent years Christmas as observed in peasant households has tended to be modified, despite everyone's enjoyment of the rituals and, among older villagers, belief in their efficacy or at least expressions of uncertainty when they are not performed.

St. George's Day

In reviewing the yearly cycle of religious events it becomes clear that most of the religious holidays have their bases in natural phenomena such as the change of seasons or placation of various types of spirits. Many such holidays, their Christian names usually after a saint who was assigned the occasion, endured intact through the middle of this century. An example is St. George's Day in early May, a rite of spring, when young people gathered in the meadows before sunrise to dance and to bathe their arms and faces in the dew-covered grass. Spring boughs were gathered and carried back to the house: willow for growth, elm for strength, dogwood for health, white beech for fertility, and spiney hawthorne to ward off the evil eye. Still today, although increasingly less so, wreaths fashioned from spring boughs are affixed above the outside door, hitched over the gatepost, and tossed down the well. Occasionally one also sees such a wreath, purchased or brought by a village relative, over the door in the hallway of a Belgrade apartment building.

Secular Holidays

The government that grew out of World War II instituted its own secular holidays which have partially displaced those of the former Kingdom of Yugoslavia, where in Serbia the Orthodox Church was, of course, the established state church. However, as in the cases of religious holidays which drew on pagan precedents, so the new state holidays incorporate aspects of traditional observances. The New Year

---

[4] Kulišić *et al.*, *Srpski Mitološki Rečnik*, pp. 29–38.

is observed in town and in the village school by the exchanging of gifts and a holiday from work and classes. The forest spirit survives in the form of a decorated New Year's tree. Like the Orthodox Christmas, for those who observe the official New Year this is a family celebration incorporating a feast with roast meat, an important part of any Serbian celebration. In town it also combines elements of the general secularization that has accompanied the merging of Christmas-New Year celebrations in western Europe and North America, where the economically important consumption of goods is associated with festivity and enjoyment. On the Orthodox Christmas and again on the Orthodox New Year, children must attend school and peasant-workers must be at their jobs. By the time the Orthodox New Year comes around on January 13, the holiday season has run its course and only a few villagers welcome the year with rifle shot at midnight.

THE FIRST OF MAY

The First of May, holiday of workers, important to socialists and communists in many parts of the world, replaces St. George's Day as a herald of spring. Here again many urbanizing families who have dropped formalized religious and customary observances "slava" on this day, with a family feast featuring roast young lamb or suckling pig. This is particularly so where the head of the household is a member of the party; by political and social definition the household no longer recognizes religious holidays. As in the case of secular New Year celebrations, observing the First of May is more common in town than in the village.

BIRTHDAYS

A completely new event is celebration of a child's birthday. Marking an individual's birthday might be seen as emphasizing a particular person over the household at large. This is not the case. The occasion serves as an excuse for a gathering of the extended kin group and another shared holiday meal. Sometimes children, especially boys, are invited to perform by reciting excerpts from the Serbian folk epics. Grandfathers who have coached them beam with pride. Relationships among kin are reinforced, as is a sense of ethnic identity. Such birthday slavas are often celebrated by workers, whether in the party or not, after they have migrated to Arandjelovac or other towns. They invite their village parents to the celebration. The fact that it is held at the home of a son or son-in-law indicates both an aspect of the decline of patriarchal focus and a new situation in which patrilineal and matrilineal kin come together. Lack of focus on the child whose birthday it is (no gifts, no special cake) preserves the traditional emphasis on the kin unit.

With increasing urbanization and the elimination of common concern over land, relationships between patrilineal kin can be more relaxed while the strong sense of mutual obligation remains. A worker can invite his brother's family to a birthday celebration; kin ties remain important, but at the same time the solidarity of the patriarchal and patrilineal structure begins to lose importance not only on the basis of secularization but also because of changes in property relationships and associated social-structural kin configurations. With these changes sharp distinctions between patrilineal and matrilineal kin also begin to diminish.

Deda Luka sees it this way:

All right, my son Toma in town is a member of the party. He's a man, he has to seek his own way. But let me tell you, it's a strange thing, to go to a slava at your own son's house. It's not a real slava, it's my grandson's birthday, but everything is there—the roast, the feast, the company. Yet I can't get over the fact that he's the host and I'm a guest.

His wife, who is more interested in the distaff preparations that go into such celebrations, says:

What do you mean, not a real slava? When you seat eighteen people, that's a slava! They slava for the child's birthday, for the New Year and for the First of May, if others haven't invited them first. And I mean slava—two sheep or one sheep and two pigs. One whole day just for making fancy little cakes. Can you imagine what this costs? I go to help my daughter-in-law. Her mother is there, too.

This older village couple takes pride in their son's achievements and possessions. When they celebrate their saint's day, however, son Toma is not among the guests. He works on that day, and besides, "Everyone knows that wouldn't be right."

Rituals of Conflict

Rituals of conflict take various forms. Within neighborhood groups and even within descent groups, long-standing antagonisms are known to exist. They rarely come to the surface because of the need for frequent joint action and mutual dependency, especially in view of the still important cooperative work groups such as those at harvest time.

Viewed in an exclusively village context, resources are finite and the progress and prosperity of one neighbor is often seen as being at the expense of another. Serbian society is verbal and thus village life takes place against a background of gossip and mutual suspicion. Much of this is discrete because of the reasons mentioned above and also in order not to attract the evil eye, especially when one wants to engage in magical rituals. Such intravillage friction has seemingly declined in the postwar period of industrialization, since the more significant opportunities for economic and social advancement now lie outside the village. Nevertheless, ritualized ways of expressing and dealing with social conflict remain.

SYMPATHETIC MAGIC: PROTECTING ONESELF

For two years tetka Mileva has been on guard against Radmila from the house over the hill. Mileva knows why her own best cow has not been producing enough milk: Clearly, Radmila is working some sort of magic to divert the milk. Mileva's cow is about to calve. This time Mileva plans a foolproof precaution to prevent the transfer of her cow's milk to Radmila's cow, to ensure the calf enough to drink, and to rid herself, finally, of the unpleasantness and uncertainty of someone else's black magic lurking in her barn. She asks her husband to bring back from

Arandjelovac a small padlock with key, making sure that no one from Orašac sees him buy it or put it in his torba. Čika Slavko doesn't believe in the nonsense his wife is up to, but if it restores their cow's productivity he is willing to give it a try. After the calf is born the "first milk" is hurriedly drawn off, mixed in a wheat batter, and baked into a small loaf. This is then crumbled in more milk, and half is fed to the cow. Urging her husband to work quickly and trying to recall what she remembers from her grandmother's remedy for a similar situation, Mileva helps her husband make an opening in the mud-brick wall of the stall. The other half of the loaf is shoved in, the lock and key are set in with it and the hole is quickly plastered over. "There," says Mileva, wiping her hands on her apron and reassuringly patting the cow's rump, "Now the milk is locked in. That ought to take care of that bitch Radmila and her tricks."

BLACK MAGIC: INFLUENCING OTHERS

Sometimes a small ritual act like this does not suffice and the services of a *vračara*, a part-time occult specialist, are needed. Both client and practitioner exercise discretion in their dealings, for one thing because the activities are officially illegal and for another because if observed the spell might be broken.

The most common services for which such a specialist are sought are curing and influencing the actions of third parties, as in the case of recalcitrant lovers. In the past when a vračara was sought to intercede in affairs of the heart, the lover to be reunited with the client was local. Therefore it was easy or at least possible to obtain from his person the snippet of hair or other symbolic item needed to initiate the magic.

Darinka, in her late thirties, seeks this kind of help on behalf of her daughter, and baba Mica in Markovac has a reputation for such work. "By God," says Darinka, "she was able to intervene with the spirits and bring a young man back to the village all the way from Kragujevac. *Joj*, God knows how she did it, but the next Sunday there was the young man, and before he knew what was happening the families were arranging a marriage."

But Darinka is skeptical as she reviews her daughter's situation:

We've really got a problem, and I don't know if baba Mica can handle it. I'm sure she's never had a case like this before. Here's the way things stand: My daughter Zvezdana had this young man. They went through school here and always liked each other. He went further, to middle technical school, and she stayed here in the village helping us at home.

They still liked each other. Both families knew it. Time was getting ripe to make marriage plans. Then what happens? One day I'm nicely walking to market with people from Gajevi, and what do they tell me?—"Oj Darinka, did you hear about wretched Velisav? Both his sons went to work in Switzerland!"

"No!" I say, "Is that possible? Not the younger one too, not Srećko?"

"The same," says Velisav's neighbor.

"*Kuku mene*, woe is me," I say to myself. And instead of continuing on to Arandjelovac I tuck the hen under my arm and return home.

Well, that's the way it is. My Zvezdana cried and cried. He's a good village boy and we were all set to arrange something. What are we to do now? She wants only him. It's already time, she's ready to marry. I don't know what else to do, so

I say to myself, without telling anyone, "Well, let's just see what that baba Mica can do."

One day in May Darinka takes a somewhat reluctant Zvezdana to Markovac to baba Mica, who learned her craft from a great-aunt famous for these skills. When they return home Zvezdana is half weeping and half laughing. Convinced of the ludicrousness of the situation she bursts out, "How can I obey her stupid instructions! I'm supposed to get a bottle filled with water that he used for washing himself!"

In June the girl goes to see baba Mica alone and asks if she can use a bit of Srečko's hair instead of the water. Baba Mica says they can give it a try. Srečko has not written to Zvezdana but she is able to get his address from one of his cousins. She writes and asks for a lock of his hair as a souvenir. By the end of the month she is able to tell baba Mica that they can get started.

Baba Mica instructs the girl to substitute water in which another man has washed, as long as it is not a man from her own family. Srečko's hair is to be put in the bottle along with some basil and incense and a white cord tied in a loop. The special properties of the cord are to bind Srečko to Zvezdana spiritually if all goes well, and to make returning irresistible. Baba Mica says that if the mixture is prepared in an empty Pepsi Cola bottle there will be a better chance of results. For three nights the bottle is to be placed on a windowsill in the direction of Switzerland, and Zvezdana, naked, is to creep outside at midnight facing Switzerland and calling Srečko's name.

In July baba Mica alters the instructions to calling for Srečko three times up the chimney at midnight. . . .

NICKNAMES

Interpersonal relationships are not easy to generalize about. The village custom of nicknames, while not a ritual, is a traditional way for identifying individuals, and since these names are sometimes inherited they are also at times a way of identifying households. In almost all cases the names are unflattering, so they are never used directly although they are known to all. "Horse-face" has a long, boney head. A woman with a wide mouth and toothy grin is called "Krokodil." A certain villager held in low esteem is "Mučak (rotten egg)." A woman with a sloppy house is known as "Djundra (manure pile)." But while expressive of some hostility and emphasizing individuals' bad habits or physical defects, the use of such nicknames is at the same time a manifestation of the village functioning as a social unit.

Blood-brotherhood and Godfatherhood

Finally, mention should be made of two ways of ritually extending kin ties, usually to establish links with someone from another village. Now somewhat archaic is the institution of *pobratimstvo*, blood-brotherhood. Two friends establish a ritual kin bond through a rite performed at the graveyard, in the presence of the initiator's ancestors. A blood-brother was often sought when a person was gravely ill, but this custom is now scorned. "We don't do this anymore. When you're ill you go to the clinic in town, you don't fool around with chains and crosses on the grave."

As has been indicated, godfatherhood has an honored position in Serbian society. It is inherited in the male line, the most important duty of the kum being selection of a name for his godchild and bestowing it at a christening ceremony. He also has the important role of witness at his godson's wedding ceremony. He may be an honored guest at the slava and at times assume the role of sponsor to his godchild. Like so many other customary observances, kumstvo is pre-Christian in origin but has been adapted into church practice.

Decline in Formalized Rituals

The decline of participation in formalized rituals, whether in the home, at the graveyard, or in church, as well as of partaking in magical practices, reflects what has often been called a trend toward secularization. As is clear from the preceding description, the decline is a relative one. Many ritual practices have been modified while others have disappeared totally. The latter is true particularly of village-wide celebrations associated with the church, especially those which involved processions through the village. These are now expressly prohibited, as is religious instruction in school, although in other ways the church functions normally.

Government Deemphasis

Consciously the government has deemphasized various religious festivals by developing its own secular ceremonial events. This is not simple replacement, as in the cases of New Year's for Christmas, and the First of May for Easter-St. George's Day. Also, not all holidays are equivalent. Just as Easter is more important than Christmas in Orthodox belief, in quite a different way the First of May represents a more ideologically significant celebration than New Year's from the point of view of the government. The Day (of the founding) of the (postwar) Republic, November 29, comes at a time when there are important slavas as well as at the beginning of the Christmas fast. New state holidays related to the Partisan struggle and communism have replaced former state holidays tied to Serbian history and Orthodoxy. In this respect the Day of the Republic is most analogous to Vidovdan, St. Vitus' Day, the anniversary of the Battle of Kosovo, and a day that also commemorates the signing of the Versailles Treaty which created Yugoslavia. Vidovdan was the biggest state holiday in prewar Yugoslavia, where Serbian influence was dominant.

If one wishes to understand the principal motivating forces shaping the lives of Serb villagers, these can be seen in part in ritual life and in part in secularized expressions of national identity. Depending on the context, a villager sees himself as a Serb, a Šumadijan, an Orašac villager, a member of a particular vamilija, and a member of a specific household. Overall, the most significant identities are being a Serb and a member of a certain vamilija and household. (Being

Yugoslav in the context of citizenship in a multiethnic state is generally important only in an international setting, as when male villagers were prisoners-of-war and currently when many are laborers in western Europe.)

Serbian Values

To be a Serb is implicitly to be Orthodox, explicitly to celebrate the slava, and importantly to associate oneself with a heroic tradition of struggle. Here the covert linking of the Partisan struggle against the Germans with earlier struggles against the Turks and later as a nation-state against the Austrians and the Germans is of great significance. This linkage becomes overt when one relates people's sentiments to the abundant memorials to the Partisans and to earlier monuments and sites of the nineteenth century currently being restored or developed in Orašac itself and in nearby Topola. In this way the memorial church of the Karadjordjević dynasty at Oplenac in Topola (built by the Kingdom of Yugoslavia), the park being created at the site of the First Revolt in Orašac, and the extensive memorial park to school children martyred by execution by German troops in Kragujevac, plus many monuments to the Partisan struggle, together form a unity reinforcing a strong sense of identity as Serbs.

Rituals associated with pre-Christian origins are particularly important. Preeminently this includes the slava which, although explicit in being distinctly Serb, is primarily a household and vamilija celebration. The slava is, of course, a symbolic representation of the vamilija as a separate entity. For the ritually pre-scribed graveyard ceremonial feasts in memory of the deceased the entire village goes to the cemetery. The vamilija concept also structures the situation here, that is, the way in which the graveyard is sectioned. Actual feasts are spread out on the grave sites of kin most closely related patrilineally to the individual households.

A decline in magical practices (those associated with curing as well as with conflict), the lessened importance of organized religion, and the falling into disuse of many ritual expressions (including those linked to the life cycle, the annual ceremonial round, and especially the yearly agricultural cycle), raise questions not of replacement but of ways in which people now meaningfully organize their lives. The importance of kin, political organization, and historical tradition provide partial answers. Recent history supplies others.

What of the future? In a political sense the contemporary Yugoslav nation faces severe challenges originating from conflicts among the various ethnic groups formalized as republics and most obviously manifest economically, particularly Serbs, Croats, and Slovenes but with other groups as well. Beyond this there seems to be a malaise, by no means unique to Yugoslavia: The war was won, the country has been modernizing, political power has been decentralized to a degree, but a satisfying modern way of life is proving elusive. A partial reaching back toward the past has already begun in terms of venerating history through monuments, museums, and cultural-historical literature, through old songs on the level of popular expression, and potentially through renewed recognition of the inherent value of generalized tradition and values associated with life on the land.

Regarding a coherent system of beliefs with respect to man, nature, and the self-created human environment, there is no easily discernible unity. Kinship and ethnicity, never discarded and now reinforced, remain vital. The latter particularly may grow stronger in new ways. It is conceivable that the role of the church may expand, but at present this seems unlikely. The situation in Orašac is not acute, as it is elsewhere; despite attempting to overcome aspects of their provincialism, people have never abandoned their roots.

6

Some Reflections on Change

THIS BRIEF STUDY HAS ATTEMPTED to examine Orašac within the framework of an historical perspective encompassing the nineteenth and twentieth centuries. In this concluding chapter we focus on the village within a narrower chronology: the postwar period and especially the years since 1953, during which we have been able to observe change within the framework of our own altering perceptions.

The Studied and the Student

There was a time when anthropologists stood apart from the people they studied. The tribe being examined clearly belonged to one cultural universe and the anthropologist to another. The whole idea of "the expedition," wherein the natives were studied along with the geological formations, flora, and fauna, presupposed these independent universes. For American anthropologists in the latter part of the twentieth century there is a growing realization that not only do the people being studied and the people doing the studying belong to the same universe and share many of the same problems, but, in addition, we are slowly becoming aware that the diverse ways in which problems of modernization are being handled in other cultures may give us some insights into our own future. We are also becoming conscious that the unsettling social transformations in our own nation may enable us to have more sympathetic insights into the kinds of problems faced by other cultures. Although the idea that we can better understand ourselves by studying remote peoples is not a new one, still its precise implications are new for each succeeding scholarly generation.

Today in America use of the word "revolution" parallels the use of "progress" in a past age, the theme implying the necessity of a radical transformation of the present to attain the possibility of a better future; yesterday's catchword seemed to express the confident feeling that things positive and purposeful were inherent in the process of development. Themes in anthropology have, of course, not always directly paralleled those in the society at large, but as the anthropologist has become more involved with peasant societies the values of our own culture have become increasingly pertinent to his research. In this connection one need only think of the tentative use of the word "development" and its related terms "under-developed" and "developing."

THE SITUATION IN THE 1950s

When our field work was begun, from the point of view of American anthropological scholarship the study of peasant communities in Europe had barely started (with the exception of a few outstanding pioneering works). The general problems involved with the study of the peasant community, as opposed to the tribe, were then still novel, and the applicability of traditional anthropological techniques to such research was much discussed. Some of these concerns still echo. On the other hand, in almost all European countries, notably including Yugoslavia and specifically Serbia, the study of their own society by local ethnologists had, at that time, a tradition going back over a century. The focuses (ethnic origins, migration patterns, material culture, folklore) of these voluminous studies were not central to the community study approach as we employed it, but many of these concerns did manifest themselves in our initial monograph. Neither sociology nor cultural anthropology then existed as academic disciplines in Yugoslavia. Due to Stalinist ideological holdovers sociology, now a prominent field of scholarship with university faculties, research institutes, journals, and monograph series, had not yet reassumed its prewar status as a legitimate field of social inquiry. (It had been only five years previously that the Yugoslav Communist party under Tito had broken with the Cominform, and at about that time the Yugoslav government had embarked on the abortive program of collectivization.)

The second world war had ended eight years earlier. In Yugoslavia the period saw, in addition to a struggle with the Germans, a large-scale civil war from which the communists emerged victorious. Many scars had barely had time to heal. Even mildly controversial political matters were discussed guardedly, and contact with foreigners, while not exactly dangerous, was still a matter to be approached with caution. There was an American military assistance mission in Belgrade and an extensive American aid program. Large quantities of surplus food were being sent, and in effect provided a cushion so that Yugoslavia could industrialize without repressive measures in the countryside.

To villagers particularly, and to many sophisticated townspeople as well, America represented something special: a land of abundance and hope and a model for emulation on many levels. Thanks were expressed for UNRRA help (United Nations Relief and Rehabilitation Administration but identified by villagers as American aid) rendered their country in recovering from the ravages of war and in resisting Soviet political pressures.

The American campus atmosphere from which we emerged in the early 1950s was one that was basically secure in the clear-cut lines drawn by the cold war. At that time Yugoslavia alone was groping toward independent action; the term "satellite," used to describe the other East European countries, was accepted with little question, as was the meaning of the Iron Curtain. Despite the activities of Joseph McCarthy, a war in Korea, and a French colonial struggle in Indochina, the term "revolution" was associated in American academia mainly with orthodox communism and past European history, and, in anthropology, with the development of agriculture, city life, and industrialization—in sum, with remote historical processes, the tactics of an opposing alliance of states, and a largely dated radical political party at home. More parochially, the concrete alternatives for anthropologists wishing to work in East Europe were field work in Yugoslavia or interviewing Soviet refugees in West Germany.

There is no question that viewed from a cumulative perspective American anthropology has more data available, increasingly sophisticated methodologies, and more highly elaborated theoretical frameworks (and, for a time, greatly increased financial support). Our successive periods of field work in Orašac have reflected these trends.

ORAŠAC IN THE 1970S

Orašac in the 1970s, with its creaking cow carts, dirt-floored cottages, and older men in peasant dress, is still sufficiently peasant-like to appeal to the traditional anthropologist. During almost two decades of our acquaintance with it, however, the village has felt strongly the impact of change and industrialization. The lignite mine in the village has closed down. Many workers commute daily to the factories in Arandjelovac. Private farming, barely tolerated in 1953, has now managed to reestablish itself. With the recently slowed pace of industrialization, jobs in towns and temporary employment in western Europe have been increasingly difficult to obtain. Private cars, no longer rare, are used to transport produce to market. An Opel station wagon is considered desirable; it can accommodate several hundred kilos of cabbage or a good-sized heifer. Individually owned tractors are also appearing in the village, and operation and maintenance courses have been set up in town for the new owners.

There are also important changes in life styles, as has been illustrated in these pages. Changing notions of prestige manifested in new patterns of conspicuous consumption make great demands. Cars have replaced carriages in village wedding processions, and order in line is now linked more to the characteristics and age of the car than to kin ties.

Orašac happens to be a Serbian historical site, and some tourism is anticipated, abetted by a paved road to the village and a park commemorating the First Revolt. At the same time, many older villagers worry about what will happen to their land since their children have moved to workers' suburbs in the growing towns.

Orašac villagers, while living better, caught up in the increasing consumption game, and in many cases working to insure a life in the city for their children, at the same time have been traumatized by fears of possible Soviet invasion and a third world war. They are troubled by the relative indifference manifested by the United States to the Russian actions in Hungary and Czechoslovakia. These worries rise and fall as political winds shift.

A car for status, cabbages, and calves

Observers of Yugoslavia today cannot help but have a new view, seeing the growing together of the rural and urban dimensions of society and the increasingly close relationship of village and market town. The rural component of Yugoslav society is still distinctive, and Yugoslavia is less industrialized than many other lands, but some of the familiar pressures are beginning to be felt: new demands of traffic in reshaping the town, and limited facilities in schooling, sewage, and other essential municipal services. And although the town is still seen by the young as an alternative to what they feel to be the mud and boredom of the village, established city dwellers are beginning to recognize the value of the countryside as an escape from city pressures.

Evaluating Revolution

How can we evaluate the Yugoslav Communist Revolution from the perspective of American anthropology almost a quarter century after the former's firm establishment at the end of the war? Intermittent study of a Yugoslav village community over two decades can shed some light on the meaning of revolutionary political change on the local level. Two important qualifications should be made. First, although there has been increasing concern among western anthropologists about the potential for and impact of radical and violent political change, for a combination of reasons virtually no field studies by western anthropologists have been done in areas in which communist governments have come into power; in large part this has been because of problems of restricted access to local communities (a state of affairs which, for example, has existed for over half a century in the Soviet Union). The second point raises the question as to how useful, analytically, are formal political designations such as communist or even socialist. The Yugoslav revolution as an indigenous peasant-based movement growing out of the second world war is in many respects more analogous to the Chinese situation than to that of Mexico. However, with its flexible ideology, permitting emphasis on local autonomy, market economy, workers' councils, and limited private ownership of both land and small-scale enterprises, certain of the details of the workings of its internal life as they have recently evolved are not too distinct from those of its noncommunist neighbors. Contemporary Yugoslav society, with its continuing socialist commitment, is also an open society with vital links to the West in intellectual terms as well as in trade and tourism.

Certain results of the revolution are clear. One is most evident in the absence of corporate groups such as competing political parties; in their place is the League of Communists with its close interrelationships with local government and industrial and commercial management. Another result is the absence of a business or commercial class 'and in its stead a group of employees and managers. This lack conditions the significance of status distinctions. Specifically in the village, there is a relative lack of overt correlation between levels of land ownership and formal village leadership. A third category is the restricted role of the church, the enlarged function of the school, the importance of medical and other social benefits, especially pensions, emphasis on industrialization, the increasing equality of women in both a formal legal and a social sense, and, finally, the presently decreasing although still vital role of the state in terms of its organs of administrative authority. Obviously a number of these items are not peculiar to communist states, and some of what might pass on first glance as due solely to the impact of communism has been attributed in other parts of the world to the general role of modernization, for example, the decline in formal religious observances.

But other aspects of change, in part clearly unplanned, are even less intimately linked to the nature of the political system and less directly tied to a revolution. Examples are the workers' suburbs in towns as well as on the outskirts of Belgrade and other major cities. Here houses are built on an individual basis on unplanned streets that will eventually be incorporated into the expanding towns. The distinctions from American suburbs are clear; these are settlements of village migrants seeking to join the town rather than of prosperous urban elements seeking to escape. The small garden plots of these new workers' homes raise not flowers and grass but vegetables and poultry, partly for economic reasons. But the conflict in relating people to land in an industrializing society like Yugoslavia, as in a "post-industrial" society like the United States, is still evident. Both adaptations would seem to be temporary solutions.

Tourism, social services, greater stress on personal consumption in the urbanizing village, and partially mechanized agriculture with accompanying shifts in traditional labor patterns—these are some of the important elements of change.

THE 1970S FROM THE PERSPECTIVE OF THE 1950S

Looking at the early 1970s from the perspective of the early 1950s, it is apparent that the villagers of Orašac have experienced a dramatic rise in their living standard. On the individual and family level there is more disposable personal income, helped by better varieties of crops and livestock and somewhat improved prices, with important supplementary sources of income from factory or white collar jobs in town and occasionally by remittances from earnings abroad. Almost all houses now have electricity. Small electric stoves and television sets are no longer rarities. Some households have built new concrete houses similar to those in town. Electric water pumps and indoor plumbing may appear in a few houses in the next several years. There is the new road, regular bus service, and weekly visits to the village by health personnel from town. On sight it is no longer possible to tell villagers, especially young people, from townsfolk. The new supermarket and department store in Arandjelovac serve villagers as well as townspeople. With increasing possibilities for private capitalization (within overall restrictions on size of landholdings and number of employed workers outside the family), work on the land and in small private businesses seems to be becoming somewhat more attractive at the same time that factory and other urban jobs are becoming harder to get.

Workers Abroad

Balancing this picture is the fact that in recent years approximately one in twenty Yugoslavs has gone to work abroad,[1] among them men from Orašac scattered in factory towns in Germany, Switzerland, France, and Sweden. Despite some reservations people see themselves today as substantially better off than twenty years ago, although earning a living continues to be a struggle.

Attitudes of those who work abroad mirror some of the ambiguities felt by peasants and workers who have matured in the postwar period. This is reflected by an Orašac man in his late twenties who completed studies at a teachers' training school and had worked as an elementary school teacher before going abroad. He is now a cook at an old people's home in Switzerland. He says he is experiencing *real* socialism in Switzerland, where all the employees eat together with the boss of the small home, and that his working relationships seem to represent a kind of equality he found lacking in his Yugoslav work experience. At the same time he clearly sees no future for himself abroad, says he resents the exclusiveness of the Swiss, and looks forward to his eventual return home with savings with which to open a small restaurant on a piece of land his family owns near the site of the proposed park.

The motivation to go abroad is overwhelmingly an economic one. Yugoslavia is the only socialist state willing to entrust its citizens with freedom of movement, and one can get a passport issued locally for travel abroad in as little as three days.

In Germany we visited the quarters of an Orašac villager who works in a tool factory. He and his wife, who accompanied him by convincing him that she could hold down two jobs (she works days in a paint factory and evenings as a char-

---

[1] As a result of wars many villagers have spent time outside the country, but voluntary emigration for temporary work abroad is a totally new pattern for Serb villagers, beginning in the 1960s.

woman at a local inn), speak proudly of the down payments they have been able to make on construction of a new house in Orašac. On a makeshift couch-bed their son puts aside his German schoolbooks and reads a Yugoslav comic book describing the heroic struggle of the Partisans against the German invaders.

Migrations to Australia and North America represent a more permanent break with the village, but occasional visits by some who have "made it" do occur. Some others, who remained in western Europe after the war (having gone there originally as prisoners-of-war) have come back to Orašac to retire comfortably on foreign pensions and savings.

The cycle continues. While watching the summer youth brigade prepare ground for monuments to be made from nearby Venčac marble, a villager who is a skilled cutter at the quarry discusses plans to leave for work abroad. He sees his departure to join a brother already in Germany as a means of taking advantage of opportunity and certainly not as rejection of the job he leaves behind: "What do I know? My brother writes that the pay is good there, and a man can save. Better to make some money now. There'll still be marble here for me to cut when I come home."

Yugoslav Socialism

Yugoslav urban intellectuals and students have a somewhat different perspective. A Yugoslav participant at an international conference held in Belgrade remarks, "If the social development is not directed energetically toward a radical change of the social role and importance of the intellectual and cultural factors, I doubt whether it will be possible to achieve on our soil anything more important than a belated, Balkan variant of modern technological consumer civilization."[2]

Such comment raises important questions that are not easily answered. Television sets and concrete and brick houses cannot be viewed as the crowning achievements of a socialist society. Socialist theorists who regard economic inequality as an ultimate evil are probably willing to accept a centralized political and economic system to enforce their ideals. They also probably would be less disturbed about investments in infrastructure such as industry, paved roads, and electricity and the provision of social services in schooling, health, and urban housing than in the increase of individual consumption and especially of capitalization of small-scale private enterprise whether in agriculture, trades, or tourism. Yugoslav ideologists and planners have been grappling with these problems and have opted for decentralization, with the participation of socially owned and managed enterprises in a market-oriented economy, along with socially owned agricultural enterprises coexisting with private agriculture and small-scale craft and service enterprises. For the Orašac villager this means that more matters affecting his welfare are now resolved within the local commune centered in Arandjelovac than centrally in Belgrade. It also means that the representatives he elects to the communal

---

[2] Quoted in Hans J. Morgenthau, "Reflections on the End of the Republic," *The New York Review of Books*, September 24, 1970, p. 39.

assembly in town can participate in a degree of meaningful decision making in which the roles of agriculture, and industrial, commercial, and tourist enterprises are all considered in the context of local planning. In the early 1970s the potential of tourism was a topic of central concern and was seen as the principal way to further the economic development of the region.

In the village the local cooperative is used extensively for marketing livestock and produce as well as for routine household purchases. The socially owned agricultural enterprise has a more limited effect on the daily lives of villagers. In August one can see its combines reaping the wheat harvest which is then loaded on trucks by the temporary labor force of teen-agers, older women, and a few older men. Younger men who are permanent employees of the enterprise drive the trucks and machines. The scale is larger and the technology superior to that of the private farmers, but work in the agricultural enterprise offers regular employment for only a few villagers in their prime working years. Because of the size of its operations and the technology involved, it does not provide a model villagers could think of emulating.[3] However, relationships between private farmers and the socialized agricultural sector continue to grow.

The peasant-workers of Orašac, burdened by commuting to factory jobs in town and after-hours work on their holdings, generally are not attracted to participation in the workers' councils management of their enterprises nor in political work in the party organization. Nevertheless a few are party members influential in local government, with activities concentrated in Arandjelovac. Political decision making rests at the level of the communal assembly which includes as well village and town representatives who are not party members. Here village representatives speak out for rural interests.

Although the feelings of most of the people of Orašac are at times ambiguous, and the struggle to earn a living remains, they feel pride in themselves and in what their country has achieved in the past quarter century of peace. The saying about turning Šumadija into a little America is no longer relevant. But the attitude toward self and community which provoked the saying is very much a part of village life in the 1970s. Orašac remains a community in which youngsters just beginning school can recite the old epic poems. Increasing participation in

---

[3] The mixed official attitude toward the private farmer is reflected in the varying nature of constitutional provisions. Article 20 states that "Land is a good of common interest." Article 21, while prescribing that "The community shall ensure material and other conditions for the establishment and development of agricultural work organizations based on the social ownership of land and on social labor, and for cooperation between farmers and cooperatives and other work organizations," also provides that ". . . Farmers are guaranteed the right to own arable land up to a maximum of ten hectares per household." Article 22 states, "Within the limits and under the conditions provided for by statute, citizens may by their personal labor engage in agriculture, exercise crafts and perform other services or similar activities with a view to earning income." It continues, ". . . No one shall hire the labor of others to earn income" and in its final section provides that ". . . within the limits and under the conditions determined by statute, the use of the supplementary labor of others may be allowed in agricultural production, crafts, and other services and similar activities carried on by citizens with their own means of production." *The Constitution of the Socialist Federal Republic of Yugoslavia,* Belgrade, 1961, Secretariat of Information of the Federal Executive Council, p. 35.

A meeting of the commune assembly in Arandjelovac

some of the amenities of contemporary Euro-American life has meant that they tend less to think of themselves as backward. "Look at us, working like mad, as though we lived in the stone age," they often apologized in the 1950s. They still slog through the mud to get to the road, haul water from water-holes for their cows, and chop trees for fuel, but they also know surely that they are becoming part of the industrialized world. Villagers do not regard being Balkan, Serbian, or Šumadijan as being provincial and, by inference, inferior (to the same extent as does the previously quoted self-conscious student in Belgrade).

Yugoslav socialism cannot easily please those who would look east or west for their models. Nor does it unequivocally please the people of Orašac, but it has become a constantly evolving life situation compatible with the pride people have in their achievements.

The Role of Conflict

The role of conflict in the functioning of society and the relationship of operation of the society to various internal pressures should be examined. For example, one learns that during the period of attempted collectivization a villager who served as a local official had an attempt made on his life. It is necessary to consider not only his personality characteristics and kin ties but the strength of feeling of the villagers with respect to government policy. In another case, an instance of attempted suicide may be more readily explicable within a traditional village context. Certain forms of conflict may not be institutionalized, but they may be treated by the villagers as expectable and in some respects as desirable (within bounds), as much a part of life as necessary patterns of cooperation. A peasant prospers in part through cooperative labor arrangements with kin and neighbors but then uses the results of his labors in a competitive contest for status.

In initially undertaking a study of Orašac, there was implicit in the observational framework a normative descriptive view; interpersonal, interfamilial data were not sought as such. The original objective, as much as one was consciously delineated at the time, was to document the village yearly agricultural round and the individual life cycle in the perspective of a well-established national historical tradition. Thus, for example, the murder of a young woman by her spurned lover, which occurred during our first stay, was seen as not particularly significant from the point of view of the overall patterning of the culture. In fact, more impressive at that time was the young man's turning himself in immediately to the local police, reflecting obedience to authority and to the strongly felt ethos for order within the village subculture. On a less serious plane restricted violence is permitted. A sign in the kafana notes the charge for broken glasses. On a Saturday night the cash drawer opens and closes while men smash their glasses as symbolic affirmations of masculinity. A young man who had drunk too much rammed his bicycle through the kafana window but was back the next day replacing it.

Orašac exists in a society where, although property is strongly respected, interpersonal relationships are officially evaluated at least in part in an ideological context. The murderer was sentenced to ten years. The court felt that the young man, an aspiring mechanic from a poor family, had been provoked by the girl's family, who had presumably treated him badly, contrasting their landed status with his marginal economic circumstances.

A more recent attempted suicide, by a man in a nearby village, illustrates the continuing importance of old values intensified in certain ways by aspects of modernization. He has eight hectares of good land in a desirable location and is a prosperous farmer by local standards. Several years ago his wife died. Being somewhat timid, he stood by quietly while his adult son blocked a potential remarriage. The son was fearful that such a union would fragment the holding he himself wished to inherit in its entirety. The land has lately increased in value, since it affords scenic and convenient possible house sites for city people wanting summer homes. Not given to seeking companionship outside, the man made advances toward his daughter-in-law. His son's wrath motivated the suicide attempt.

American anthropologists live in a postindustrial society, where individual physical violence often has been glorified historically, and where competitiveness and aggressive behavior are considered norms. Some of our universities, with their medieval patina, have been settings for a degree of toleration of violence somewhat on the pattern of factories in the 1930s when unions were organizing. Here, within home territory, has been played out the confrontation between state authority and dissident student groups, and violent death has occurred. On a national scale urban riots have become commonplace. Anthropologists living within this situation must to at least some degree be affected not only in their own life styles but also, even if unconsciously, in their evaluation of the role of conflict and violence in the foreign society being studied.

The Revolution and Second World War

The Yugoslav revolution during the second world war was an extremely violent and bloody struggle against a foreign occupier and at the same time a political and ethnic civil war. In American terms it combined aspects of our Revolutionary War (struggle against the foreign occupier), our Civil War (contest for state power), and our racial strife (interethnic hostility). There were the communist Partisans led by Tito, the Serbian nationalist group (Četniks), and Croatian fascists (Ustaši) linked with the German and Italian occupiers, all fighting one another. All three Yugoslav groups had considerable peasant support. There were other groups as well. In the latter stages of the war the British and Americans aided the Partisans, whom they deemed the most effective in fighting the Germans. At the end of the war Russian land armies entered Yugoslavia and together with the Partisans undertook the final battle against the Germans.

After the war the revolutionary government consolidated its position by eliminating the opposition. Their property was confiscated and their organizations abolished. In the villages all land holdings over ten hectares became socialized property. In 1948, with Yugoslavia's expulsion from the organization of East European communist states, there was an open threat to the existence of the nation. Foreign domination again became a feared possibility. At about this time the abortive program of collectivization was instituted, only to be subsequently withdrawn. These events followed a bitter war which had been preceded a generation earlier by the destructive first world war. All this understandably traumatized the population.

Some western observers, including some social scientists, appear intrigued with the idea of political, economic, and social revolution as a means of solving critical development problems of nonwestern countries. It is difficult for outsiders viewing the postrevolutionary scene in Yugoslavia to fully understand the extent of the pain and blood that went into the making of the particular Yugoslav experience which grew out of events of the German occupation. An official history of the Šumadijan district center of Kragujevac relates:

> Strong elements of occupation troops went into action in the middle of October 1941. They started by savagely killing several hundred peasants in the villages of Grošnica, Maršić, and Ilićevo. On the morning of October 20 they blockaded Kragujevac and launched a mass roundup. . . . During that day they caught and locked up about 10,000 inhabitants, who had been most brutally dragged out from their homes, offices, shops, schools, or pounced upon in the streets. Nearly all male inhabitants . . . between 15 and 60 years were arrested. On the same date a group of 50 hostages . . . was shot.
>
> Next day, October 21, from the huge mass of prisoners they took about 7,000 citizens and shot them all. The victims included also three hundred pupils. . . .[4]

In June 1941 the first Partisan resistance against the Germans was organized in the Arandjelovac area at a meeting in the woods in a village adjoining Orašac, recalling the similar secret meeting 137 years earlier, in Orašac itself, when revolt

---

[4] *Socialist Republic of Serbia,* Secretariat of Information of the Assembly of the Socialist Republic of Serbia, Belgrade, 1970, p. 299.

against the Turks was first organized. The earlier revolt had also seen massacres of the Serb population. Struggle against a threatening enemy was thus very much part of the tradition of this area, repeated in the early twentieth century in the Balkan War of 1912, the Serbo-Bulgar War of 1913, and World War I from 1914–1918. The Partisan movement saw itself not only leading the fight against the Germans but also establishing a new state order. According to the official history, "In the place of the old authority, the people elected a new one—the people's liberation committees, whose members included the most prominent anti-fascists." This was in the early stages of the war in temporarily held territories. Later, when the hilly regions of Šumadija were occupied on a more permanent basis, the Communist party and the Young Communist League formed local branches, and party materials were printed and distributed. In the spring of 1944, when a final push toward Belgrade was underway, "Partisan units were joined by large numbers of brave peasants, workers, and intellectuals from Arandjelovac and surrounding villages."[5]

Economic development in the postwar period is seen as a continuation of the wartime struggle:

> The enthusiasm of working people, particularly of youth, was demonstrated during the rehabilitation work immediately after the war. Organized into work brigades, the people constructed economic installations in which they were to become protagonists of productive work and later on, self-managers. Between 1947 and 1957 two large factories were constructed [in Arandjelovac]: the Factory of Refractories [the fire-brick plant] and the Factory of Electric Porcelain [the electro-porcelain insulators plant].[6]

This ideological spirit is still present in the youth brigades working in Orašac during the summers of 1970 and 1971. The plan to build a park commemorating the First Revolt thus combines a formalization of memories of historical struggles against foreign occupiers with a sense of the value of labor and ideological commitment; it is also an indication of the practical recognition of the potential of tourism.

Our happening to arrive in Orašac in 1953 was fortuitous. That year was a quiet one in Yugoslavia compared to preceding events and political turbulence ahead. It was a period of hope and building. Serb villagers were just beginning to become factory employees and become more amenable to a cash economy. Interpersonal and interfamilial hostility and conflict can best be appraised within this broader framework. Greater contact with the towns and migration out of the village by many of the more ambitious young people suggest that conflict and cooperation within the village become less vital in individual lives as the arena of interaction of the villagers takes on wider scope. This would also apply to the meaning of intravillage organizational structures and status differentiations.

[5] *Socialist Republic of Serbia*, p. 252.
[6] *Socialist Republic of Serbia*, p. 253.

Results of Revolution

Judged in its own contemporary broad terms (and not within a rigid pre-1948 dogmatic framework), the Yugoslav Communist Revolution has had a great measure of success. The state provides security for its citizens; there is an increasingly higher standard of living, growing equality between the sexes, and a great deal of social mobility. Gone now are the aspirations of prewar peasant parties. A prewar observer noted:

> Balkan Peasant Party Collectives propose to go further than all this and to extend cooperation into production: they would reorganize on a grand scale the old peasant customs of collective labor while preserving individual property. At the same time, these new cooperatives are to be peasant schools for general education and political self-government. To sum it all up, what they want is to conserve the ancient peasant character and folk-culture and to blend it with modern technical knowledge and equipment.[7]

Most land remains in private hands, but no one thinks seriously about the conservation of "ancient peasant character and folk-culture." In part because of government limitations on the size of private holdings and the capitalization of private agriculture, most young people have serious doubts about following in parental footsteps. Most also reject the traditional village economy, and there is a decline in the prestige of the hard labor required to wrest a living from the soil. The revolution in Yugoslavia has been successful in destroying the folk society as a future-oriented model of development. Perhaps this might have happened without revolution, as in western Europe. But by its progress the revolution has raised vital questions such as the future meaning of labor in an advancing society. The peasant subculture is clearly in the process of becoming something else, but then so is the urban worker's subculture. The growing urbanization of the village combined with the impact of the peasant migrant on the town brings closer together two formerly distinct ways of life.

The post-peasant age was entered with the cooperation of all. Even those who opposed communism as an ideology felt positively about industrialization, increasing standards of living, health and education, and the role of the state as the guarantor of a degree of economic security.

The growing overlap of rural and urban subcultures, both in the process of altering, nevertheless does not eliminate old conflicts. We are accustomed to viewing these as dualities; cultural coherence requires continuity in pattern but cannot continue to exist without innovation. New futures are meaningful only in relation to past patterns. Culture in its cumulative sense and the desire for variety make imperative the large scale complexity of modern nation-states. These units can function only if there is standardization and a degree of uniformity. But with personal labor, especially sheer physical effort, increasingly redundant, there is now more room for innovation in individual life styles. These life styles are most

---

[7] Stoyan Pribichevich, *World Without End: The Saga of Southeastern Europe*, New York, Reynal and Hitchcock, 1939, p. 273.

meaningfully carried out, however, within a restricted social context where inter-personal relations are maximized.

The traditional peasant subculture is in the process of disappearing but not of being forgotten. Cooperative work groups and the cyclical religious observances are rapidly becoming antique. Urban centers offer both personal stimulation and subjugation in the performance of daily tasks; rural villages have fresh air, vistas, and cultural stagnation. Parks in the city and motels in the country no longer suffice. New patterns are sought. The nineteenth-century philosophies of communism and capitalism are irrelevant. Postrevolutionary Yugoslavia, Serbia, and the village of Orašac are grappling with many of the same problems that beset the contemporary American scene. The diffusion of technology is not so far advanced, and certain Serbian behavior patterns and kinship structures may seem old-fashioned to an American. On the other hand, the Yugoslavs have displayed more ability to experiment in political-administrative and organizational forms. This is perhaps one of the most important heritages of their revolution. Cultural conservatism is many-faceted. Yugoslav and American societies provide instructive contrasts in this regard.

Reciprocal Rural and Urban Influences

It is of considerable significance that various nationalist movements, including that of the South Slavs, have turned to village cultures in attempting to understand what has made them, as a people, distinctive in a modernizing world. This has been partly romantic in the sense that rural values have been idealized from an urban perspective. Partly, too, it is a substantial acknowledgement that the processes of industrialization and urbanization do not represent simply a one-way influence of urban values on the village. This is particularly true in Serbia, where the state evolved from a peasant base. Hostility between town and village, which increased economically and socially as the state developed, did not in any way diminish the importance of the rural subculture in shaping the nation. The fact that the prewar ideals of the peasant parties have not been realized should not be confused with the more subtle role these values have continued to play, even in the context of a socialist state.

The persistence of these values can be seen in a number of ways. Kin ties provide a bridge over which villagers migrate temporarily or permanently to town for education or a job. They also make it possible for city people to return to the village as a haven in time of war, to vacation in summer, or to retire in old age. Through these contacts goods are exchanged and labor rendered. Peasant culture contributes to urban traditions in the form of literary themes, folk song and dance, crafts revivals, and rich ethnographic museums. Urban restaurant decor borrows romanticized folk art.

Fresh air and the peace of the countryside are taking on increasing value even though the escape from the village mud is a fresh memory. A growing mani-festation of renewed interest in the village, and of prosperity, is the innovation of the small weekend home (*vikendica*) causing land prices to climb in Orašac and elsewhere. On the part of urban Serbs a general interest in plants, puttering with the soil, and pet animals is still not as developed as in western Europe or North

America, but there are signs that it is growing. Of more significance is the nature of workers' settlements in Arandjelovac and other Serbian towns. A small private house with kitchen garden and a few fruit trees is infinitely preferred to living in an apartment. Plum brandy remains the national drink and lard the basis of cooking. The urban-organized Communist party, following the *hajduk* tradition of struggle against the invader, formed its base of resistance in the countryside. This did not make it a peasant movement as such, but it did affect the nature of its organization. The retention of private property in land is not unrelated to the wartime experience.

Some rural influences on the town have been modified over time. An example is the pig-in-the-bathtub theme (in which, after the war, some urbanites ridiculed new migrants by accusing them of using unfamiliar bathtubs to pen pigs in, or balconies to raise chickens on). However, ties with the village tend to attenuate only over the generations. On the other hand, the very success of the city in population growth, industrial development, and prosperity of its citizens in terms of number of cars and increased leisure makes the countryside increasingly attractive for a second home. Folk music, art, and history are rediscovered in different ways by each succeeding generation. As rural and urban subcultural differences decrease, the perception of the past changes from an embarrassed consciousness of an anachronism to be discarded in the march toward the future to a loving recall of one's roots. This is part of the change we have observed in Orašac and in Serbia in the period from the 1950s to the 1970s.

Social and Private Sectors in the Village

In Orašac one can get a sense of this change by standing at the bend of the road and looking right toward the massive *zadružni dom* (the cooperative building) and then left toward work in progress on the First Revolt Memorial Park. The barracks-like building was inaugurated in 1954, at which time it was hailed by guest political speakers as a command base for expanding socialism on the village level. It has not fulfilled this vision. Its yellow paint flaking and its windows streaked, today the big building is only partially utilized, housing little more than the office of the village clerk and a small first-aid clinic used for the doctor's weekly visit. The auditorium is often used for storing grain. Combines belonging to the agricultural enterprise rest beside it. Socialized agriculture has become a limited corporate farm, larger than any single private holding but of secondary importance in the village's overall agricultural economy. The socialized sector is prime in Orašac only in the context of the incomes of peasant-workers who daily commute to the Arandjelovac factories.

In the village the socialized and private sectors coexist in a mutually supportive and at times conflicting relationship. The dom is a monument of sorts to the ineffectiveness of massive programs of instant social transformation. The emerging memorial park, with its planned esplanade of busts of heroes of the First Revolt and paths leading to the glen where the uprising was plotted, glorifies Orašac's moment in Serbian history and reinforces the enduring past.

The idea of social ownership, in which factory employees collectively have control of the enterprise and through a workers' council are responsible for its management, makes the work relationship one in which the economic status of the employees is linked directly to decisions made by the workers' councils. It also tends to make for job stability and relatively low labor turnover. The autonomy of the enterprise and its need to show profit does, however, put it in a position of competition with other organizations.

On the rural level the general consumer and marketing cooperative in Orašac provide villagers with an alternate mode of disposal for their products (other than the open daily and weekly markets and seasonal fairs in Arandjelovac, where fruits, vegetables, and livestock are sold). Generally bulk sales, for example, grain, grapes, and major livestock, tend to be sold to the social sector. This may be done either directly through the cooperative in the village or through agencies of socially owned enterprises that come to the major fairs, from Belgrade and other towns, with their large trailer trucks. The peasant-worker generally views his wage as an economic supplement to his farm economy but highly values the fringe benefits of being a state employee: medical care, disability benefits, and pension rights. Paid vacation time usually means a chance to put in more work on his holding.

From the villager's point of view the existence of alternate outlets for his produce lends a certain stability to the market and enables him to plan his production with a degree of assurance. The system hardly works perfectly. Farmers are frequently dissatisfied with prices. Wages are felt to be low, and the option to strike has not been used (although labor unrest has occurred in other parts of Yugoslavia). The main industries of Arandjelovac have enjoyed a degree of stability although there does not appear to be much prospect for expansion of the work force. A mineral water bottling plant, including the preparation of Pepsi Cola under license, has, however, undergone development with the opening of a new branch not far from Orašac.

There is a surplus of labor, including a growing number of young, educated workers, since most villagers now finish the eight-year elementary school and many subsequently complete trade schools. Freedom to migrate abroad for work has been an important safety valve. Also, by means of some relative increases in the prices of agricultural products and by making it easier for farmers to purchase machinery such as tractors, farm life has become somewhat more attractive by the early 1970s. Vigorous development of the potential for tourism, based on the pleasant rolling hills, the Bukovička Banja spa, and local historical attractions such as Orašac, Topola, and Oplenac, is a current goal of local commune governments.

Agriculture in Orašac: Flexibility and Social Policy

Orašac farms, with their small-scale and highly diversified production and use of marginal labor, from very old people to the very young, seem destined to change into more specialized types of farms as the overall economy develops. A few sheep and pigs, chickens, some cows, possibly a horse, combined with wheat and corn fields, a vegetable garden, a vineyard and orchards, all on a few hectares,

The general store of the marketing cooperative in Orašac

does not seem to be the kind of agriculture with a future, especially when quality production is desired. Superior production is also unlikely from the part-time efforts of peasant-workers and their wives. The population of the village is an aging one (although more young people may be remaining at home in the early 1970s than in the preceding two decades). There are relatively few young people. At the traditional cooperative labor pools for threshing wheat, most of the participants are now women and older men.

From this perspective the Yugoslav government's plans for the ultimate socialization of private agriculture appear plausible. (The other alternative, increasingly capitalized farms on an expanding land base, does not arise in a socialist context.) It is possible that Orašac may specialize its production, as has happened in Vinča (see pp. 83–84).

The contemporary mixed system under which Orašac villagers live is not ideal. It is more in the nature of a transitional economy, but it is one in which governmental coercion has been minimized, although the socialized sector is obviously favored with economic support, technical equipment, and professional staff. The present Yugoslav scene and specifically the situation in Orašac may not excite those who look for dramatic solutions to pressing social problems, but the flexible approach of its evolving political structures does offer encouragement to those who favor a multilineal approach to modernization and the management of technology. The innovations in and relative openness of Yugoslav society attract the interest of those who realize that future violent revolutions may occur but who also are aware of the human price that must be paid in attempts to forcefully direct socioeconomic change.

The part-subsistence family farms of Orašac do serve an important social function; although unspecialized and inefficient in terms of labor utilization, they provide a wide range of roles including some for old people and for the disabled and mentally incompetent. There is work for people in their sixties, seventies, and even eighties, and the village idiot still exists in Orašac. He provides fun for himself and a butt for the jokes of more fortunate men at the village kafana, but it is an important fact that he continues to tend his family's cows. The network of kin ties and responsibilities combined with peasant small holdings relieve the state of some primary responsibility for the aged and the infirm. Public welfare in the village context is virtually nonexistent, since even a minimum holding provides basic subsistence. The number of old couples and widows or widowers is increasing. They are looked after either by close relatives in the village or kin in town or often a combination of both. Thus tolerance and even occasional encouragement of private diversified, semi-subsistence agriculture by the Yugoslav socialist state has had concrete advantages. Underemployment (as with seasonal laborers) or unemployment of peasant-workers has a built-in cushion. It makes possible the return to the family farm by those who have not succeeded in the town and also has given Yugoslav socialism room to experiment in the 1960s (in the late 1940s and 1950s private holdings had been viewed almost entirely as an obstacle to progress).

The relationship between private farmer and the state, while reciprocal, is not altogether stable. As the transitional status of the peasant-worker indicates, the trend continues to be out of agriculture for the young and able. The scale, techniques, and capitalization of private agriculture will have to increase to provide long-range attraction for the young, or, as seems more likely, relationships with the socialized sector in agriculture will increase. A development in this direction is the leasing of private farm land by the agricultural enterprise. In Orašac the prospect for expansion of employment opportunities in socialized agriculture does not appear to be substantial.

The Peasant-Worker in Socialist Planning

In all these trends the peasant-worker is the key figure, although from the viewpoint of the socialist planner not a very satisfactory one. The planner would prefer a more clearly defined commitment from the worker, with economic ties to the village severed. The planner would also like to see faster expansion of the socialized sector of agriculture. Returning migrant workers from western Europe bring back with them acquired tastes for increased private consumption and often desires to enter into small private businesses. This will necessitate a rather delicate politics of accommodation in the future. An important element here is the continuing migration to the city. In the five year period 1961–1966, more than

In private farming traditional ways continue, but boys replace men.

10 percent of the population left Orašac (225 individuals out of 2187), most of them people in their prime working years and their young children. By 1966 considerably less than half the village households were headed by an individual who was a full-time farmer or who had children or the potentiality to produce heirs to maintain the household as a farming unit. Exodus from the village was motivated by the disparity between rural and urban living patterns, the limitations on private holdings and investment in farming, the educational system's emphasis on the progressive role of the urban working class, and a general desire to be modern. The impact of these factors lessened somewhat by the late 1960s, but fulfillment of youthful aspirations continues to be found in town and not in the village.

Certainly not the least of the advantages of long study of a village community is the mirror that long-term observations provide for changing values in

The state farm has invested heavily in capital equipment.

the course of alterations in the observer's own perspective. If analogy is made with a photograph, not only does the scene being photographed change but so does the kind of camera, its focus, and the quality and sensitivity of the film.

The Observer and His Perceptions

Finally, there is a need to confront directly certain factors implicit in the background of the observer and to relate them to the people being studied. American anthropologists who set out to study foreign peasant communities are not randomly selected from the American population. They are products of American higher education, occupying or aspiring toward the particular functional and social niche occupied by university professors of the social sciences. Most seem to be products of urban or suburban background, probably of middle-class origins. In coming to understand rural people of improving but still restricted means, part of the culture shock of field experiences relates not only to cultural differences but also in part to an attempt to reach across barriers of occupation, status, and class.

American anthropologists, however ambivalent in their regard for the values of their own culture, are nevertheless members of that culture. There has been pride in the technical sophistication of anthropology as it has evolved in the United States and to an important degree an unquestioned self-assurance, especially as far as scholarly motives are concerned. Until now we have not really thought through the important implications of the obvious fact that we go abroad to study peasant folk to an infinitely greater degree than foreign scholars come to research our rural populations. Studies of foreign rural cultures have been oriented more toward documenting distinctive cultural patterns than toward interest in exploring the extent of a common concern with problems linked to the progressive worldwide elimination of traditional rural subcultures. This is not a question of the role of American or Yugoslav models or even of formulating contemporary cross-cultural models of modernization processes. It is a matter of attempting to evaluate the Yugoslav experience while conscious of the extent to which the peculiarities of the American situation determine the structure of the lens through which we do our viewing. Certainly an important objective should be an attempt to discover the significant common parameters, if any, that will structure future developments in both countries. In this connection terms such as "rural," "urban," "peasant," and "poverty" very much need to be reevaluated.

Villagers viewing the anthropologist's view of the village

Interpreting Change in Orašac·

Trends in Orašac can be interpreted from the point of view of sociocultural change and the related problems of development within the context of an evolving socialist state. It is also possible to look at contemporary Orašac and its interaction with its market town, cities, and work opportunities abroad from the perspective of the meanings of life in a modern technological consumer civilization. The importance of the changing but still close ties to the soil and the village are apparent.

As we have seen, even in urban areas few Serbs are more than one or two generations removed from a village background. But it is an illusion to look at Orašac from the perspective of a developed nation where the emotional and psychological importance of rural life ways has largely receded into the distant past. In America the existence of suburbias with private houses on small green plots seems to be in part an abortive effort to create instant villages or at least certain values associated with a rural provincial past in the context of large-scale urbanization and industrialization. Orašac represents for Yugoslavia an example not only of the slowly modernizing productive resources of agriculture but also of an ethnic heartland from which the modern state derives. In Yugoslavia, social evolution in a technological context is occurring in terms of vigorous interaction with the still existing although greatly modified traditional rural subculture. It is out of this dynamic and reciprocal interaction, where urban-derived ideologies and technologies affect rural life, and where village values temper the ways in which towns grow, that the future is being shaped.

7

1986
Perspectives on Long-Term Research

Introduction to the Research Approaches

On the level of personal relationships there is perhaps no need to pose a question regarding long-term research. The ongoing research experience has been tremendously enriching for the investigators and our now adult children, who first arrived in the village as toddlers and as an infant. From what our village friends convey, satisfactions with this enduring relationship have been a two-way process. But beyond personal affect, what is the intellectual value of long-term study of a single community?

Over thirty years ago the opportunity to document European village life, in this case a village in Serbia, presented itself as a challenging academic endeavor. From the perspective of Anglo-American scholarship at that time, the only significant works on Balkan peasant society were Sanders' pioneering *Balkan Village* and the writings of Moseley on the structure of the zadruga. Their researches were based on pre-war investigations and were important statements for earlier points in time. Apart from our analyses of wide-ranging sociocultural, economic and demographic changes over time, the ongoing nature of our work as it continues to evolve over several decades in the village of Orašac in Šumadija affords simultaneous appreciations of dynamics of transformation discerned on a human scale.

Glimpses of Change

The first scholarly publication resulting from the research (*A Serbian Village* 1958) is a base-line against which to assess subsequent observed changes. Taking as an example a complex of changes related to easier access to material goods and new values, there is much to contrast between the first version, the later edition (1967) and the present. The 1967 edition described a situation in which villagers traveling by cow-drawn cart faced the novelty of choice: to take the familiar pot-holed *drum* (mud and stone highroad from Turkish times) or a just completed, longer asphalt-surfaced connector road. Vans, autos and motorcycles are beginning to appear in the villages. The bucolic vision of plum blossoms is now often sullied by clouds of dust.

By the early 1970s we observe (*A Serbian Village in Historical Perspective* 1972) that the rural scene retains its aura of "time immmorial" — but this appearance of constancy is deceptive, on the surface only. Up close the village is seething with change. By the late 1970s Šumadija's rolling landscape is laced with all-weather roads, and new drivers careen along them with disregard for the still extant creaking carts piled high with hay. They speed past unaware pedestrians, shepherds and spinners who amble on the dangerous roads as though on quiet village lanes. Plastic floral memorial wreaths placed along the verges are poignant testimony to the frequency of auto and pedestrian tragedies in a society experiencing the first generation of automobile drivers.

Village houses were usually built *daleko od druma,* "far from the road," another legacy from Turkish times, but now it is fashionable to build directly along the road. A few householders plan for a windowless side or rear elevation to face the road, thereby eliminating some of the intrusive dust and noise which by now is commonplace. For most households in the process of constructing new homes, however, the village ethic of presenting a proud facade to the world is more important. New houses are staked out as soon as the plot is inherited or acquired. The first item erected is a chain-link fence and stone portals, announcing symbolically to all passersby, "This is mine!" Sometimes these fences enclose a patch of grass, or simply piles of bricks and sand awaiting construction. Observations during a 1984 visit reinforce an increasing concern with statement of self.

This attitude carries over to the village graveyard, formerly relatively egalitarian in terms of community access and with limited variation in types of grave markers. Today we see massive polished slabs, commissioned monuments and new manifestations of a need to bound off what is one's own. These slabs with their elaborate ornamentation in the form of photographic likenesses of recently deceased kin, combined with the engraved names of the relatives who erected the monument, are a symbol of the conscious desire to unite past and present members of a lineage. The manifestation of this desire is not only an

New tombstone style, with photo-engraving of deceased on tractor.

assertion of long-standing cultural values but an overt expression of "status" in a newly competitive context.

Some of these large new investments result from the fact that many households have an able-bodied member temporarily working "in Europe" (Western Europe), sending home remittances. The workers return annually, and as labor and funds are available new brick houses go up slowly over a period of years. Here is the zadruga in new form: father, titular head of household, remains on the land; son goes to work abroad; together they construct and own a joint household which is physically two structures: the old house on the land and the new home on the road.

Frequently we see a hand-lettered sign, *plac na prodaj*, "plot for sale," nailed to a tree. Such land is often offered by older villagers who can no longer farm. Some of them may have moved to join urban kin if there are no immediate kin in the village. Or the land may be offered by daily commuters who now have jobs in town. These social changes reflect the complexity of migration patterns. Some former villagers prefer to move to towns or overcrowded Belgrade rather than remain on the land their fathers and grandfathers tilled so assiduously. They explain that they are tired of "tramping the village mud" as their reason for leaving the land they inherited. Some return, not to reside in the village as peasants but to convert the former homestead to a *vikendica*, a week-end house on the land which is their patrimony.

When a new vacation house is started on purchased land, a nostalgia for the virtues of village life is seen in the planting of fruit trees and the laying out of a garden even before construction starts. This kind of leisure time agriculture only partially compensates for a displaced wheat field or vineyard. In many cases, the variation in architectural styles between houses of local peasant-worker and vacationing urbanite are indistinguishable. New A-frame dwellings rise near old-style sheep hutches.

A country home in the village, whether owned by a returned village son or an individual with no kin ties in the village, is enhanced by contemporary ease of access to Bukovička Banja, a landscaped spa located in a wooded area on the far side of the market town of Arandjelovac. This spa is also the source of Knjaz Miloš, a highly acclaimed mineral water. The firebrick and insulator factories in town represent initial industrialization of this area in the late 1950s and 1960s. Along with the spa founded in the mid-19th century, and the marble quarry in the nearby village of Venčac predating the present period of industrialization, they represent the non-agricultural parts of the regional economy. A local official sums up the situation: "We take advantage of all our resources — we sell our mud [clay for firebrick and insulators and local potters], rock [marble for gravestone markers, sculpture and monumental architecture], water [mineral water] and even our air [for tourists]."

When we first started going to town we walked in with villagers bringing produce to barter or to sell at the weekly Friday market. Then, the long, single cobbled street (*dug kao ženski jezik*, "long like a woman's tongue" was lined with craftsmens' shops and rows of the pruned and whitewashed acacia trees characteristic of every Šumadijan small town. On market day one walked its length while leading sheep to the livestock market. In the afternoon village boys and girls (who had hiked barefoot, carrying their shoes) strolled up and down in groups looking each other over before joining in *kolo* dancing on the grass near the church. That cobblestone street, and its beige and peach and soft green-tinted craftsmen's shops, like a watercolor from another era, has been gone for almost 20 years. It is replaced by a wide paved road marked with pedestrian crossings and parking spaces. The old craft shops have given way to specialty stores, department stores, supermarkets, cafes and a potter's studio which caters to domestic tourists.

Is this the same town where Danica used to trek in *preko brda* ("over the hill") to sell a single basket of eggs? Where grandfather Radovan took up his staff and spent a day walking there and back to transact a few minutes of business at the county office? Today regularly scheduled buses operate between Orašac and the town. Arandjelovac also boasts a bypass to accommodate large trailer trucks and keep heavy traffic off the main street. Both new roads are lined with modern apartment buildings. Vestiges of the old small-town architecture diminish each time we visit. The old spa, refurbished, is now regarded as the town cultural center and its formally laid out park surrounded by renovated and new hotels is the scene of an annual international sculpture festival. The local mineral water has become the base for Pepsi Cola, bottled under license. "B.B.," as the state enterprise is known, has expanded its line to include carbonated fruit drinks and diet colas. Like the factories, this large enterprise provides continuing employment opportunities for many villagers. Fleets of B.B. trucks move from the bottling plant to distribution points throughout Serbia. Litter seems to come with modern life. Discarded Knjaz Miloš bottles and the yellow plastic shipping cases are testimonies to Šumadija's participation in the larger world.

Despite these links to the town and beyond, Orašac village itself continues to display a characteristic dispersed pattern, not only in settlement but in lack of a crossroads-type center, a direct result of mid-19th century edicts restricting development to towns. Events in recent years reverse this earlier pattern of town centralization. Some of the shops and services formerly found only in town now appear in the village. These include a general merchandise store, a modest medical clinic, a post office. Federal law presently permits small-scale private enterprise (owner and total number of employees not to exceed five), and there are *privatnici* here and there along the road. On the way to Arandjelovac one passes an auto repair service, a stone-cutter's workshop and a few cafe-restaurants. One *kafana* features a folk ensemble on weekends. The name of the establishment (on a metal sign provided by the Yugoslav Pepsi Cola franchise) is *Složna Braća* ("The Compatible Brothers"), a sentimental ploy on the valued zadruga ideal of brothers sharing common roof and hearth. In fact, the establishment is owned and operated by an enterprising couple from Mladenovac, a nearby town. Up the hill on the left is a large new shed housing an auto body shop. Chassis parts are spread about, some overlapping surrealistically into the adjacent plum orchard.

And yet, when you reach the top of the hill and gaze at the village panorama below, there it all is: the sweeping view, the hills, the familiar undulating fields of corn and wheat. There are the patches of acacia woods, the hedgerows along the lanes, the weathered tile roofs, the plum orchards, the vineyards. On the horizon Mt. Kosmaj reaffirms its purple contours. Sentimental? Yes. A better setting could not be contrived for the old folk song, *"Šumadijo, rodni kraju"* ("Šumadija, My Birthplace"). From that height and distance it is the same scene we saw when we jounced up the hill in the back of a cow-cart over 30 years ago and had our first glimpse of Orašac village below.

In sum, our impressions of Orašac seem to represent three chronologically placed themes. These reflect what we observed directly in the field but also grow out of our own backgrounds. We have changed, as have our observational frameworks, affected by evolving scholarly concerns which in turn relate to shifting societal dynamics. In our first years in Orašac, 1953-54, we were impressed overwhelmingly by the predicatble, repetitive and self-sufficient aspects of village life. (This was before we had lived in Asia.) The rural East European setting contrasted strongly with the cosmopolitan world in which we grew up. At the time of that initial visit agricultural work depended mainly on human and animal power. The village was a conscious social unit. Discrete courtship centered on village dances held on local festivals and after special market days. The rituals of Christmas and Easter were shared as family events. Women chanted the poetry of mourning at graveyard feasts. When old men played the *gusle* and recited oral epics they were eagerly listened to and did not have to compete with soccer matches on TV.

The village, of course, had never been isolated nor culturally static, but we were understandably impressed by "timeless tradition," reflecting as much our own inexperience and the state of sociocultural anthropology at the time, with its emphasis on the value of documenting ways of life previously unstudied in the West. The reality of Yugoslavia at that period reflected initial stages of implementation of a socialist society, just several years removed from the horrors of German invasion and a simultaneous civil war. When we arrived in rural Serbia the socialist revolution had recently tried to undertake collectivization of the land. This policy was withdrawn in 1952, following Yugoslavia's 1948 break with the Cominform.

In the mid-1960s and early 1970s many unique events of change were highlighted for us. In addition to improved roads were innovations altering village life, particularly electrification and bus service. Local government services began to appear in Orašac, e.g., the postal station and the clinic.

The village as a whole was beginning to feel strongly the impact of migration by the young. Migration was not new, but it had never been so massive. Along with this trend was the coming into prominence of a new kind of villager, the peasant-worker. This meant that more heavy farm work fell to the women who remained at home. The construction and expansion of factories in Arandjelovac went along with the appearance of non-recyclable plastic garbage beside the roads and its persistent and unfamiliar accumulation on the scattered homesteads. The detritus of rusting auto parts became increasingly obvious and made us feel less in a "traditional" peasant milieu. Above all, this was a period of expansion and the opening up of a range of economic possibilities.

The late 1970s and mid-1980s impress us as a time of consolidation and a period of assimilating achieved change. It is also a time of dealing with limited options. It appears less a matter of achieving socialist goals as such, but rather of dealing with inflation, limited urban job opportunities and difficult international trade possibilities. Other serious considerations which have recently become increasingly important in the village are the costs of industrialization as reflected in the need for pollution control, and the necessity to maintain the market town infrastructures expanded in the 1960s and '70s. From the villagers' point of view now is a time of investment, to affirm enduring values inherent in family relationships and ties to the land. This perhaps accounts for the newly elaborate and massive grave markers with their inscriptions of family members specifying explicit kin links to the deceased. These material monuments to the past are balanced by monuments to the present and future in the form of very substantial houses constructed with surplus capacity. Such spacious and partially-used rural housing can be contrasted with cramped urban apartments, usually obtainable only with great difficulty. (Since contemporary Yugoslavia provides limited opportunity for the investment of private capital in small-scale familistic enterprises, monies earned abroad tend to be invested in kin-oriented consumption.)

The Community Study Approach

As a research method, community studies have been somewhat justly criticized for being myopic in their view, concentrating on local society to the exclusion of national trends or, more precisely, failing to articulate the two levels in a meaningful way. Further, such studies have been intellectually eclectic, with differing focii. This makes comparative work difficult. It is not appropriate to pursue that specific discussion here but rather to note that when fieldwork in Orašac was begun, documentation of a way of life until then not represented in the Western scholarly literature made sense and filled a need. In retrospect, it has turned out that observations we made then, because our emphases were different from those of local scholars, also have proven to be of interest to contemporary Yugoslav ethnographers and social historians.

While community studies of segments of nation-states have, by definition, been studies of sub-cultures, it is important that the community study approach is an integrated one, seeing the village as a cultural unit. This is not mindless or indiscriminate collecting of data but, at best, a considered attempt to document value cultures in full complexity against a background of particular research interests.

Longitudinal Studies

Advantages of long-term research are manifold. The most obvious is the value of repeated field visits and subsequent reflection in the intellectual context of evolving theoretical perspectives. (This is evident to the reader who peruses the Suggested Readings at the end of this book and notes items published since 1972, the date of its first edition.)

Long-term research further provides the possibility of undertaking longitudinal studies, where the same population is followed over time with specific investigative interests in mind. Such studies are demonstrably valuable in fields such as psychology, sociology and biology as well as in anthropologically based community studies. Our research has emphasized demographic content and thus has ties to all these fields. As the research has progressed over the years and we have observed and participated in the life of the village community during repeated visits, we simultaneously pursued written documentation and analyzed oral tradition reflecting folk perspectives on history. From an anthropological viewpoint, our longitudinal studies have thus linked developments in oral traditional studies to historical demography. In population studies the results of long-term observation and analyses of demographic variables combine to provide a view of trends in the community as a whole as well as to offer case study data based on empirical observation, often focused on selected individuals and families. An important and obvious concommitant is that statistical materials from the local setting can be compared with regional and national trends. This has been done for the Orašac data, rendering it possible to judge which trends in the community reflect more general developments in the society as a whole (Halpern and Wagner 1984). Against that approach, viable oral tradition and a wide range of oral genre studies (Kerewsky-Halpern listings in Suggested Readings) provide a view to the past. The ways in which people interacted within the social structure are delineated by historical demography. Autobiographies and lineage histories collected over the 30-year research period have been invaluable for that purpose.

Applying Diverse Theoretical Perspectives

Using a variety of theoretical perspectives in an interdisciplinary team approach in a single community, research has been carried out in several Yugoslav communities (Halpern and Wagner 1980). Both social and biological science methodologies were employed. Our variation on this approach in Orašac has been smaller in scale; primarily, only the two of us were involved, with occasional aid by others (Kerewsky-Halpern and Halpern 1977, Halpern and Wagner 1981, 1982). Three American anthropological dissertations have come out of the research in Orašac: *Social and Cultural Change in a Serbian Village* (Halpern 1956); *Speech as Ritual and Process: Aspects of the Ethnography of Communication in Rural Serbia* (Kerewsky-Halpern, Department of Anthropology, University of Massachusetts, 1979); and recently a demographic profile, *Children and Change in a Serbian Village, 1870-1975* (Wagner, Department of Anthropology, University of Massachusetts, 1984). All three focus on the same site. The approaches and data bases overlap. The initial work fits the pattern of the community study approach and descriptive ethnography, with subsequent restudies (published in revised form as Halpern 1958, 1967). The second dissertation is grounded in changing forms of oral tradition using a sociolinguistic approach, and the third, using computer-generated data sets based on our source materials, is concerned with demographic processes.

Integrative Approaches

A jointly edited monograph (Kerewsky-Halpern and Halpern 1977) integrates these diverse perspectives in order to shed light on the dynamic interrelationships of social structure, oral tradition and demography. For example, by appreciating and analyzing the "epic pulse" by means of which some elders retain details of their lineage history (Kerewsky-Halpern 1981 based on 1979 work), we have been able, in turn, to comment on the evolution and transformations in the zadruga-based household (Halpern and Kerewsky-Halpern 1980). We have dealt with ways in which quantitative measurements of kin ties relate to the means by which individuals perceive these same ties in a diachronic framework, as discussed earlier in Chapter 2. Vital rates and specific social structural frameworks, as in household size and family-household structures, are elucidated on the basis of administrative records (birth, marriage and death registers, landholding, tax and other population lists including census records preserved by the local administrative offices and the Serbian State Archives). (Examples of the use of these records appear in Halpern 1977, 1981 and Halpern and Wagner 1982.)

Depicting the nexus of social relationships as defined by villagers themselves reflects a sense of collective identity. Combining approaches from historical demography and the study of oral tradition has made possible the interpretation of a multidimensional model of Serbian village society. This has been implemented by the explicit interrelating of computerized demographic and social structural data bases with sociolinguistic analyses of communicative competences and speech patterns which are the gifted legacy of members of an oral traditional culture. This has enabled us to "map" a community's kin relationships and associated social structures over a period of 200 years. Orally recollected lineages of eight to twelve generations have provided points of departure. By this means we have been able to look at the various forms of household structures experienced by an individual over the life course (Chapter 2). Our intentions have been to combine oral tradition and historical demographic records in mutually informative ways to stimulate new insights into the social structural and cultural dynamics.

Linear and Cyclical Time: A Theoretical Construct

Connected to these approaches are efforts in recent years to explore ways of integrating the data by applying concepts of linear and cyclical time. It becomes possible to posit an understanding of how Serbian village culture and its social system alters over time and how resultant changes affect the ecological setting. A point of departure is to consider cultural ideologies based on cycles, as in the case of values associated with the extended family system or the values reinforced over generations by the protagonists in the well-loved oral epics. Individual experience, however, must always deal with linear (historical) change, as in the unique and non-recurrent experiences encountered by ordinary individuals during the course of a lifetime.

For men in Orašac this has often involved leaving family and village to serve their country in one or several of the many wars Serbia has experienced over the last century, both as an independent state up to World War I and subsequently as a constituent republic of Yugoslavia. Motivations for fighting for one's country may be similar in each period, but the specific forms of warfare and their consequences have been quite different. The two time frames are not systems apart; rather, they are in continuous interaction, producing adaptive sequences. In this instance, the cultural ideal is continuity of the South Slav extended family undergoing a series of predictable sequences of household formation. The reality is that cyclical time ideals must adapt to linear time changes, e.g. the war loss of a father/husband household head or of a sole son, projected inheritor of the patrimony. There exists a felt bond between the patriarchal heroism portrayed in the epics, such as the one cited in Chapter 1, and a more contemporary depiction of the tragedy of war and human experience, with its reality of social structural consequences, which is not part of the epic tale.

An initial distinction can be made between recurrent family cycles in process, whose dynamics are tied to individual life cycles, and the particular linear time frameworks or historical moment. Some social structural features are recurrent, and others clearly are not replicable. Precise categorizations of those phenomena which are cyclical and repetitive, and those which are discrete and linear, are not made easily. All persons are born and die. Most people mature. The exact sequence of intervening events is nevertheless unique for each individual. These phenomena can be looked at from the point of view of individuals in the same age cohort and those from different generations. While all share similar expectations, timing remains idiosyncratic. Sometimes individuals share the consequences of cultural disasters, as in the case of the death toll in Orašac as a result of the influenza epidemic during World War I. But the outcomes are unique to the individual in a linear time framework while the ideals based in cyclical time represent, at best, options or possibilities.

Cyclical time perspectives refer both to occurrences in the life course and in the processes of the family-household cycle. The sequence of events in the latter is propelled by changes in individual vital events — birth, marriage, migration and death and the social consequences of these events. The cyclical concept we apply refers to a typology of predictable, sequential events whose beginning and end points can be defined with precision. Family cycles can end, as when an elderly couple dies in the village leaving no descendants. Or the family's experience as part of the village community can close when all migrate out. In these cases parental homes are sometimes maintained, at least for a period, as vacation residences.

Pure cyclical time can be envisioned as a closed circle. In graphic form it can be depicted as a helix with a series of circles interlocking around a straight line representing linear time. This line of linear time extends infinitely but can change direction and thus can respond to cyclical time values, analogous to an electrical field. Cycles can also alter and be viewed as the varying form and diameter of the circles, representing elapsed time in a particular cycle. It is possible to choose arbitrary starting and terminal markers on a cycle but they must always exist with reference to a specific process, whether in physiological aging or the annual seasonal progression. A logical point of departure is a new season, a new life with built-in replicability. In linear time each event is unique and fits into an unalterable order. Here process is not reinforcing. The disappearance from Šumadija ("Woodlands") of the dense oak forests during the 19th century is a case in point, and we have explored its specific ecological consequences in Chapter 3. Only a little more than a century earlier travelers from Western Europe reported that the area was so thickly wooded that they never emerged from the shade. Today the trees most in evidence in much of the region are clumps of fast growing acacia, maintained as woodlots.

It is characteristic of the value distinctions between the two time processes that it is much easier to define linear time in negative terms and cyclical time in positive ones. As explained, linear time has no fixed terminus. It can be projected back into the past but it is not readily predictable from past events. From a cultural perspective, linear time occurs in a secular rather than sacred context. When viewed as an arbitrarily defined point of departure, linear time can be seen as always in the process of by-passing any chronologically fixed cultural setting. This may be balanced by an alternative perspective which conceives change as experiential content, reflected in the cumulative aspect of culture especially with respect to the technical order. In this latter sense, linear time has no precedent, and the consequences of developments based in linear time can be assessed in terms of probabilities only. Thus the linear time ecological change cited above can also be considered from the perspective of environmental degradation involving both the loss of non-renewable resources and the advent of environmental pollution. We think of the cycles of seasonal change on another level, that is, parts of man-made and unnatural as opposed to natural worlds, or pollution versus decay and rebirth.

Links between past and future exist, but their relationship is neither implicit nor readily predictable. Modernization, processes of industrialization and urbanization call forth images of specific kinds of changes exemplified here. To take an example of a linear time event in the local context, look at the demise of local crafts. In the 1950s Arandjelovac supported extensive crafts especially oriented toward serving the adjacent peasant population. Craftsmen included potters, blacksmiths, wheelwrights, furriers (mainly sheep skins for hats and vests), candlemakers, sandal makers (from pigskin), dyers (of wool), tailors (men's peasant costume from locally raised wool), makers of rope (hemp was a local crop) and harness makers, among others. Today they are almost completely gone. Those that survive, such as the potter, have reoriented their trade. Villagers want factory-made goods now, not ceramic jugs and crocks. The ending of these crafts not only lessened the material distinctiveness of peasant culture but also, for many peasant sons, eliminated a possible life stage as apprentice to a craftsman. This change is an event in linear time which affects cyclical patterns. There are other dimensions. Items of clothing no longer produced by local labor from the products of agriculture has meant obvious greater dependence on a cash economy as well as a decreasing tie-in with the cyclical aspects of the local agricultural economy which featured diversification, e.g. food, fiber and traction uses for animals and animal products. Such needs now are linked to national and international economic patterns which function more in linear time dimensions, as in the case of petroleum and its subsidiary products, all of which must be imported.

Sacred observances engage cyclical time and are related to the natural world as represented in daily and seasonal activities. Ritual events associated with birth, marriage and death are sacred time markers in the life course. Since the past is replicated, it is replenished or reaffirmed by such ritual. Cyclical time is sanctioned by rituals of affirmation of achieved stages. Rituals can be seen as giving expression to biological processes and the annual seasonal cycle.

Ceremonies for the dead at the village graveyard function in this manner. These are of two types. There are annual calendrical memorial ceremonies participated in by the whole community, and there are individual funeral rites and subsequent prescribed periods of commemoration of an individual's death. Simply to visit the graveyard is to identify not only with the deceased but with the patriline, since placement of burial areas in the village cemetery mirrors by lineage groups the distribution of houses in village neighborhoods. Women's lamenting in formulaic patterns reaffirms kin links with the deceased. This cyclical time process remains potent even as the contemporary graveyard setting amidst radically changed styles of tombstones reflects linear time developments in enhanced technology and greater disposable income. The oral traditional component has also reformulated as skills in modes of verbal expression alter in response to growth in mass communication in a linear time frame. Values rooted in cyclical time remain dominant in the graveyard; the fancy new tombstones still symbolize kin links between the living and the dead emotionally, and as mentioned earlier, visually as well. A broader look around the graveyard is revealing of an altered cycle. The older graves of individuals with whom living kin could not have been acquainted are vitually ignored, neither weeded nor tended. The time span of effective recall has obviously shortened and with it the universe of remembered kin. Cycles still operate, but they are abbreviated.

Idealized futures always contain cyclical elements replicating the past, as in anticipated stages of an individual's life course. Events in linear time need a cyclical time referent to make them intelligible. It is apparent that historical anniversaries, as in the commemoration of significant events in the founding or development of the nation-state, can be said to be anchored in linear time, i.e. they occurred only once. Yet their reinforcement in an annual calendrical observance does situate them in a cyclical time frame. In this case it is necessary to distinguish between the original event and its process of commemoration. Postwar state holidays such as the First of May are examples of a process which has been adapted into village culture. However, this process is not cumulative, for some of the prewar holidays are no longer celebrated. This feature is part of Yugoslavia's process of revolutionary social change (but similar dynamics are also present in countries which have not gone through political revolution).

There is an analog to developments at the graveyard, with the selective overlooking of the more remote past and greater embellishment of the proximate past. The cyclical process continues as its content alters, affecting specifics of the cyclical stages.

In the kinds of change observed over the course of an individual lifetime as encapsulated in a biography, cycles can be seen as measures of linear time. Specific cycles always involve particularized events in keeping with the constellation of elements in an individual's experience and, as a consequence, bear a degree of unpredictability. Examples are the kinds of sociocultural changes in linear time discussed above. Such changes help interpret the ways in which individual life course and household cycles do not fit ideal expectations. The perception of these events as discontinuities is, in turn, a product of cultural values grounded in cyclical time experience. Autobiography is always composed of a blending of the two time elements.

When asked to define their lives in this type of structured format, Orašac villagers identify simultaneously with the distinct time dimensions. It is the lineage ideology which marks the beginning of personal time. Male villagers will frequently say the equivalent of "This I remember" as a preface to recounting events of their grandfathers' time. This cyclical time value is still fresh among the present generation. People in their 50s speak of events of World War II in the direct manner of relating a personal experience. The verb tense they select for such narration is the historical present. For women in this agnatically based society cyclical time values are linked consistently to the postmarital residential group of their husbands. It is through the descending generations which involve their sons, and to a lesser extent their daughters, that the focus of their identity lies. The birth of a son is important to both husband and wife but for different reasons. For the father it is a manifestation of the continuing cycle and for the mother the creation of a new cycle. Secondarily, for women there is a link to the past through their brothers, a theme often present in folk epic and lyric poetry. Young men may also have a special kin bond with their mother's brother (*ujak*), one founded in a history of positive affect while devoid of possible material conflict as could be the case with father's brother (*stric*). This is the explanation for the prominent role of mother's brother as ritual witness in a marriage ceremony, as described in Chapter 4.

Value complexes composing kinship ideologies, grounded in cyclical time, tend to be modified at a slower rate than events and even ideas concerning technological and related economic phenomena occurring in linear time. Ideologies concerning social structure derive their credibility from repetition, not innovation. Cyclical concepts manifest a conservatism which only slowly assimilates ideas based in linear time. Overall, any ideological system attempts to make sense of both time dimensions in that there are always ways to encounter and deal with unanticipated events.

A Link Between Orality and the Written Record

America has been defined as a society in which nuclear family values predominate. But we are also a society with ramified kin linkages and one with a historical consciousness, both on the national level and on local and family levels, at least potentially. Orality can function in two linear time dimensions, each intersecting with the cyclical processes of family time. In Yugoslavia, especially in the southern and eastern areas such as Serbia, Montenegro and Macedonia, up to the present a culture ideal has been to preserve and transmit oral history, thereby transposing experience from a cyclical time (oral) context to a linear (written) one.

There is reversibility in that process as played out in America, one which may become more the case in Yugoslavia in the future. An American historian concerned with Balkan affairs decided, in the course of work on the Balkans in a major U.S. library, to look up his family's published genealogy. He has numerous kin in a Midwestern rural area, and they were all aware that they traced descent to early 19th century settlers from New England. Specific links to the past ceased at the grandparental generation of those who are now the oldest generation. In the published record the historian located a remembered kin link. He photocopied that section for his relatives, and this launched local kin on a voyage of discovery to locate the ancestral homestead through court records and to find family photographs in local published sources. These explorations have not transformed values, but they have created new heirlooms for the group: the newly found linear time links are becoming part of family lore in cyclical time. This incident is taking place at the same time that younger Orašac villagers and their urban relatives are losing oral links to the past and coming to rely more on written documents.

Applying Time Concepts to Demographic Data

How do these theoretical notions apply to the research data from a Serbian village? For long-term fieldwork they yield productive results. In looking at population data from Orašac there are expected linear time changes over the period 1784-1984. This time span coincides approximately with the existence of Orašac as a named settlement. During these two centuries the population grew from some 30 household at the beginning of the 19th century to about 500 by the mid-20th century, with a subsequent decline of about 20% in the ensuing quarter-century, caused largely by migration to expanding urban areas. The five-fold increase in the population of Orašac in the 19th century (from about 330 to 1,600) coincided with another linear time event, the ecological trans-formation of the area from that of densely wooded forest to one of open farm land. This important change is representative of developments in all of Serbia proper. There are also the expected social structural changes, with the decline in average household size from eight persons at the beginning of the period to about four in recent times. There are, too, expected transformations in vital rates over the past century (the period for which we have full records). Birth rates have declined by more than half, from a high of 48 per 1,000 in the 1870s to 25 in the 1950s while death rates have decreased more than three-fold (35 per 1,000 in the 1870s and 12 per 1,000 in the 1950s).

The age structure of the population of Orašac has undergone a similar transformation. This is most evident in the category age 50 and over, where both in absolute and relative terms the numbers were negligible: 5% in the 1860s. In the 1960s the category grew consistently and increased to 30% by the 1970s, reflecting a large migration of the younger age groups and parallel increase in the expected life-span.

Using Computerized Data Bases

Using concepts of linear and cyclical time in consonance with computer-generated data bases we can also discuss changes in internal household struc-tures, in prime kin dyads and in age structures. Within the extended household structure until the mid-20th century, the key relationship was the father/son dyad. A newer pattern of husband/wife as the numerically prime dyad reflects the lessening importance of the extended family household structure of two co-existing marital pairs. Along with these linear time changes in the village (which also reflect socioeconomic transformations throughout Yugoslavia in the postwar period), there are other quantitative affirmations of the continuing importance of cyclical time perspectives in kinship structures. For the last century (1870-1970) the average age at marriage for women remains constant at about 20. For most of the two-century period (here defined as 1760-1949), the age of the father at the birth of his first son (no data exist for female births for the 18th and early 19th centuries) also remains constant at about age 25. (These data are based on the father's decade of birth.) Birth intervals between the first and second child are also constant at about 2.5 years for the period 1850-1950 (based on the birth decade of the mother).

In Orašac and in Šumadija generally, despite transformations in the age structure of the population and the halving of the average household size, the percentage of the population living in extended or multiple households interestingly remains stable at 72% in the period 1863-1975. The percentage of nuclear family households also remains almost identical at 36% (1863) and 34% (1975) for the two end points of the same period, as has the percentage of extended and multiple households (48%). The multiple household category subsumes diverse household types. Units comprised of two married couples including a married father and his married son has doubled between 1863 and 1975, from 19% to 36% of all households. In 1863 18% of all household units contained married brothers (with or without a parental couple). By 1948 that type of structure essentially disappeared. In 1975 only 43% of the people of Orašac lived in households of six or more members (as contrasted with 89% in 1863).

These data are significant. They reveal that in terms of life experience most Orašac villagers still live in complex households, i.e. within kinship structures more complex than that of the nuclear family. Today, however, households are smaller because they contain fewer children and lack multiple family units within the same generation. Because of increased longevity, contemporary households are now likely to include an aged parent, and interactions between three and even four generations are a more common experience. The latter situation represents a new category of social experience. There are also new social structures of older couples and elderly individuals living alone. Formal structural categories, however, are not sufficient to determine interaction. Thus there are possibilities of multigenerational interaction if the elderly person is "alone" in a physically separate house but resides near (often next to) close kin. Periodic prolonged visits to children in town or city also preserve the vitality of the relationship.

The cyclical time values inherent in the one-to-two century continuity in initial stages of family formation (age at marriage, timing of first child and interval to subsequent birth) correlate well with the persistence of multigenerational household structures. Linkage between the two can be seen as potentially causal and mutually reinforcing. The interaction pattern is not simple since these family formation patterns apply to couples living in nuclear and extended family households, but both exist within a universe of agnatic kin of which older couples or individuals living alone are most frequently a part.

Time Frames and the Myth of Achieved Change

When we first began our work in the early 1950s it appeared from both Yugoslav and American perspectives, however varied, that "modernization" was a state to be achieved, that we in the United States had largely arrived there and that the Yugoslavs were taking steps in that direction. From the perspective of the mid-1980s and the intervening wars, revolutions, technological disasters and economic uncertainties, the notion of achieving a stage of being fully modern seems less sure and less meaningful. The increase in living standards since the 1950s is real for Yugoslavs. Changes evident on the village level are dramatic, but there is hardly satisfaction. Some nostalgia for a selectively remembered past exists, and there is much concern about resolving the problems of the present. The socialist revolution in Yugoslavia has solved some of the problems found elsewhere in the world: there are assured social benefits in health and retirement; the towns and cities lack slum areas; and clearly while there are many inequities some Orašac village migrants to Belgrade live as well as do families of those who have been high officials. At the same time, the considerable earnings of villagers who work abroad do not appear to have been put to the most productive use. There is a surplus of new housing in villages and a lack of adequate housing in towns. As discussed, problems connected with economic development have not permitted adequate investment in urban infrastructure, including adequate environmental controls. Recent conditions appear to be somewhat better in the countryside than in the cities. This may restore to agriculture its needed priority in the interests of the nation. Private agriculture and socialized industry continue to coexist. Orašac villagers are secure in a materially better life which has evolved over the past third of a century. But however clear the problems are, the means for their resolution are not readily apparent.

Concluding Reflections

By using materials based on extant oral traditions our investigations pose some orienting concerns: How do individuals structure recall of their collective pasts? Is the transmitted information affected by the form of recall? How do the values of the narrator condition the data being presented? To what degree does oral recall match archival and other written records? To what extent is the research of the field investigator limited by the communicative competence and reference frame of informant (and by the communicative competence and reference frame of the researcher)? Examining such questions is feasible when there is a viable oral tradition combined with significant archival records, as is the case for Orašac. Oral tradition encompasses many domains of culture and historically has provided the basic material for classic ethnographic accounts. In our discussion, in illustrating the importance of long-term fieldwork, we have chosen to refer to but a few examples specifying the complementarity of the study of oral tradition to our other approaches (the scope is self-explanatory in the listing of our anthropological writings on Orašac).

Finally, it is worth mentioning that the approaches to research discussed here are from the perspectives of two sociocultural anthropologists married to one another but linked neither by kin ties nor by ethnic heritage to Serbia. We regard the long period of fieldwork there as a privilege. All aspects of a given culture are constantly in flux, of course, with different features undergoing changes at varying rates. During the long course of participant-observation it has been satisfying to note how our views have become refined over time. More recent insights derived from continued fieldwork and the use of new and revised theoretical approaches appear to reflect deeper levels of comprehension of processes of change than those we were able to understand earlier.

Ongoing anthropological research with a given population represents a constant challenge to universalize the particular in innovative ways. There is also the challenge of preserving context, all within the convergence of altering time frames. The end-product of fieldwork and reflection, a written statement such as this one, reflects a synthesizing of many levels of consciousness. Data derived from new observations are interpreted by an interacting anthropological team. There are the differing perspectives within the anthropological discipline, influential in forming impressions at the time of each revisit to the village. Also significant are factors of gender, varying reactions to the aging process and the diverse ways we interact with people in the village community.

In addition to new data from the field, there is constantly fresh information from a variety of sources such as archival materials, published census data, new researches by Yugoslav scholars and the further discovery of published sources not previously used, e.g. materials on the deforestation of Šumadija. The altering disciplinary environment both in terms of evolving theoretical approaches and methodological techniques (more sophisticated computer programs, for example) are also essential to the ongoing process of discovery. Our objective is not to up-date for the purpose of producing more data. Rather, the aim is to try to arrive at new kinds of understanding. The process of "doing anthropology" is as important to exemplify as is the fieldwork itself. Augmenting the published record reflects a way of generating ideas about the observers as well as the observed.

Over the years the people being studied have observed changes in the investigators. Villagers have guided our family through village age and gender stages with the rural-based inventory of knowledges, responsibilities and competences that each stage encompasses. The endeavor is reciprocal, involving mutual learning within friendships. That feature in itself is rationale enough for ongoing work in Orašac.

Glossary

Serbian Terms

Are: Unit of land measurement; .01 part of a hectare.
Baba: Grandmother, or any village woman over 45–50
Badnjak: Yule log.
Brat: Brother generally, and also cousin, depending on kin term modifiers used.
Deda: Grandfather, or any villager over 50.
Dinar: Yugoslav currency; the official exchange rate in 1970 was 12.5 dinars to $1.00.
Dizelke: Diesel engines.
Domaćin: Householder, household head.
Gazda: Prosperous peasant.
Gimnazijum: Academic high school.
Gotov: Finished, ready
Gusle: Single-stringed folk instrument played with a bow; accompanies chanting of heroic epics.
Hajduk: Highwayman in Turkish times.
Han: Inn in Turkish times.
Hectare: Unit of land measurement; 1 hectare = 2.47 acres.
Kafana: Formerly coffee-house, now usually tavern.
Kolo: Characteristic circle folk dance.
Komišanje: Cooperative corn-husking.
Kuća: House, household, or, literally, hearth.
Kum: Godfather.
Kumstvo: Godfatherhood.
Majstor: Master craftsman.
Miran: Peaceful, quiet
Moba: Cooperative labor pool for hoeing corn or for threshing.
Pobratimstvo: Blood-brotherhood.
Pozajmica: Cooperative labor loan.
Prelo: Spinning bee.
Prijatelji: In-laws, very close friends.
Rakija: Brandy, especially local plum brandy (*šljivovica*).
Rodjen: Adjective, "born"; a classifier distinguishing immediate kin from those more distant.
Sarma: Stuffed cabbage leaves.
Seosko dete: Village child, one born in village.
Sestra: Sister generally, and also cousin, depending on kin term modifiers used.
Slatko: Sweet preserves offered guests as formal gesture of hospitality.
Slava: Feast day of vamilija's patron saint (verb *slaviti,* to glorify).
Sna (snaha, snaja): Female in-law marrying into the zadruga; generally used to refer to son's wife, brother's wife, or grandson's wife.
Sofra: Low, round Turkish-style table.
Sprega: Recriprocal livestock loan.
Starešina: Zadruga headman.

Starojko: Honorary wedding witness, preferably groom's ujak.

Stric: Uncle (father's brother).

Strina: Aunt (father's brother's wife).

Tetka: Aunt (father's or mother's sister), or any young or middle-aged woman older than speaker.

Torba: Woven wool carrying sack.

Ujak: Uncle (mother's brother).

Vajat: Outbuilding formerly used as sleeping quarters for married couple.

Vamilija: Group of families with common descent; coincides with lineage but lacks clearly defined corporate functions.

Veze: Personal connections, contacts.

Vikendica: City-dweller's weekend house in the country.

Vračara: Part-time female occult practitioner.

Zadruga: Characteristic South Slav extended family household; today also marketing cooperative.

Zadružni Dom: Cooperative building.

Zajednica: Local term for zadruga.

Zdravo: Hello, greetings.

Zet: Classificatory affinal kin term for daughter's husband, sister's husband, or husband's

Social Anthropological Terms

AFFINAL: Relation by marriage (as opposed to *consanguineal,* relation through descent).

AGNATIC: Pertaining to the male line of descent.

CORPORATE: A group organization concerned with socioeconomic interests.

DISTAFF: A wooden spinning board from which women spin raw wool by hand; in English, refers to women's work generally.

DOWRY: Substantive property in land or in cash that a bride's family contributes to a marriage contract; *ruvo* (trousseau) is the bride's personal effects only.

DYADIC: Kin ties between two related individuals.

EXTENDED FAMILY: A nuclear family plus other kin sharing a household.

FRATERNAL ZADRUGA: An extended household consisting of two or more nuclear families headed by brothers.

LINEAGE: Kinship group tracing descent from a common, named ancestor and sharing some corporate functions.

MIR: Institution of rule by consensus in the traditional Russian village.

NUCLEAR FAMILY: A married couple and their children.

PATRIARCHAL: Authority vested in the father specifically and adult males generally.

PATRILINEAL: Descent through the father's line (as opposed to *matrilineal,* descent through the mother's line).

PATRILOCAL: Residence in the household of husband (as opposed to *matrilocal,* in the household of the wife's family).

Suggested Readings

Anthropological Writings by the Authors on Orašac

Halpern, Joel M.
1956 *Social and Cultural Change in a Serbian Village.* New Haven: Human Relations Area Files (Original version of doctoral dissertation).

_____,
1958, 1967 *A Serbian Village.* New York: Columbia University Press (Revised edition, New York: Harper & Row, Colophon Books; incorporates updated data and photos from the 1960s).

_____,
1977 "Individual Life Cycles and Family Cycles," In *The Family Life Cycle in European Societies,* J. Cuisenier ed. The Hague: Mouton, 353-380. (Analysis of historical demographic materials on Orašac from the census of 1863).

_____.
1981 "Demographic and Social Change in the Village of Orašac: A Perspective Over Two Centuries," *Serbian Studies,* Part I, 1 (3): 51-70.

_____ and Eugene A. Hammel.
1977 "Serbian Society in Karadjordje's Serbia," *University of Massachusetts Papers in Anthropology,* 17: 1-36 (Perspectives on early 19th century social structure using census data).

_____ and Barbara Kerewsky-Halpern.
1980 "Yugoslav Oral Genealogies and Official Records: An Approach to Their Combined Use," *World Conference on Records,* Utah Genealogical Society, Salt Lake City: 7, Local History Series 530, 1-31.

_____ and Richard A. Wagner.
1982 *Microstudies in Yugoslav (Serbian) Social Structure and Demography,* University of Massachusetts: *Program in Soviet and East European Studies, Occasional Paper,* No. 8.

_____.
1982 "Demographic and Social Change in the Village of Orasac: A Perspective over Two Centuries," *Serbian Studies,* Part II, 1 (4): 65-92; Part III, 2 (1): 33-60.

_____.
1984 "Time and Social Structure: A Yugoslav Case Study," *Journal of Family History,* 9 (3): 229-244.

Kerewsky-Halpern, Barbara.
1981 "Genealogy as Genre in Rural Serbia," in *Oral Traditional Literatures (Fetschrift in Honor of Albert B. Lord).* J. Foley ed. Columbus: Slavica Publications, 301-325 (Examples of epic pulse recollection and transmission of Orašac lineage information).

_____.

1981 "Text and Context in Ritual Lament," In *Canadian-American Slavic Studies*, 15 (1): 52-60 (Sociolinguistic analysis of an annual mourning event).

_____.

1983 "Watch Out for Snakes! Ethnosemantic Misinterpretations and Interpretation of a Serbian Healing Charm," *Anthropological Linguistics* Fall: 309-325 (Linguistic analysis of a healing charm performed by a male acting as a ritual female).

_____.

1985 "*Rakija* as Ritual in Rural Serbia," *East European Quarterly*, 18 (4): 481-494 (Drinking behaviors as illustrated by analysis and anecdotes).

_____.

1985 "Trust, Talk and Touch in Balkan Folk Healing," *Social Science & Medicine*, 21 (3): 319-325 (Discussion of communicative modes in patient/practitioner interactions).

_____ and J. Foley.

1976 " 'Udovica Jana': A Case Study of Oral Performance," *Slavonic and East European Review* 14 (1): 11-23 (Linguistic and prosodic examination of theme of "unfaithful mother" in Serbian epic).

_____.

1978 "The Power of the Word: Healing Charms as an Oral Genre," *Journal of American Folklore*, 91 (362): 903-924 (Examination of social and linguistic aspects of the phenomenology of a healing rite).

_____ and J. Halpern eds.

1977 *Selected Papers on a Serbian Village: Social Structures as Reflected by History, Demography, and Oral Tradition.* University of Massachusetts, Department of Anthropology, *Research Reports*, No. 17.

Other Pertinent Publications

Bičanić, Rudolf.

1981 *How the People Live: Peasant Life in Southwestern Croatia, Bosnia, and Hercegovina; Yugoslavia in 1935.* University of Massachusetts, *Research Report* 21, J. Halpern and E. Despalatovic eds.

Byrnes, Robert F. ed.

1976 *Communal Families in the Balkans: The Zadruga. Essays by Philip E. Mosley and Essays in His Honor.* Notre Dame: University of Notre Dame Press (Collection of articles by first American social scientist to study the zadruga in 1930s, with accompanying essays by Yugoslav and American researchers).

Denich, Bette.

1974 "Sex and Power in the Balkans," In *Women, Culture, and Society.* M. Rosaldo and L. Lamphere eds. Stanford: Stanford University Press, 243-262.

_____.

1977 "Women, Work and Power in Modern Yugoslavia," in *Sexual Stratification: A Cross-Cultural View.* A. Schlegal ed., New York: Columbia University Press.

Erlich, Vera Stein.

1966 *Family in Transition, a Study of 300 Yugoslav Villages.* Princeton: Princeton University Press (Based on interview data from rural teachers, a particularly good source for gender-defined roles in prewar period).

Filipović, Milenko.
1982 *Among the People, Selected Writings.* E.A. Hammel et al eds. *Papers in Slavic Philology,* 3 (English translation of selected works of the outstanding Serbian ethnologist of the mid-20th century).

Halpern, Joel M.
1963 "Yugoslav Peasant Society in Transition — Stability in Change," In *Anthropological Quarterly,* 36 (3): 136-182.

―――――.
1965 "Peasant Culture and Urbanization in Yugoslavia," in *Human Organization,* 24 (2): 162-174.

―――――.
1967 *The Changing Village Community.* Englewood Cliffs: Prentice-Hall (Dynamics or rural-urban relationships).

―――――.
1967 "Farming s a Way of Life: Yugoslav Peasant Attitudes," In *Soviet and East European Agriculture.* J. Karcz ed. Berkeley: University of California Press, 356-381.

―――――.
1969 "Yugoslavia: Modernization in an Ethnically Diverse State. In *Contemporary Yugoslavia,* W.S. Vucinich ed., Berkeley: University of California Press, 316-350.

―――――.
1975 "Some Perspectives on Balkan Migration Patterns (with particular reference to Yugoslavia (Serbia)). In *Migration and Urbanization: Modes and Adaptive Strategies.* B. du Toit and H. Safa eds., Chicago: Aldine, 77-115.

―――――.
1980 "Memories of Recent Change: Some East European Perspectives," In *The Process of Rural Transformation: Eastern Europe, Latin America and Australia.* I. Voglyes et al eds., White Plains: Pergamon Press, 242-268 (Biographical account from the 1960s of a young woman from a village in central Serbia).

――――― and Eugene A. Hammel.
1969 "Observations on the Intellectual History of Ethnology and Other Social Sciences in Yugoslavia," *Comparative Studies in Society and History,* 11 (1): 17-26 (historical background on the development of ethnology in Yugoslavia).

――――― and Barbara Kerewsky-Halpern.
1979 "Changing Perceptions of Roles as Husbands and Wives in Five Yugoslav Villages," In *Europe as a Culture Area.* J. Cuisenier ed., Chicago: Aldine, 159-72 (Considers the diverse national groups that compose the Yugoslav state).

――――― and David A. Kideckel.
1983 "Anthropology of Eastern Europe," in *Annual Review of Anthropology;* 12: 377-402 (Evaluation of contemporary research including detailed bibliographical survey).

――――― and Richard A. Wagner.
1978 "Anthropological and Sociological Research on the Balkans During the Past Decade," In *Balkanistica,* 4: 13-62.

Hammel, Eugene A.
1969 *Alternative Social Structures and Ritual Relations in the Balkans.* Englewood Cliffs: Prentice-Hall (Key source on kinship, with emphasis on godparenthood).

―――――.
1972 "The Zadruga as Process," In *Household and Family in Past Time.* P. Laslett and R. Wall eds. Cambridge: Cambridge University Press: 335-73 (Useful analysis of kinship dynamics).

_____.

1984 "The Yugoslav Family in the Modern World: Adaptation to Change," In *Journal of Family History,* 9 (3): 217-228.

Hofer, Tamas.

1968 "Anthropologists and Native Ethnographers in Central European Villages: Comparative Notes on the Professional Personality of Two Disciplines," *Current Anthropology,* 9: 311-315 (Essay by Hungarian ethnologist comparing research styles of American anthropologists and European ethnographers).

Horecky, Paul L. ed.

1969 *Southeast Europe, a Guide to Basic Publications.* Chicago: University of Chicago Press.

Jensen, J.H.

1968 "The Changing Balkan Family," *National Archives of Ethnography* 51: 20-48 (Comparative analysis of *Balkan Village* by Sanders and *A Serbian Village* by Halpern).

Lampe, John R. and Marvin R. Jackson.

1982 *Balkan Economic History, 1550-1950, From Imperial Borderlands to Developing Nations.* Bloomington: Indiana University Press.

Lockwood, William G.

1975 *European Moslems: Ethnicity and Economy in Western Bosnia.* New York: Academic Press, (Community study and marketing patterns in an ethnically diverse area, useful for a comparative perspective on Serbia).

Lodge, Olive.k

1941 *Peasant Life in Yugoslavia.* London: Seeley, Service and Co. (Best general prewar account of village life).

Mitrany, David.

1951 *Marx Against the Peasant.* Chapel Hill: University of North Carolina Press. (Valuable for exposition of fates of peasant parties in pre-World War II Eastern Europe).

Obrebski, Jozef.

1976 *The Changing Peasantry of Eastern Europe.* J. Halpern and B. Kerewsky-Halpern eds. Cambridge: Schenkman.

Petrovich, Michael B.

1977 *A History of Modern Serbia.* New York: Harcourt, Brace, Jovanovich.

Rheubottom, David B.

1980 "Dowry and Wedding Celebrations in Yugoslav Macedonia," In *The Meaning of Marriage Payments,* J.L. Comaroff ed. New York: Academic Press, 221-249.

Sanders, Irwin T.

1949 *Balkan Village.* Lexington: University of Kentucky Press (Classic monograph on a Bulgarian village near Sofia).

Simić, Andrei.

1972 *The Peasant Urbanites: A Study of Rural-Urban Mobility in Serbia.* New York: Seminar Press (Study of kinship in Belgrade).

_____.

1978 "Winners and Losers: Aging Yugoslavs in a Changing World," In *Cultural Variations on Growing Old.* B. Meyerhoff and A. Simic eds. Beverly Hills: Sage, 77-105.

_____.

1983 "Adaptive and Maladaptive Aspects of Traditional Culture in Yugoslav Modernization. In *Urban Life in Mediterranean Europe.* M. Kenny and D. Kertzer eds. Urbana: University of Illinois Press (Critical survey of urban anthropological research in Yugoslavia).

————.

1983 "Machismo and Cryptomatriarchy: Power, Affect and Authority in the Contemporary Yugoslav Family," In *Ethos* 11 (1-2): 66-86.

Singleton, Fred.

1985 *A Short History of the Yugoslav Peoples.* New York. Cambridge University Press, 1985 (Background on contemporary Yugoslav society, with useful references).

Stoianovich, Trian.

1967 *A Study in Balkan Civilization* New York: Alfred Knopf (Insights by a social historian using anthropological sources).

Sugar, Peter F. ed.

1980 *Ethnic Diversity and Conflict in Eastern Europe.* Santa Barbara: Clio Press (Perspectives by Balkan historians).

Tomasevich, Jozo.

1955 *Peasants, Politics and Economic Change in. Yugoslavia.* Stanford: Stanford University Press (Source for the economic history of Yugoslav peasantries from the Middle Ages to 1941).

Vucinich, Wayne S.

1975 *A Study in Social Survival: Katun in Bileca Rudine.* Monograph Series in World Affairs, No. 13, Denver: University of Denver (Study of a highland community by an American historian who grew up there).

Warriner, Doreen.

1965 *Economics of Peasant Farming,* 2nd edition. New York: Barnes and Noble (Essays on peasant problems in Eastern Europe in the 1930s).

————.

1965 *Contrasts in Emerging Societies: Readings in the Social and Economic History of Southeastern Europe in the Nineteenth Century.* Bloomington: Indiana University Press (Collection includes translations from original sources).

West, Rebecca.

1941 *Black Lamb and Grey Falcon: A Journey Through Yugoslavia.* New York: Viking Press, 1941 (Classic travel account of Yugoslavia in the interwar period; politically biased but sensitive and perceptive).

Winner, Irene and Thomas Winner eds.

1983 *The Peasant and the City in Eastern Europe, Interpenetrating Structures.* Cambridge: Schenkman.